OKLAHOMA
FUTURE HOMEMAKERS
of
AMERICA
COOKBOOK

75 YEARS of PRIDE and HERITAGE

FAVORITE RECIPES PRESS

©Favorite Recipes Press, A Division of Great American Opportunities, Inc. MCMLXXXIV
P. O. Box 77, Nashville, Tennessee 37202
Library of Congress Catalog Card No. 84-081315
ISBN 0-87197-180-1

EDNA CROW
State Adviser, 1975-84
Oklahoma Association
FHA/HERO

Dear FHA/HERO Adviser,

Future Homemakers of America throughout the nation say "Happy 40th Birthday" with this beautiful FHA/HERO Cookbook! FHA/HERO Advisers have always been contributors to the welfare of the family. You will be delighted to add this cookbook to your series of favorite recipe cookbooks.

Much appreciation is due the FHA/HERO Adviser for all the many worthwhile projects they sponsor but a very special "Thank You" is given for this fabulous cookbook. Many vital school projects will be benefited by this project.

Edna Crow

Dedication

Edna Crow has devoted most of her professional life to the field of education in Oklahoma, serving for over 36 years.

Edna served for over 25 years as a vocational home economics teacher and local FHA adviser in Hollis. Nine years ago Edna joined the state staff of home economics with the State Department of Vocational and Technical Education serving as a district supervisor, providing assistance to numerous home economics teachers in the Northwest and Southwest districts.

Edna has served as FHA/HERO State Adviser for nine years, providing leadership to several thousand students and attracting nationwide recognition to Oklahoma FHA/HERO.

Edna is a life member of the Oklahoma Vocational Association and American Vocational Association and has been an active member of the Oklahoma Association of Vocational Home Economics Teachers. She has served as president of OVA and received the 25-year *OVA Silver Key Award* and numerous other awards in professional organizations. At the National FHA Convention in Chicago, Illinois, July, 1984, Edna received the *National Distinguished Service Award in Future Homemakers of America.*

Edna's life has had a positive and beneficial influence on the lives of many people, both youths and adults. Her influence and contributions will long be remembered in Oklahoma and by the Future Homemakers of America.

Expression of Appreciation

Even though I only had the opportunity to serve under Mrs. Crow for two months, she has proven to be the backbone of our organization. Her courage and strength have helped me to get through the best — and worst — of times. Words simply cannot express the love, admiration and respect I feel for this great lady. Our time together has been short, but I feel lucky for having the time we did have.

Thank you, Mrs. Crow, for all you've done to build FHA/HERO into what it is today. May this be a small token of our everlasting appreciation. I will NEVER forget you!!! I love you so very much.

Lesa Jennings
1984-85 State President

I can't begin to express what Future Homemakers of America and Mrs. Crow mean to me. FHA has become a way of life for me. The leadership training I have gained, the places I have gone, and the people I have met have enriched my life and given me memories forever. This has been one of the most exciting years to serve as Oklahoma's State President. It was very meaningful to cut the ribbon at the dedication ceremony at the national headquarters in Reston, Virginia, after an outstanding fund raising project to make Oklahoma number one in the nation. Through working with Mrs. Crow in various ways, I have grown to love and appreciate her untiring effort and dedication to the young people of Oklahoma. She is the best friend anyone could have, and her ready smile is an inspiration to everyone.

Love always,
Jennifer Walsh
1983-84 State President

When I first received my letter from the State Department, it brought back several wonderful memories of being a Future Homemakers of America State Officer.

One of the most memorable parts of my year was having Edna Crow for a State Adviser. Mrs. Crow's patience, planning, organization, and loving care are what has made Oklahoma Future Homemakers of America the very best in the nation.

I am saddened at Mrs. Crow's retirement be-cause the State Department is losing one of their most valuable workers. But I am proud for Mrs. Crow that she will finally be able to spend the time she desires with her husband and family.

Thank you, Mrs. Crow, for all you did. I will never ever forget you or FHA!

You will be missed greatly!

Much love,
Dede Speed
1982-83 State President

When I was a freshman in high school, I took our freshman FHA quiz and one of the questions on it asked who the GHA Adviser was. I answered it without a blink of the eye, but little did I realize that in two years, I would be working closely with you and grow to love you more with each passing year. It is such a comfort to me to know that if I ever need anything, you are just a phone call away in Stillwater.

During my year as state president, I would often comment that even in the busiest and worst of days, you would always have a smile on your face and only had concern for others and not yourself. The perfect example of this was the day we were working on the state convention and trying to plan for the big change to the Myriad. In the midst of all the problems, you pulled out enough little red and white bear key chains for every state officer. That little outpouring of love and concern for us is what is so characteristic of you — giving of yourself to others. I love you.

Sue Sokolosky
1981-82 State President

In Mrs. Crow's time as State Adviser, she gave what would be equal to over one hundred years of service, because she invested herself into the future of America — its youth. She never told us what to do; she helped us to discover new ideas and new methods on our own, and we grew. We shared, we learned, and we loved. We looked always to her for treasured friendship, and we will never forget her unconditional support. She is a rare and priceless friend.

Stacia Long
1980-81 State President

So much has happened since I last wrote you in college. I am now happily married of one and a half years. We're expecting our first child in January. At the present I'm working for a bank in downtown Dallas, and I'm loving every minute of it. That is just a brief account of the past two years. In a nutshell, my dreams are becoming realities, and I owe so much to you. Thank you seems so inadequate for the gratitude I wish to express to you for the love, understanding, teaching, encouragement, support and warming personality you befriended me with. You're one in a million. You've given so much of yourself to others, and you deserve so much in return. May God's Richest Blessings Be Bestowed Upon You.

Love,
Ranita Smitherman (Sprouse)
1979-80 State President

Words cannot begin to express the gratitude within my heart for all you have done as a great leader of the Future Homemakers of America Organization and as a friend. You have made the Oklahoma FHA what it is today. Much dedication is needed for a job such as yours, and we are all so thankful for your devotion and inspiration through the years. We hate to see you leave, but we know that you leave with great pride in our organization and will continue to keep us in your heart. I personally want to thank you for all your guidance and instruction during my term as state president. Our team would not have succeeded as well if it weren't for your many smiles and loving heart. I will miss you but will continue to think of you always as FHA's most devoted and sincere adviser.

Love always,
Sherree (Walsh) Orrell
1978-79 State President

Mrs. Crow is a perfect example of dedication to FHA/HERO. Without true dedication like hers, an organization of this type could not survive. During my year as FHA/HERO state president, Mrs. Crow was a tower of strength to me. She was always there with her cheerful smile and those special words to keep me going. Thank you, Mrs. Crow,

for the outstanding way you dedicate yourself to serving young people through the Future Homemakers of America.

With love and admiration,
Abby Hartsell King
1977-78 State President

As a state president of the Oklahoma Association of Future Homemakers of America, I had the opportunity to work in close contact with Mrs. Crow in her capacity as state adviser. In this role, she strived at all times to exemplify the purposes of the organization and was a model of dedication to those of us who worked with her. I personally benefited from her efforts to insure that students found opportunities for personal growth and received positive recognition for their efforts. I think I speak for many state officer alumni when I say that Edna Crow was much more than an adviser; she was, and is, a great friend and a role model, as well. There is no doubt this personal involvement with students is largely responsible for the continued support Oklahoma FHA/HERO members show to the organization, even after their graduation from high school.

Debbie Vincent
1976-77 State President

Mrs. Edna Crow led the Oklahoma Association, Future Homemakers of America, to the No. 1 position in the United States, not only in the drive for the National Leadership Center, but in spirit as well. I am so proud to have served under her leadership on her first state officer team. That is an experience that I will cherish forever. Her influence has had a lasting effect on my life. Probably the most valuable lesson she taught me was the desire for excellence in work. Her teaching style was unique in that each helpful suggestion was sincere and came from her heart. *Positive* advice and guidance were definitely her trademarks. She always put others first and never once did she forget that FHA/HERO is a student organization.

She is one in a million and Oklahoma FHA/HERO is very fortunate to have had nine years of her dedicated service.

Best wishes in your retirement, and always remember you are loved by all those that you have touched with your many rays of sunshine.

Linda Raines Thompson
1975-76 State President

Contents

BAKED ALMOND DOUGHNUTS, recipe on page 100.

A-OK Commodity Cook-Off

The A-OK Commodity Cook-Off was established in the summer of 1983 by the Oklahoma Agricultural Commodity groups, Oklahoma Department of Agriculture, Farmer-Stockman Magazine, and Oklahoma Future Home-makers of America.

The main purpose of this unique contest is to give secondary students an opportunity to recognize and creatively promote the agricultural products produced and/or processed in their state.

Each recipe is an original recipe and 50% of the ingredients (excluding herbs and spices) are Oklahoma agricultural products. The Oklahoma agriculture products are indicated by an asterisk in the recipe.

The contestants entered their original recipe in Division I (Freshmen and Sophomore) or Division II (Junior and Senior) at the sub-district level. The first place and possibly second place dishes in each division met for competition at the district level. Then the first place dishes from each district in both divisions competed in the state finals. The state contest was held Saturday, May 5, 1984 at the Oklahoma Farm Show on the Oklahoma Fairgrounds.

Each contestant and the steering committees of the 1984 Annual A-OK Commodity Cook-Off would like to recognize the following organizations for making the contest possible. The contributors are:

**Hydro Insurance, Alvin Davis
**Oklahoma Beef Commission
**Oklahoma Wheat Commission
*Fort Gibson State Bank
*Guthrie Cotton Oil Co.
*Oklahoma Farm Bureau
*Oklahoma Sheep & Wool Producers
*Rohm & Haas Chemical Co.
 Bank of Hydro
 Eastern Oklahoma Production Credit Assoc., Muskogee
 Estes Chemical Co., Oklahoma City
 First National Bank of Coweta
 Wayne and Fern Krehbiel, Hydro

*Oklahoma Agricultural Products

Oklahoma Peanut Growers
Security National Bank of Coweta
Shanks Trucking and Brokerage, Webbers Falls
Oklahoma Cowbelles, Inc.
American Soybean Assoc.
AMPI Ladies Auxiliary, Oklahoma Division
Grayson Beekeeper Supply, Owasso
Phil Carter Insurance Agency, Coweta
Billy Smith, Mustang
Junior and Alpha Tillman, Hinton
Massey Ferguson, Muskogee
Oklahoma Soybean Ladies Assoc.
Tulsa Farm Equipment, Inc.
Wheeler-Cummins, Hinton
Oklahoma Wheathearts
Farmers Co-Op, Broken Arrow and Coweta
Farmer's Produce, Wagoner
Farmer's Union Insurance, Coweta
First National Bank of Muskogee
Fort Smith Farmers Co-Op
Hinton Gin, Lee Entz
Kremers Equipment, Fort Smith
Sids Farm Supply, Porter
Bower Equipment, Muskogee
Mannings Insulation Specialists, Inc., Broken Arrow
Stockyards Equipment and Supply, Tulsa
Hamby Electric, Tulsa
Jerry and Jimmie Jamison, Coweta
Eakly Gin
Acco Feeds, Oklahoma City
Agland USA, Inc., Austin, Texas
Agri-Sales Associates, Inc., Oklahoma City
C.S.I. Chemical Corporation, Greensburg, Kansas
Coba/Select Sires, Inc., Choctaw
Dinsmore Truck and Equipment Company, Shawnee
Farm Data Services, Inc., Stillwater
Jerry's Fine Honey, Oklahoma City
Knutson Irrigation Design, Yukon
Stucky Sales Company, Moundridge, Kansas

Cook-Off Recipes

⬥ STATE WINNERS

FIRST PLACE		SECOND PLACE	
Division I	Michelle Charles	Division I	Donna Thornburg
Division II	Amy Hajek	Division II	Connie Jo Bierig

SOUTHWEST
DISTRICT WINNERS

HARVEST CHICKEN PIE
First Place State Winner

* *4 med. potatoes, chopped
* *3 med. carrots, chopped
* 1 lg. stalk celery, finely chopped
* *1 sm. onion, finely chopped
* *1   4-lb. chicken, cooked, boned
* 1 1/4 tsp. salt
* 1/4 tsp. coarse pepper
* 1/8 tsp. minced garlic
* *1   4 1/2-oz. can mushrooms, drained
* *1/4 c. chopped crisp-cooked bacon
* *1   10-oz. package frozen peas,
    partially thawed
* *1   10-oz. package frozen corn,
    partially thawed
* *1 can cream of chicken soup
* *1 can cream of mushroom soup
* *1 c. chicken broth
* *1/2 c. milk
* *3 c. flour
* *2/3 c. shortening
* *1/2 c. butter

Boil . . . . potatoes, carrots, celery and onion in water to cover in saucepan for 35 minutes; drain.
Combine . . . . with chicken, 1/4 teaspoon salt, pepper, garlic, mushrooms, bacon, peas and corn in bowl; toss to mix.
Blend . . . . . . soups, broth and milk in bowl.
Add . . . . to chicken mixture, mixing well.
Sift . . . . flour and 1 teaspoon salt into bowl.
Cut . . . . in shortening and butter until crumbly.
Add . . . . 2/3 cup ice water gradually, stirring until pastry clings together; shape into ball.
Roll . . . . 2/3 of the pastry into rectangle on floured surface.
Fit . . . . into 7 x 12-inch glass baking dish.
Spoon . . . . . . in chicken mixture.
Top . . . . with remaining pastry; crimp edges.
Bake . . . . at 400 degrees for 55 minutes.
Yields . . . . . . 8 servings.

Michele Charles, Gotebo
District II, Division I

OKIE-DOKIES
First Place District Winner

* *4 eggs, beaten
* 1/2 tsp. salt
* 1 tsp. vanilla extract
* 1   1-lb. box brown sugar
* *1 c. chopped pecans
* *1 1/2 c. flour
* *3 tbsp. butter
* 1 c. confectioners' sugar
* 3/4 tsp. cinnamon
* 1/8 tsp. each nutmeg, mace
* *1 1/2 tsp. milk

Beat . . . . eggs, salt, vanilla and brown sugar together in large mixer bowl.
Add . . . . pecans and flour, mixing well.
Spread . . . . . in greased and floured 10 x 13-inch baking pan.

*Oklahoma Agricultural Products

8

Bake . . . . at 325 degrees for 25 to 30 minutes or until dry around edges.
Melt . . . . butter in saucepan.
Add . . . . confectioners' sugar and spices, mixing well.
Add . . . . milk.
Spread . . . . . over hot cookies.
Cool . . . . for 10 minutes.
Cut . . . . into squares; cool on wire racks.
Garnish . . . . . with additional confectioners' sugar.
Yields . . . . . . 24.

Marsha Manar, Apache
District II, Division II

Sub-District Winners

CURRIED CHICKEN SALAD
Sub-District Winner

* 2 whole chicken breasts
* 2 tbsp. butter
  1/3 c. long grain rice
* 2/3 c. chicken broth
* 1 red Delicious apple, cut into chunks
  2 stalks celery, chopped
* 1/2 c. dry roasted peanuts, chopped
* 3 tbsp. sliced green onion
  1/2 c. raisins
* 1 c. sour cream
  2 tbsp. brown sugar
  1 1/2 tsp. curry powder
  Juice of 1 lemon
  1/2 tsp. salt
  1/4 tsp. pepper
  1/8 tsp. ginger
  1/2 tsp. MSG
  1/4 c. coconut, toasted

Place . . . . chicken breasts on baking sheet; dot with butter.
Bake . . . . at 350 degrees for 30 to 35 minutes or until tender; cool and bone.
Cut . . . . chicken into bite-sized pieces.
Cook . . . . rice in broth in covered saucepan for 20 minutes.
Combine . . . . chicken, rice, apple and next 4 ingredients in bowl.
Blend . . . . . . sour cream and remaining ingredients except coconut in bowl.
Pour . . . . over chicken mixture; toss to mix.

Chill . . . . covered, for 1 hour or longer.
Serve . . . . on spinach or lettuce-lined plates topped with coconut.

Deedra Abbott, Frederick
District I, Division I

SOUFFLE SUPREME
Sub-District Winner

* 7 slices bread, cubed
* 1 c. chopped cooked ham
* 3/4 lb. process, cheese spread, cubed
* 1/4 c. margarine, melted
* 7 eggs, beaten
* 2 1/2 c. milk
  1 tsp. prepared mustard
  3/4 tsp. salt

Layer . . . . . . bread, ham and cheese in 9 x 13-inch glass baking dish.
Drizzle . . . . . margarine over top.
Beat . . . . eggs, milk, mustard and salt in bowl.
Pour . . . . over layers.
Chill . . . . covered, overnight.
Bake . . . . uncovered, at 300 degrees for 1 hour.

Miriam Larson, Granite
District I, Division II

OATMEAL-PECAN PIE
Sub-District Winner

* 2 eggs, well beaten
  1 c. sugar
  3/4 c. light corn syrup
* 1/2 stick margarine, melted
* 1/2 c. milk
  1/2 tsp. vanilla extract
  1/4 tsp. salt
  3/4 c. oats
  1/2 8-oz. can flaked coconut
* 1/2 c. chopped pecans
* 1 unbaked 9-in. pie shell

Combine . . . . first 10 ingredients in bowl in order listed, mixing well.
Pour . . . . into pie shell.
Bake . . . . at 350 degrees for 45 to 60 minutes or until set.

Sharla Rhodes, Grandfield
District III, Division I

*Oklahoma Agricultural Products

9

Cook-Off Recipes

APPLE PUDDING
Sub-District Winner

* 1/2 c. shortening
  2 c. sugar
* 1 egg
* 2 lg. cooking apples, peeled, chopped
* Flour
  2 tsp. cinnamon
  1 tsp. soda
  Dash of salt
* 1/2 c. pecan halves

Cream . . . . . . shortening and 1 cup sugar in bowl.
Beat . . . . in egg.
Stir . . . . in apples.
Sift . . . . in 1 cup flour, 1 teaspoon cinnamon, soda and salt; mix well.
Fold . . . . in pecans.
Spread . . . . . in 8 x 8-inch baking pan.
Bake . . . . at 275 degrees for 1 hour.
Combine . . . . 1 cup sugar, 3 tablespoons flour, 1 teaspoon cinnamon and 1 cup boiling water in saucepan.
Cook . . . . until thickened, stirring constantly.
Serve . . . . over pudding.
Yields . . . . . . 6 servings.

Aimee Stoll, Chattanooga
District III, Division II

CAROL'S APPLE DUMPLINGS
Sub-District Winner

* 1/2 c. shortening
* 1 c. flour
* 3 yellow apples, peeled
  Sugar
* 2 tbsp. butter
  3 drops of red food coloring
  Cinnamon

Cut . . . . shortening into flour in bowl until crumbly.
Mix . . . . in 2 tablespoons water with fork to make dough.
Shape . . . . . . into 6 balls.
Roll . . . . into circles on floured surface.
Cut . . . . apples in half lengthwise; remove core.
Place . . . . 1 apple half, 1 tablespoon sugar and 1 teaspoon butter on each circle; fold dough to enclose filling, sealing seams.
Place . . . . in 9 x 13-inch baking dish.
Mix . . . . 1 cup sugar with 2 cups water and food coloring.
Pour . . . . over dumplings.
Sprinkle . . . . generously with sugar and cinnamon.
Bake . . . . at 350 degrees for 30 minutes; baste.
Bake . . . . for 15 minutes longer.

Tressia Scott, Ryan
District IV, Division I

MEXICAN BEEF CREPES
Sub-District Winner

  3/4 c. flour
  1/2 c. cornmeal
  Salt
* 1 3/4 c. milk
  3 eggs
  1 tbsp. melted butter
* 2 lb. ground chuck
* 2 tsp. onion flakes
* 1 8-oz. package cream cheese, softened
  3 4-oz. cans chopped green chilies
* 1 lb. American cheese

Combine . . . . flour, cornmeal, 1/8 teaspoon salt, 1 1/4 cups milk, eggs and butter in mixer bowl.
Beat . . . . at medium speed until smooth.
Pour . . . . a small amount at a time into lightly greased crepe pan, tilting to cover bottom.
Cook . . . . until lightly browned on both sides.
Brown . . . . . . ground chuck with onion and 1/2 teaspoon salt in skillet, stirring frequently.
Mix . . . . with cream cheese and 1 can green chilies.
Spoon . . . . . . onto crepes and roll to enclose filling; arrange in baking dish.
Heat . . . . cheese and 1/2 cup milk until cheese melts.
Stir . . . . in 2 cans green chilies.
Pour . . . . over crepes.
Bake . . . . at 350 degrees until heated through.

Penny Jackson, Ringling
District IV, Division II

EAST
DISTRICT WINNERS

MARVELOUS MEAT LOAF
First Place District Winner

* * 1 c. saltine cracker crumbs
* * 1/2 c. chopped onion
* * 1/2 c. chopped red pepper
* * 1 8-oz. can tomato sauce
* * 1 egg, slightly beaten
* 1 tsp. salt
* 1/4 tsp. pepper
* 1 tbsp. celery seed
* 1 tsp. garlic powder
* * 1 1/2 lb. ground chuck
* * 1 c. catsup
* * 3 slices bacon

Combine .... first 10 ingredients in order given in bowl, mixing well.
Shape ...... into loaf in loaf pan.
Make .... 4 diagonal indentations on top.
Fill .... with catsup.
Bake .... at 350 degrees for 40 minutes.
Arrange ..... bacon slices between indentations.
Bake .... for 20 minutes longer.
Garnish ..... with parsley.

Cindy Drake, Pocola
District IV, Division I

A-OK MEAT PIE
First Place District Winner

* 1 pkg. dry yeast
* 1 tbsp. sugar
* Salt
* * 2 tbsp. peanut oil
* * 2 3/4 to 3 1/4 c. flour
* * 1 lb. ground beef
* * 1/2 lb. sausage
* * 1/2 c. chopped onion
* * 1 tbsp. butter
* * 1 10 3/4-oz. can tomato puree
* 3/4 tsp. oregano
* 1/8 tsp. garlic salt
* 1/4 tsp. each thyme, basil

Dissolve .... yeast in 1 cup warm water in bowl.
Stir .... in sugar, 1 1/2 teaspoons salt, oil and 1 1/2 cups flour, beating until smooth.
Add .... enough remaining flour to make stiff dough.
Knead ...... on floured surface for about 5 minutes or until smooth and elastic.
Place .... in greased bowl, turning to grease surface.
Let .... rise, covered, in warm place for 45 minutes or until doubled in bulk.
Punch ...... dough down; divide into 4 portions.
Roll .... out.
Fit .... into individual baking dishes.
Bake .... at 350 degrees for 10 minutes; cool.
Brown ...... ground beef and sausage in skillet; drain.
Saute ...... onion in butter in skillet.
Combine .... tomato puree, seasonings and 1/8 teaspoon salt in bowl.
Add .... sauteed onion and ground beef mixture.
Spoon ...... into shells.
Bake .... at 425 degrees for 20 to 25 minutes.
Sprinkle .... with cheese.
Garnish ..... with parsley.
Yields ...... 4 servings.

Lori Hopcus, Jones
District I, Division II

*Oklahoma Agricultural Products

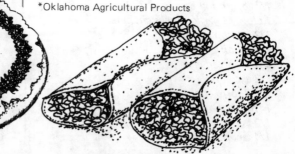

Cook-Off Recipes

Sub-District Winners

CHEESY LASAGNA
Sub-District Winner

* * 2 lb. ground beef
* * 1/4 c. finely chopped onion
*   1/4 tsp. salt
*   1/8 tsp. pepper
* * 2 4-oz. cans mushrooms
* * 4 oz. Cheddar cheese, grated
* * 4 oz. Swiss cheese, grated
* * 1 8-oz. box lasagna noodles, cooked
* * 1 15-oz. can tomato sauce
* * 4 1-oz. slices American cheese
* * 1 c. small curd cottage cheese
* * 4 oz. mozzarella cheese, grated

Brown . . . . . . ground beef and onion in skillet; drain.

Add . . . . salt, pepper and mushrooms.

Simmer . . . . . for 15 minutes.

Reserve . . . . . a small amount of Cheddar and Swiss cheese.

Alternate . . . layers of 2 noodles, 1/5 of the ground beef and tomato sauce and 1 of the cheeses in oiled 2 1/2-quart baking dish until all ingredients are used, ending with mozzarella cheese.

Sprinkle . . . . reserved cheeses on top.

Bake . . . . at 325 degrees for 25 to 30 minutes.

Garnish . . . . . with whole sauteed mushrooms and parsley.

Yields . . . . . . 4-6 servings.

Sally LaPratt, Meeker
District I, Division I

STUFFED ZUCCHINI BOATS
Sub-District Winner

* * 3 zucchini
* * 1/4 lb. ground beef
* * 1 clove of garlic, finely chopped
* * 1/2 c. chopped onion
* * 2 tbsp. oil
* * 6 tbsp. bread crumbs
* * 1/2 egg yolk
*   1 1/2 tbsp. chopped dill
*   1 tbsp. chopped parsley
*   1/2 tsp. salt
*   1/4 tsp. pepper
* * 2 tbsp. Parmesan cheese
* * 1 6-oz. can tomato sauce
* * 1 1/2 tsp. butter
*   3/4 tsp. thyme
*   1/2 bay leaf

Slice . . . . zucchini in half lengthwise.

Scoop . . . . . . out to make shells, reserving pulp.

Brown . . . . . . ground beef with half the garlic and 1/4 cup onion in 1 tablespoon oil in skillet, stirring frequently.

Stir . . . . in reserved pulp.

Cook . . . . for 3 minutes.

Add . . . . 1/4 cup crumbs, egg yolk, dill, parsley, 1/4 teaspoon salt and 1/8 teaspoon pepper.

Cook . . . . until slightly thickened, stirring constantly.

Spoon . . . . . . into zucchini shells in baking dish.

Top . . . . with 2 tablespoons crumbs and cheese.

Drizzle . . . . . 1 tablespoon oil over tops.

Bake . . . . at 375 degrees for 40 minutes.

Mix . . . . tomato sauce, butter, 1/4 cup onion, remaining garlic, thyme, bay leaf, 1/4 teaspoon salt and 1/8 teaspoon pepper in saucepan.

Cook . . . . for 10 minutes, stirring frequently.

Serve . . . . over zucchini boats.

Edith Gibson, Weleetka
District II, Division I

MEAT LOAF ROLL
Sub-District Winner

* * 1/2 10-oz. package frozen chopped broccoli
* * 1/2 10-oz. package frozen chopped cauliflower
* * 2 lb. ground beef
* * 2 eggs
*   3/4 c. oats
* * 1/4 c. catsup
* * 1/4 c. milk
* * 1/4 tsp. pepper
* * 1/4 tsp. oregano

*Oklahoma Agricultural Products

1 1/2 tsp. salt
*1 3-oz. package smoked sliced ham
*5 3 x 3-in. slices Cheddar cheese,
    cut in half diagonally

Rinse ...... broccoli and cauliflower under cold running water to separate; drain.

Mix .... ground beef with next 6 ingredients and 1/2 teaspoon salt in bowl.

Pat .... into 10 x 12-inch rectangle on foil.

Spread ..... broccoli and cauliflower on rectangle to within 1/2 inch of edges.

Sprinkle .... with 1 teaspoon salt.

Arrange ..... ham over top.

Roll .... as for jelly roll from short side, sealing seam and ends.

Place .... on rack in shallow pan.

Bake .... at 350 degrees for 1 1/4 hours.

Arrange ..... overlapping cheese slices on top.

Bake .... for 1 minute longer.

Garnish ..... with celery leaves and candied apple rings.

Tracy Lowe, Weleetka
District II, Division II

SKILLET GUMBO
Sub-District Winner

*1 1/2 c. frozen cut okra
 Cornmeal
*1 lb. ground beef
*1 med. onion, finely chopped
 1 tbsp. shortening
*1 6-oz. can tomato paste
*4 c. stewed tomatoes
*1 c. frozen corn
*1 c. macaroni

1 tsp. salt
1/2 tsp. garlic flakes
*1/2 c. grated cheese

Dust .... okra with cornmeal.

Brown ...... ground beef with onion and okra in shortening in skillet, stirring frequently.

Add .... remaining ingredients except cheese, mixing well.

Simmer ..... for 20 minutes or until macaroni is tender.

Sprinkle .... cheese over top.

Yields ...... 4 servings.

Sharon Funburg, Checotah
District III, Division I

STRAWBERRY BREAD
Sub-District Winner

*3 1/2 c. flour
 2 c. sugar
 1 tbsp. cinnamon
 2 tsp. soda
 1 tsp. salt
*1 1/4 c. oil
*4 eggs
*2 16-oz. packages frozen strawberries, thawed
*1 1/4 c. chopped nuts

Mix .... flour, sugar, cinnamon, soda and salt in large bowl.

Add .... oil and eggs, mixing well.

Stir .... in strawberries and nuts.

Pour .... into 2 greased and floured loaf pans.

Bake .... at 350 degrees for 1 1/4 hours.

Denise Baxter, Checotah
District III, Division II

*Oklahoma Agricultural Products

Cook-Off Recipes

FRESH APPLE CAKE
Sub-District Winner

1 c. sugar
* 1/2 c. shortening
* 1 egg
* 1 c. flour
1/2 tsp. soda
1/4 tsp. salt
1/4 tsp. each nutmeg, cinnamon
* 2 c. chopped apples
1 tsp. vanilla extract
* 1 c. chopped pecans

Cream . . . . . . sugar and shortening in bowl.
Beat . . . . in egg.
Add . . . . sifted dry ingredients gradually, mixing well.
Fold . . . . in apples and vanilla.
Pour . . . . into greased and floured 9 x 13-inch baking pan.
Top . . . . with pecans.
Bake . . . . at 350 degrees for 30 minutes.

Darla Shrum, Poteau
District IV, Division II

SOUTHEAST
DISTRICT WINNERS

A-OK CHEF SALAD SANDWICH
First Place District Winner

* 1   1 to 1 1/2-lb. round loaf French bread
* 3/4 c. creamy Italian dressing
* 2 c. spinach leaves
* 1/2 lb. ham, thinly sliced
* 1/2 sm. onion, thinly sliced
* 1/4 lb. Monterey Jack cheese, sliced
* 1/2 lb. turkey, thinly sliced
* 1 sm. tomato, sliced
* 1/4 lb. Colby cheese, sliced

Slice . . . . bread into 3 layers.
Spread . . . . . cut sides with dressing.
Place . . . . spinach, ham, onion and Monterey Jack cheese on bottom layer; cover with center bread slice.
Layer . . . . . . spinach, turkey, tomato and Colby cheese on top.

Place . . . . top slice on sandwich.
Yields . . . . . . 6 servings.

Andrea Leatherwood, Colbert
District II, Division I

GOOD-FOR-YOUR-EYES PIE
First Place District Winner

* 1 1/4 c. mashed cooked carrots
* 3/4 c. packed brown sugar
* 1 c. evaporated milk
1/2 tsp. vanilla extract
* 2 eggs, well beaten
1 tsp. cinnamon
1/2 tsp. ginger
1/4 tsp. each nutmeg, salt
* 1 tsp. flour
* 1 unbaked 9-in. pie shell

Combine . . . . carrots, brown sugar, evaporated milk, vanilla and eggs in bowl.
Mix . . . . cinnamon, ginger, nutmeg, salt and flour in small bowl.
Add . . . . to carrot mixture, mixing well.
Pour . . . . into pie shell.
Bake . . . . in preheated 425-degree oven for 40 to 45 minutes or until set.
Garnish . . . . . with whipped topping and pecan halves.

Karen Carter, Colbert
District II, Division II

Sub-District Winners

SAVORY CHICKEN WITH CHEESE (POLLO SABROSO CON QUESO)
Sub-District Winner

* 1   3-lb. chicken, cooked, boned
* 1 lb. Cheddar cheese, grated
* 1 med. onion, chopped
* 1 can Ro-Tel
* 2 cans cream of chicken soup
1 tsp. each garlic salt, chili powder
* 10 flour tortillas
* Chicken broth

*Oklahoma Agricultural Products

14

Cut . . . . chicken into bite-sized pieces.
Mix . . . . with half the cheese and remaining ingredients except tortillas and broth.
Dip . . . . tortillas in broth.
Layer . . . . . . 5 tortillas and half the chicken mixture in greased 9 x 13-inch baking dish.
Repeat . . . . layers with remaining ingredients; top with remaining cheese.
Bake . . . . covered, at 350 degrees for 35 minutes.
Yields . . . . . . 8 servings.

Robin George, Dickson
District I, Division I

CHERRY-PECAN BREAD
Sub-District Winner

3/4 c. sugar
* 1/2 c. butter, softened
* 2 eggs
1 tsp. almond extract
* 2 c. flour
1 tsp. soda
1/2 tsp. salt
* 1 c. buttermilk
* 1 c. chopped pecans
1 10-oz. jar maraschino cherries, drained, chopped

Cream . . . . . . sugar, butter, eggs and flavoring in mixer bowl.
Add . . . . mixture of dry ingredients and buttermilk alternately, beating until blended after each addition.
Fold . . . . in pecans and cherries.
Pour . . . . into greased loaf pan.
Bake . . . . at 350 degrees for 55 to 60 minutes or until bread tests done.
Remove . . . . from pan to cool.

Kim Harvey, Marietta
District I, Division II

PARSLEY-CHEESE BISCUITS
Sub-District Winner

* 2 c. flour, sifted
1/2 tsp. cream of tartar
1/2 tsp. salt
2 tbsp. sugar
4 tsp. baking powder
* 1/2 c. grated Cheddar cheese
1/2 tsp. parsley flakes
* 1/2 c. shortening
* 1 egg, beaten
* 2/3 c. milk

Sift . . . . first 5 dry ingredients into bowl.
Stir . . . . in cheese and parsley.
Cut . . . . in shortening until crumbly.
Add . . . . mixture of egg and milk, mixing until just moistened.
Knead . . . . . . 10 to 12 strokes on floured surface; roll 1 inch thick.
Cut . . . . out with floured biscuit cutter; place on baking sheet.
Bake . . . . at 450 degrees for 12 to 15 minutes or until brown.
Yields . . . . . . 1 dozen.

Donna Wilson, Haworth
District III, Division I

CHICKEN PEPPERED BALLS
Sub-District Winner

* 2 lg. green peppers
* 1 c. chopped cooked chicken breast
Pinch of onion salt
2 tbsp. lemon juice
* 2 hard-boiled eggs, chopped
* 2 tbsp. pimento
* 1/4 c. sweet relish
* 1/4 c. mayonnaise
Dash of paprika
* 2 tomatoes, sliced
* 6 radishes
Sprigs of parsley

Remove . . . . tops and seeds from green peppers; rinse and drain.
Combine . . . . chicken, onion salt, lemon juice, eggs, pimento, relish and mayonnaise in bowl, mixing well.
Spoon . . . . . . into green peppers; sprinkle with paprika.
Garnish . . . . . with tomatoes, radishes and sprigs of parsley.
Serve . . . . with crackers.
Yields . . . . . . 2 servings.

Cindy Edmondson, Idabel
District III, Division II

*Oklahoma Agricultural Products

Cook-Off Recipes

JANA'S SURPRISE LOAF
Sub-District Winner

* * 2 eggs
* * 1 c. milk
* * 2/3 c. dry bread crumbs
* * 2 lb. ground beef
* * 1/4 c. chopped onion
* 1 tsp. salt
* 1/2 tsp. garlic salt
* 1/2 tsp. dry mustard
* 1/4 tsp. pepper
* 2 tsp. Worcestershire sauce
* * 1 c. baking mix
* * 4 slices American cheese

Combine . . . . eggs, milk, bread crumbs, ground beef, onion, salt, garlic salt, mustard, pepper and Worcestershire sauce in bowl, mixing well.

Shape . . . . . . into 5 x 8-inch loaf in shallow baking dish.

Bake . . . . at 375 degrees for 1 hour; drain.

Mix . . . . baking mix and 1/4 cup water in bowl.

Beat . . . . 20 strokes.

Shape . . . . . . into ball on floured surface; knead 5 times.

Roll . . . . into 12-inch circle; cut into 4 wedges.

Arrange . . . . . cheese slices and dough quarters on loaf; prick dough with fork.

Bake . . . . at 375 degrees for 15 minutes.

Yields . . . . . . 6-8 servings.

Jana Cook, Wilburton
District IV, Division I

TURKEY AND WILD RICE CASSEROLE
Sub-District Winner

* * 1/2 c. chopped onion
* 1/2 c. sliced celery
* * 1/4 c. margarine
* * 1/4 c. flour
* 1 chicken bouillon cube
* * 1 1/2 c. half and half
* * 1   4 1/2-oz. jar mushrooms
* * 3 c. chopped cooked turkey
* 1/2 c. wild rice
* 1/2 c. rice
* 1 tbsp. chopped pimento
* 1 tbsp. parsley flakes
* 1 tsp. salt
* 1/8 tsp. white pepper
* 1/2 c. sliced almonds

Saute . . . . . . onion and celery in margarine in saucepan until tender.

Blend . . . . . . in flour.

Stir . . . . in bouillon dissolved in 1 cup water, half and half and liquid from mushrooms.

Cook . . . . for 1 minute or until thickened, stirring constantly.

Add . . . . mushrooms and remaining ingredients except almonds, mixing well.

Spoon . . . . . . into 2-quart casserole.

Bake . . . . at 350 degrees for 45 minutes.

Sprinkle . . . . almonds over casserole.

Bake . . . . for 15 minutes longer.

Yields . . . . . . 4 servings.

Kim Cecil, Wilburton
District IV, Division II

PEANUT BUTTER AND HONEY CAKE
Sub-District Winner

* * 1 pkg. yellow cake mix
* 1   3-oz. package vanilla instant pudding mix
* * 3/4 c. oil

*Oklahoma Agricultural Products

16

* 4 eggs
* 1/3 c. peanut butter
* 1/3 c. honey

Combine .... first 4 ingredients and 1/2 cup water in mixer bowl.
Beat .... for 2 minutes.
Pour .... 1/3 of the batter into greased bundt pan.
Mix .... peanut butter and honey in bowl.
Spoon ...... half the mixture over batter.
Repeat ..... layers with remaining ingredients, ending with batter.
Bake .... at 350 degrees for 45 to 55 minutes or until cake tests done.
Cool .... in pan for 10 minutes.
Serve .... warm or cool.

Sally Speed, Latta
District V, Division I

SAUSAGE CAKE
Sub-District Winner

1 c. raisins
2 c. sugar
* 1 lb. sausage, softened
* 2 eggs
1 tsp. each cloves, cinnamon, nutmeg, allspice
1 tsp. each baking powder, soda
1/2 tsp. salt
* 2 1/2 c. flour
* 1 c. buttermilk
* 1 c. nuts
* 1 3-oz. package cream cheese, softened
* 1/4 c. butter, softened
1 tsp. vanilla extract
2 c. sifted confectioners' sugar

Cover ...... raisins with 1 1/2 cups boiling water; set aside.
Cream ...... sugar and sausage in bowl; beat in eggs.
Add .... sifted dry ingredients alternately with buttermilk, mixing well after each addition.
Fold .... in drained raisins and nuts.
Pour .... into greased tube pan.
Bake .... at 350 degrees for 60 to 70 minutes or until cake tests done.

Beat .... cream cheese, butter and vanilla in mixer bowl until fluffy.
Add .... confectioners' sugar gradually, beating until smooth.
Spread ..... over cooled cake.

Julie Thomas, Allen
District V, Division II

NORTHEAST DISTRICT WINNERS

BEEF-BISCUIT ROLL
First Place District Winner

* 1 1/2 lb. ground beef
* 1 med. onion, chopped
* 1 16-oz. can stewed tomatoes, drained
* 1/2 c. catsup
1 tbsp. chili powder
* 1 12-biscuit recipe biscuit dough
* American cheese, grated
* 1 c. milk, scalded
2 tbsp. cornstarch
Salt and pepper to taste

Brown ...... ground beef with onion in skillet, stirring until crumbly; drain.
Stir .... in tomatoes, catsup and chili powder.
Bring .... to a boil; cool.
Roll .... biscuit dough into 1/2 inch thick rectangle on floured surface.
Spoon ...... ground beef mixture onto center; fold dough to enclose filling, sealing seams.
Place .... on 9 x 13-inch baking dish.
Bake .... at 375 degrees for 18 to 20 minutes or until golden.
Stir .... cheese into milk gradually until melted.
Blend ...... cornstarch with 1/3 cup water.
Stir .... into cheese mixture gradually.
Cook .... until thick, stirring constantly.
Season ..... with salt and pepper.
Serve .... sauce over slices of beef roll.

Tammy Keeton, Bristow
District I, Division I

*Oklahoma Agricultural Products

17

Cook-Off Recipes

BEEF AND BROCCOLI ESCONDIDO
First Place District Winner

* 1 10-oz. package frozen broccoli
* 2 lb. lean ground beef
* 2 eggs
* 3/4 c. soft bread crumbs
* 1/4 c. catsup
* 1/4 c. milk
  1/2 tsp. pepper
  1/4 tsp. oregano
  1/2 tsp. Worcestershire sauce
  2 1/2 tsp. salt
* 1 3-oz. package luncheon meat
  1 lb. peeled potatoes, cooked, drained
  1 egg yolk
  2 tbsp. melted butter
* 3 3 x 3-in. slices Mozzarella cheese, cut diagonally

Separate .... broccoli under cold running water; drain.
Mix .... ground beef with next 7 ingredients and 1/2 teaspoon salt in bowl.
Pat .... into 10 x 12-inch rectangle on foil.
Spread ..... broccoli over rectangle to within 1/2 inch of edges.
Sprinkle .... with 1 teaspoon salt.
Arrange ..... luncheon meat over top.
Roll .... as for jelly roll from short side, sealing seam and ends.
Place .... on rack in shallow pan.
Bake .... at 350 degrees for 1 hour.
Mash .... potatoes with 1 teaspoon salt, egg yolk and butter.
Pipe ...... around meat roll.
Bake .... for 20 minutes longer.
Arrange ..... overlapping cheese slices on roll.
Bake .... for 1 minute longer or until cheese melts.
Yields ...... 8 servings.

Galien McClellan, Sapulpa
District I, Division II

Sub-District Winners

LAORA SPECIAL
Sub-District Winner

* 2 slices bacon, cut into 1-in. pieces
* 3 cloves of garlic, mashed
* 1/2 lb. round steak, thinly sliced
* 3 tbsp. soy sauce
* 5 green onions, chopped
* 1 med. green pepper, cut into strips
* 6 lg. fresh mushrooms, sliced
* 1 med. cucumber, cut into strips
* 1 tomato, sliced
  Salt and garlic salt to taste
* Rice, cooked
  Chow mein noodles
* Cherry tomatoes

Stir-fry ..... bacon in skillet until nearly crisp.
Cook .... garlic with bacon in pan drippings for 1 minute.
Add .... steak, soy sauce and 2 tablespoons water.
Cook .... until nearly tender.
Stir .... in next 5 vegetables.
Cook .... until tender-crisp.
Season ..... with salt and garlic salt.
Serve .... over rice, garnished with chow mein noodles and cherry tomatoes.

Catrina Wallace, Muldrow
District II, Division I

PREACHER'S MEAL-IN-ONE
Sub-District Winner

* 2 lb. ground beef
* 2/3 c. chopped onion
* 2/3 c. chopped green pepper
* 1 tbsp. shortening
  1/2 tsp. salt
  Pepper to taste
  2 tsp. chili powder
* 3 lg. white potatoes, thinly sliced
  2/3 c. rice
* 2 16-oz. cans tomatoes
  1 can Manwich
  2/3 c. catsup
* American cheese, sliced

Brown ...... ground beef, onion and green pepper in shortening in skillet, stirring frequently.
Season ..... with salt, pepper and chili powder.
Layer ...... potatoes, ground beef mixture, rice, tomatoes and Manwich in casserole.

*Oklahoma Agricultural Products

Blend ...... catsup with 2/3 cup water.
Pour .... over top.
Bake .... at 350 degrees for 45 to 60 minutes or until potatoes and rice are tender.
Top .... with cheese.
Bake .... until cheese melts.

Michelle Galloway, Ft. Gibson
District II, Division II

WEST DISTRICT WINNERS

CHEESE BALL
Second Place State Winner

* *2 8-oz. packages cream cheese, softened*
* *1/4 c. chopped green pepper*
* *2 tbsp. minced onion*
  1 8-oz. can crushed pineapple, drained
* *1/4 c. ground ham*
* *1 c. chopped pecans*

Mix .... all ingredients except pecans in bowl.
Chill .... for 15 minutes.
Shape ...... into ball.
Roll .... in pecans to coat.
Store .... in refrigerator until ready to use.
Yields ...... 15 servings.

Connie Jo Bierig, Okeene
District IV, Division I

A-OK PEANUT CASSEROLE
Second Place State Winner

* *1 lb. ground beef*
* *1 c. chopped onion*
* *Green pepper*
* *2 tbsp. peanut oil*
  2 tsp. salt
  1/2 tsp. pepper
* *1/2 c. evaporated milk*
  1 tbsp. Worcestershire sauce
* *4 to 5 oz. shell macaroni, cooked*
* *1 c. grated Cheddar cheese*
* *3/4 c. chopped roasted peanuts*
* *1/8 tsp. red pepper*

Brown ...... ground beef with onion and 1/2 cup chopped green pepper in oil in skillet.
Stir .... in next 5 ingredients and 1/2 cup cheese.
Simmer ..... covered, for 20 minutes, stirring occasionally.
Pour .... into greased 1 1/2-quart casserole.
Top .... with peanuts, 1/2 cup cheese, green pepper rings and red pepper.
Bake .... at 350 degrees for 30 minutes.
Yields ...... 4-5 servings.

Donna Thornburg, Alex
District II, Division II

*Oklahoma Agricultural Products

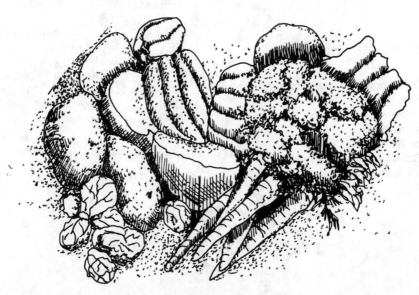

Cook-Off Recipes

Sub-District Winners

OKLAHOMA VEGETABLE-CHEESE BREAD
Sub-District Winner

* 4 c. flour
  2 tbsp. baking powder
  2 tsp. salt
* 1/2 c. margarine
* 1 1/2 c. milk
* 1 c. chopped green peppers
* 1 c. chopped onion
* 1 c. butter
* 1/2 lb. bacon, crisp-fried, crumbled
* 1/2 c. Parmesan cheese
* 1 c. shredded Cheddar cheese

Mix . . . . first 3 dry ingredients in bowl.

Cut . . . . in margarine until crumbly.

Add . . . . enough milk to make soft dough, mixing well.

Knead . . . . . . lightly 20 to 25 times on floured surface; cover and set aside.

Saute . . . . . . green pepper and onion in butter in skillet.

Roll . . . . biscuit dough 3/4 inch thick; cut into 1 x 1 1/4-inch pieces.

Stir . . . . into skillet with bacon and cheeses, coating well.

Spoon . . . . . . into greased bundt pan.

Bake . . . . at 350 degrees for 40 minutes.

Amber Cash, Tuttle
District II, Division I

BAKED CHICKEN DIVAN
Sub-District Winner

* 2   10-oz. packages frozen broccoli spears, cooked
* 2 cans cream of chicken soup
  1 tbsp. nutmeg
  2 tbsp. Worcestershire sauce
* 1 c. Parmesan cheese
* 4 lg. chicken breasts, cooked, sliced
* 3/4 c. whipping cream, whipped
* 1/3 c. mayonnaise

Arrange . . . . . drained broccoli spears in 8 x 12-inch shallow baking dish.

Blend . . . . . . soup, nutmeg and Worcestershire sauce in small bowl.

Layer . . . . . . half the soup mixture, 1/3 cup cheese, chicken, remaining soup mixture and 1/3 cup cheese over broccoli.

Bake . . . . at 400 degrees for 25 minutes.

Fold . . . . whipped cream into mayonnaise.

Spread . . . . . over layers.

Top . . . . with 1/3 cup cheese.

Broil . . . . for 2 to 3 minutes or until golden.

Debbie Eischen, Okarche
District IV, Division II

NORTH DISTRICT WINNERS

AMY'S FANTASTIC FUDGE
First Place State Winner

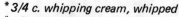

* 1 8-oz. package process cheese
* 1 c. butter
  5 1/2 c. confectioners' sugar
  3/4 c. cocoa
  1 tbsp. vanilla extract
* 1/2 c. chopped pecans

Melt . . . . cheese and butter in saucepan; mix well.

Stir . . . . in confectioners' sugar, cocoa and vanilla.

Beat . . . . at medium speed of electric mixer; stir in pecans.

Spread . . . . . in buttered 7 1/2 x 12-inch pan.

Chill . . . . for 2 hours or until firm.

Yields . . . . . . 3 1/4 pounds.

Amy Hajek, Medford
District III, Division II

*Oklahoma Agricultural Products

CHICKEN AND DRESSING DINNER DELUXE
First Place District Winner

* *1   2 to 3-lb. fryer, cooked, boned
* *1   16-oz. package frozen chopped broccoli, thawed, drained
* *1   16-oz. package frozen cauliflower, thawed, drained
* *2 cans cream of potato soup
* *3/4 c. milk
* *1 1/2 c. melted process cheese
* *1   6-oz. box chicken-flavored stuffing mix
* *1 3/4 c. chicken broth
* *1/2 c. bread crumbs
* *1/4 c. butter

Layer ...... chicken, broccoli and cauliflower in 9 x 13-inch baking dish sprayed with cooking spray.

Pour .... mixture of soup and milk over top.

Spread ..... cheese over soup.

Prepare ..... stuffing mix according to package directions using broth; spread over cheese.

Sprinkle .... bread crumbs over stuffing; dot with butter.

Bake .... at 375 degrees for 45 minutes.

Janetta Gay Berry, Chandler
District IV, Division I

Sub-District Winners

LEAH'S MICROWAVE SURPRISE
Sub-District Winner

* *4 eggs
* *2 c. half and half
* *1/2 tomato, sliced
* *1 c. cooked chopped broccoli
* *1/4 c. thinly sliced onion
* *1 c. shredded mozzarella cheese
* *5 slices crisp-fried bacon, crumbled
* *1 c. shredded Cheddar cheese

Blend ...... eggs and half and half in bowl.

Stir .... in tomato, broccoli and onion.

Sprinkle .... mozzarella cheese and a small amount of bacon in quiche pan.

Pour .... in egg mixture; sprinkle remaining bacon on top.

Top .... with Cheddar cheese.

Microwave .. for 20 minutes or until firm, turning every 2 1/2 minutes.

Yields ...... 6 servings.

Leah Gayler, Boise City
District I, Division I

FOUR TIMES FOUR CASSEROLE
Sub-District Winner

* *1/2 lb. ground beef
* *1/2 lb. ground pork
* *3/4 c. finely chopped onion
  2 med. cloves of garlic, finely chopped
* *1   10-oz. can tomato sauce
  1 tsp. sweet basil
  1/2 tsp. each oregano, salt
* *1   10-oz. package frozen chopped spinach, thawed, drained
* *1 pt. small curd cottage cheese, drained
* *2 tbsp. Parmesan cheese
* *1 egg, slightly beaten
* *1/2 lb. Swiss cheese, grated
* *4 c. cooked curly macaroni

Brown ...... ground beef and pork in skillet; add onion and garlic.

Cook .... until onion is tender; add tomato sauce and seasonings.

Simmer ..... for 5 minutes.

Combine .... spinach, cottage cheese, Parmesan cheese and egg in small bowl.

Reserve ..... 1/2 cup Swiss cheese.

Layer ...... half the macaroni, Swiss cheese and meat sauce in greased 2-quart baking dish.

Cover ...... with spinach mixture.

Layer ...... remaining macaroni, Swiss cheese and meat sauce over top.

Bake .... at 375 degrees for 40 minutes or until bubbly.

Sprinkle .... reserved 1/2 cup Swiss cheese over top.

Bake .... for 3 to 4 minutes longer or until cheese melts.

Let .... stand for several minutes before serving.

Yields ...... 8-10 servings.

Tangee Hughes, Boise City
District I, Division II

*Oklahoma Agricultural Products

21

Cook-Off Recipes

NUTTY WHEAT MUFFINS
Sub-District Winner

　　1/2 c. sugar
　　1 c. packed brown sugar
　* 1/2 c. wheat germ
　* 1/2 c. oil
　　1 tbsp. cinnamon
　* 1 c. buttermilk
　　1 tsp. soda
　* 1 1/2 c. flour
　* 1/2 c. chopped pecans

Combine . . . . sugars, wheat germ, oil and cinnamon in bowl; mix well.
Reserve . . . . . 1/2 cup for topping.
Stir . . . . in mixture of buttermilk and soda; blend in flour.
Spoon . . . . . . into greased muffin cups.
Add . . . . pecans to reserved sugar mixture; sprinkle over batter.
Bake . . . . at 400 degrees for 20 to 25 minutes or until muffins test done.

Sharon Roberts, Alva
District II, Division I

CAREFREE CASSEROLE
Sub-District Winner

　* 1 c. canned chicken
　　1 can cream of celery soup
　* 1/2 c. sliced canned mushrooms
　* 1 c. shredded Cheddar cheese
　　2 c. cooked rice
　* 1/2 c. crushed potato chips
　* 1 c. shredded mozzarella cheese

Combine . . . . chicken, soup, mushrooms and Cheddar cheese in 2-quart casserole.
Add . . . . rice, mixing well.
Sprinkle . . . . with potato chips and mozzarella cheese.
Bake . . . . at 350 degrees for 15 to 20 minutes or until cheese melts.
Yields . . . . . . 6 servings.

Sherri Olson, Waynoka
District II, Division II

POTATO PILLOWS
Sub-District Winner

　* 2 med. red potatoes, cooked, peeled, quartered
　* 1/4 lb. American cheese, grated
　　1/4 tsp. pepper
　　Salt
　* 2 to 2 1/2 c. flour
　* 4 egg yolks
　　1 tsp. tapioca
　* 1 lg. onion, thinly sliced
　* 4 tbsp. margarine
　* Sour cream (opt.)

Mash . . . . hot potatoes with cheese, pepper and salt to taste in bowl; set aside.
Combine . . . . 1 cup flour, egg yolks, tapioca, 1 teaspoon salt and 1 cup water in bowl, mixing well.
Stir . . . . in enough remaining flour to make stiff dough.
Roll . . . . 1/8 inch thick on floured surface; cut into 2-inch squares.
Spoon . . . . . . 1 tablespoon potato mixture onto half the squares; top with remaining dough, sealing edges.
Cook . . . . in simmering water in saucepan for 4 to 6 minutes or until firm; remove with slotted spoon.
Saute . . . . . . onion in 2 tablespoons margarine in skillet; drain on paper towel.
Brown . . . . . . pillows in remaining 2 tablespoons margarine and pan drippings; drain on paper towel.
Serve . . . . with onion and sour cream.
Yields . . . . . . 4-6 servings.

Crystal Shellhammer, Wakita
District III, Division I

PORTUGUESE CHICKEN WITH POTATOES
Sub-District Winner

　* 2 chicken breasts, split
　* 2 med. potatoes, cut in half lengthwise
　* 1/2 c. catsup
　　1 tsp. vinegar
　　1/2 tsp. each paprika, parsley flakes
　　1/4 tsp. each salt, cinnamon

*Oklahoma Agricultural Products

Arrange . . . . . chicken breasts and potatoes in 9 x 13-inch baking dish.
Combine . . . . catsup, vinegar, 1/4 cup water and seasonings in bowl.
Pour . . . . over chicken and potatoes.
Bake . . . . covered, at 350 degrees for 45 minutes.
Bake . . . . uncovered, for 15 minutes longer.
Yields . . . . . . 4 servings.

Kim Kay, Drummond
District III, Division II

LASAGNA DELICIOSO
Sub-District Winner

  * 2 1/4 lb. ground chuck
  * 1 sm. onion
  * 1 sm. green pepper
  1 stalk celery
  2 cloves of garlic
  1 bay leaf
  * 4 c. tomato sauce
  * 1 8-oz. can tomato paste
  1 tsp. oregano
  1/2 tsp. pepper
  * 1 16-oz. package lasagna noodles, cooked
  * 2 c. drained cottage cheese
  * 1 c. Parmesan cheese
  * 1 lb. mozzarella cheese, grated

Brown . . . . . . ground chuck in skillet, stirring until crumbly; drain.
Place . . . . vegetables, garlic and bay leaf in blender container; grind coarsely.
Add . . . . to skillet with tomato sauce, paste and seasonings.
Simmer . . . . . for 1 hour, stirring occasionally.
Spread . . . . . a small amount of sauce in 9 x 12-inch baking dish.
Layer . . . . . . 3 noodles, sauce, cottage cheese, Parmesan and mozzarella cheese alternately in prepared dish until all ingredients are used.
Bake . . . . at 325 degrees for 30 minutes.
Let . . . . stand for 20 minutes before serving.

Robyn Shea Wonn, Chandler
District IV, Division II

POOR BOY STEW
Sub-District Winner

  * 1 lg. onion, chopped
  * 5 med. potatoes, chopped
  * 8 carrots, sliced
  * 3 med. tomatoes, peeled
  * 1 1/2 lb. lean ground beef
  6 beef bouillon cubes
  Dash of pepper
  Pinch of salt

Place . . . . onion, potatoes and carrots in large saucepan filled 2/3 full with water.
Simmer . . . . . for 30 minutes. Add tomatoes.
Bring . . . . to a boil.
Add . . . . remaining ingredients.
Simmer . . . . . for 30 to 45 minutes or until vegetables are tender.

Amber Boyles, Lenapah
District V, Division I

KIM'S KRAZY ONE-POT DINNER KREATION
Sub-District Winner

  ' * 1 lb. ground beef
  * 1 c. chopped onion
  * 1 10-oz. can corn
  * 1 c. cooked brown beans
  * 1 10-oz. can pork and beans
  1/4 c. packed brown sugar
  * 1 c. chopped potatoes
  1/8 tsp. each salt, pepper
  1/2 tsp. garlic salt
  * 1 c. catsup
  * 1 c. tomato juice
  1 tbsp. liquid smoke
  3 tbsp. white vinegar

Brown . . . . . . ground beef and onion in skillet; drain.
Place . . . . in 6-quart Crock-Pot.
Add . . . . remaining ingredients 1 at a time, mixing well after each addition.
Cook . . . . on Low for 1 1/2 to 2 hours or to desired consistency.
Yields . . . . . . 12 servings.

Kim James, Lenapah
District V, Division I

*Oklahoma Agricultural Products

Cook-Off Recipes

CRAFTY CRESCENT LASAGNA
Sub-District Winner

* *1/2 lb. sausage
* *1/2 lb. ground beef
* *3/4 c. chopped onion
* *1   6-oz. can tomato paste
* 1/2 tsp. minced garlic
* 1 tbsp. parsley flakes
* 1/2 tsp. each basil, oregano, salt
* Dash of pepper
* *1 c. creamed cottage cheese
* *1 egg
* *1/4 c. Parmesan cheese
* *2 cans refrigerator crescent dinner rolls
* *1 c. shredded mozzarella cheese
* *1 tbsp. milk
* 1 tbsp. sesame seed

Brown . . . . . . sausage and ground beef in skillet, stirring until crumbly; drain.
Add . . . . onion, tomato paste and seasonings.
Simmer . . . . . for 5 minutes.
Mix . . . . cottage cheese, egg and Parmesan cheese in bowl.
Unroll . . . . . . dough; place on cookie sheet, overlapping edges.
Seal . . . . perforations and edges.
Spread . . . . . half the meat mixture down center.
Layer . . . . . . cheese mixture and remaining meat mixture over top.
Top . . . . with mozzarella cheese.
Fold . . . . in edges to enclose filling.
Brush . . . . . . with milk; sprinkle with sesame seed.
Bake . . . . at 375 degrees for 20 to 25 minutes or until deep golden brown.
Yields . . . . . . 6-8 servings.

Kelli McEldonny, Grove
District VI, Division I

CHICKEN EGG ROLLS
Sub-District Winner

* *1 med. chicken, cooked, boned, chopped
* *1 med. head cabbage, shredded
* *2 carrots, chopped
* 2 stalks celery, chopped
* *1/2 onion, chopped
* 1 can water chestnuts, chopped
* *1 can mushrooms chopped

* *1/2 c. chicken broth
* *1/2 c. soy sauce
* *Oil
* 1 tsp. each salt, pepper
* *1 pkg. egg roll wrappers

Place . . . . chicken in saucepan.
Add . . . . next 6 vegetables.
Stir . . . . in broth, soy sauce, 3 tablespoons oil, salt and pepper.
Simmer . . . . . until vegetables are tender, stirring constantly; cool.
Spoon . . . . . . onto egg roll wrappers.
Fold . . . . to enclose filling; seal.
Deep-fry . . . . at 350 degrees for 3 minutes or until golden brown; cool.

Kim Haynes, Fairland
District VI, Division II

ORIENTAL BEEF
Sub-District Winner

* *1 1/2 lb. boneless steak, cubed
* *1/2 c. flour
* 1 tsp. salt
* 1/2 tsp. pepper
* *1/2 c. minced onion
* *2 tbsp. oil
* 1 c. red cooking wine
* *1   4 1/2-oz. can mushroom caps
* 1   8-oz. can bamboo shoots
* *2 tbsp. Parmesan cheese
* 1/4 c. slivered almonds
* 1 1/2 c. minute rice, cooked
* *1/4 c. chopped green peppers

Coat . . . . steak with mixture of flour, salt and pepper.
Brown . . . . . . with onion in oil in skillet over medium heat.
Stir . . . . in 1/2 cup water and wine.
Simmer . . . . . covered, for 1 hour or until steak is tender.
Add . . . . mushrooms, bamboo shoots, Parmesan cheese and almonds.
Simmer . . . . . for 15 minutes.
Serve . . . . . . over rice mixed with green pepper.
Yields . . . . . . 6-8 servings.

Debi McBride, Adair
District VII, Division I

*Oklahoma Agricultural Products

Appetizers & Beverages

PIQUANT CHEESE LOG, recipe on page 27. CHILI-YOGURT DIP, RED BEAN DIP, recipes on page 28.

Appetizers

CANADIAN CHEESE SOUP

1/2 c. each finely chopped onion,
    carrots, celery
1/4 c. butter
1/4 c. flour
1 1/2 tbsp. cornstarch
1 qt. chicken stock
1 qt. milk
1/8 tsp. soda
1 c. grated Cheddar cheese
Salt and pepper to taste
2 tbsp. parsley

Saute . . . . . . onion, carrots and celery in butter in stock pot.
Blend . . . . . . in flour and cornstarch.
Cook . . . . until bubbly.
Add . . . . chicken stock and milk gradually.
Cook . . . . . . until thickened, stirring constantly.
Stir . . . . in soda, cheese and seasonings.
Cook . . . . over low heat until cheese melts, stirring constantly.
Add . . . . parsley.
Yields . . . . . . 4-6 servings.

Amy Fogleman
Locust Grove H. S., Locust Grove

CREAM CHEESE BALL

1 8-oz. package cream cheese, softened
3 tbsp. sour cream
1 tsp. chopped onion
1 tbsp. chives
1 sm. jar chipped beef
1/2 tsp. seasoning salt

Combine . . . . cream cheese and remaining ingredients in bowl, mixing well.
Shape . . . . . . into ball.
Chill . . . . until firm.

Karen Durkee
Waynoka H. S., Waynoka

MAKE-AHEAD CHEESE LOGS

1 lb. Velveeta cheese, softened
1 8-oz. package cream cheese, softened
Worcestershire sauce to taste
Garlic salt to taste
1 c. chopped pecans
Chili powder

Blend . . . . . . first 4 ingredients in bowl.
Stir . . . . in pecans.
Shape . . . . . . into logs.
Roll . . . . in chili powder to coat; wrap.
Freeze . . . . . . until firm.
Thaw . . . . . . slightly before slicing.

Winona Vaughn
Dewar H. S., Henryetta

CHILI CHEESE LOGS

1/2 lb. process American cheese, grated
1 8-oz. package cream cheese, softened
1/2 tsp. each salt, garlic salt
1/2 tsp. instant minced onion
1/8 tsp. red pepper
2 tsp. lemon juice
3/4 c. finely chopped nuts
3 tbsp. chili powder

Mix . . . . all ingredients except chili powder in bowl.
Shape . . . . . . into 1-inch thick logs.
Roll . . . . in chili powder.
Serve . . . . with crackers.

Tina Cantwell
Checotah H. S., Checotah

MOMMA'S CHEESE BALL

4 3-oz. packages cream cheese, softened
6 oz. Roquefort cheese, crumbled
1 10-oz. jar Old English cheese spread
2 tbsp. chopped onion
1 tsp. Worcestershire sauce
1 c. chopped pecans
Parsley

Mix . . . . cheeses with onion and Worcestershire sauce in bowl.
Chill . . . . for 1 hour.
Shape . . . . . . into ball.
Roll . . . . in pecans and parsley.
Serve . . . . with crackers.

Wendy Freed
Moore H. S., Moore

HAM-CHEESE BALL

2 8-oz. packages cream cheese, softened
1/2 lb. sharp cheese, shredded
2 tsp. grated onion
2 tsp. Worcestershire sauce
1 tsp. lemon juice

1 tsp. mustard
1/2 tsp. paprika
1/3 tsp. salt
1 2 1/4-oz. can deviled ham
2 tbsp. parsley flakes
2 tbsp. chopped pimento
2/3 c. chopped pecans

Mix . . . . cream cheese, sharp cheese and onion in bowl.
Add . . . . . . remaining ingredients except pecans, mixing well.
Chill . . . . for several minutes or until nearly firm.
Shape . . . . . . into ball; roll in pecans.
Chill . . . . wrapped in foil, overnight.
Sprinkle . . . . with additional paprika. Chili powder, toasted sesame seed or finely chopped dried beef may be substituted for pecans.

Ruth Lindsey
Westville Schools, Westville

PARTY CHEESE BALL

2 8-oz. packages cream cheese, softened
2 c. shredded Cheddar cheese
1 tbsp. chopped pimento
2 tbsp. chopped green onion
2 tsp. Worcestershire sauce
1 tsp. lemon juice
Dash each of salt, cayenne pepper,
    garlic powder
1 tbsp. chopped green pepper
Finely chopped pecans

Blend . . . . . . cream cheese and Cheddar cheese in bowl.
Add . . . . remaining ingredients except pecans, mixing well.
Shape . . . . . . into ball; roll in pecans.
Serve . . . . with crackers.

Wendy Been
Howe H. S., Howe

SALMON LOG

2 16-oz. cans salmon, drained, flaked
2 8-oz. packages cream cheese, softened
1/2 sm. onion, grated
2 tbsp. lemon juice
2 tsp. horseradish
2 tsp. liquid smoke

1/2 tsp. salt
Chopped pecans

Combine . . . . all ingredients except pecans in bowl, mixing well.
Chill . . . . for several hours.
Shape . . . . . . into logs; coat with pecans.
Serve . . . . with crackers.
Yields . . . . 2-4 logs.

Preston Balmain
FHA Recreation Leader, Westville Schools, Westville

PIQUANT CHEESE LOG

1 8-oz. package cream cheese, softened
2 oz. blue cheese, crumbled
2 tbsp. instant minced onion
2 tbsp. parsley flakes
1 tsp. garlic powder
1/3 c. chopped radishes
1/4 c. toasted sesame seed

Combine . . . . first 5 ingredients in mixer bowl, beating until well blended.
Stir . . . . in radishes.
Chill . . . . covered, for 1 hour.
Shape . . . . . . into log.
Roll . . . . in sesame seed; wrap in plastic wrap.
Store . . . . in refrigerator.
Let . . . . stand at room temperature for 15 minutes before serving.
Serve . . . . with toasted bread rounds or crackers.

Photograph for this recipe on page 25.

JEZEBEL SAUCE

1 18-oz. jar pineapple preserves
1 18-oz. jar apple jelly
1 sm. can dry mustard
1 5-oz. jar horseradish
1 tbsp. coarsely ground pepper
1 pkg. cream cheese, softened

Combine . . . . first 5 ingredients in bowl, mixing well.
Chill . . . . in refrigerator.
Pour . . . . over cream cheese.
Serve . . . . with crackers. May serve with beef, lamb, ham or pork.

Zelda Sue Flowers
Highland West Middle School, Moore

Appetizers

PIZZA FONDUE

1 c. chopped onion
1/2 lb. ground beef
2 tbsp. butter
1 tbsp. cornstarch
1 tsp. oregano
1/4 tsp. garlic salt
2 10 1/2-oz. cans pizza sauce
10 oz. Cheddar cheese, grated
1 c. grated mozzarella cheese

Brown . . . . . . onion and ground beef in butter in fondue pot over medium heat, stirring until ground beef in crumbly.
Blend . . . . . . cornstarch and seasonings with pizza sauce in bowl.
Stir . . . . into ground beef mixture.
Cook . . . . until thick, stirring constantly.
Add . . . . cheeses 1/3 at a time, mixing well after each addition.
Serve . . . . warm with garlic bread cubes, fresh vegetable dippers or toasted English muffin cubes.
Yields . . . . . . 10-12 servings.

Jennifer Walsh
Oklahoma State FHA President, Union City

BLACK-EYED PEA DIP

1 can black-eyed peas, drained
2 sticks margarine, melted
1 canned jalapeno pepper
1 1/2 tsp. jalapeno pepper juice
1 onion
1 clove of garlic
1 4-oz. package shredded Cheddar cheese
1 c. milk

Combine . . . . black-eyed peas and margarine in food processor container.
Process . . . . . until smooth.
Add . . . . next 4 ingredients.
Blend . . . . . . for 4 seconds.
Combine . . . . with cheese in saucepan.
Cook . . . . over low heat until cheese melts, stirring constantly.
Stir . . . . in milk.
Heat . . . . to serving temperature.
Serve . . . . with vegetables and corn chips.
Yields . . . . . . 2 1/4 cups.

Sonja Tyree, Adviser
Tomlinson Jr. H. S., Lawton

RED BEAN DIP

1 15-oz. can red kidney beans
1 tbsp. onion powder
1 tsp. oregano
1 tsp. garlic powder
1/2 tsp. salt
Dash of pepper
3 tbsp. oil
1 tbsp. sweet pickle relish

Drain . . . . . . beans, reserving 2 tablespoons liquid.
Reserve . . . . . 1/4 cup beans.
Combine . . . . remaining beans with reserved liquid and remaining ingredients in blender container.
Process . . . . . for 1 minute or until smooth.
Spoon . . . . . . into serving dish.
Chill . . . . covered, for 1 hour.
Garnish . . . . . with reserved beans and fresh vegetable sticks.

Photograph for this recipe on page 25.

CHILI-YOGURT DIP

1 c. yogurt
1/2 c. creamed cottage cheese
2 tsp. chili powder
1 tsp. each salt, onion powder
1/2 tsp. garlic powder
1/8 tsp. pepper
1/2 c. chopped cucumber
1/2 c. chopped tomato, drained

Combine . . . . all ingredients except cucumber and tomato in bowl, mixing well.
Stir . . . . in cucumber and tomato.
Chill . . . . covered, for 1 hour or longer.
Garnish . . . . . with additional chopped cucumber and cherry tomato.
Serve . . . . with fresh vegetable sticks or crackers.

Photograph for this recipe on page 25.

DIP FOR FRESH VEGETABLES

1 c. mayonnaise
1 8-oz. carton sour cream
2 tbsp. minced onion
1 lg. clove of garlic, minced
1 tsp. salt

1/2 tsp. freshly ground pepper
1/2 c. chopped parsley
1 tbsp. prepared Dijon mustard

Combine .... all ingredients in bowl, mixing well.
Chill .... for 2 to 3 hours.
Serve .... with fresh vegetables.
Yields ...... 2 1/2 cups.

Tammy Jones
Checotah H. S., Checotah

CREAMY ONION DIP

1 8-oz. carton sour cream
1/2 c. mayonnaise
2 tbsp. dry onion soup mix
2 tbsp. chopped parsley

Combine .... all ingredients in bowl, mixing well.
Chill .... in refrigerator.
Serve .... with assorted chips and crackers.
Yields ...... 1 1/2 cups.

Joann Collins
Moore H. S., Moore

DIETER'S CHIP DIP

1 16-oz. carton cottage cheese
1/4 c. mayonnaise
1/4 tsp. garlic salt
1/4 tsp. Worcestershire sauce

Combine .... cottage cheese, mayonnaise, garlic salt and Worcestershire sauce in blender container.
Process ..... until smooth.
Pour .... into serving bowl.
Serve .... with chips or fresh vegetables.

Robin Renee Johnson
Moore H. S., Moore

CREAM CHEESE-ROASTED PEPPER DIP

1 sm. green pepper
4 oz. cream cheese, softened
1/2 c. sour cream
1/4 c. thinly sliced onion
1 clove of garlic, thinly sliced
4 drops of hot pepper sauce
1/4 tsp. Worcestershire sauce

1 tbsp. finely chopped chives
Salt to taste
1 sweet red pepper

Prick .... green pepper with fork.
Broil .... green pepper until skin is charred, turning frequently.
Cool .... pepper in tightly closed paper bag.
Peel .... cooked pepper; cut in half, discarding seeds.
Chop .... finely.
Combine .... cream cheese and next 5 ingredients in blender container.
Process ..... until smooth.
Add .... chopped green pepper, chives and salt, mixing well.
Spoon ...... into hollowed-out red pepper.
Sprinkle .... with additional chopped green pepper.

Sheila Nightengale
Ringwood H. S., Ringwood

DILL DIP

1 c. mayonnaise
1 8-oz. carton sour cream
1 tsp. horseradish
1 tbsp. each dillweed, parsley
1 tbsp. instant minced onion
1/2 tsp. salt

Combine .... all ingredients in bowl, mixing well.
Chill .... for 24 hours or longer before serving.
Serve .... with fresh vegetables.

Denise Johnson
Barnsdall H. S., Barnsdall

TOFU DILLY DIP

1 8-oz. cake tofu, crumbled
4 tsp. dry mustard
1 tsp. basil
1 tsp. dillweed
3/4 tsp. salt

Blend ...... all ingredients with 1/3 cup water in bowl.
Serve .... with fresh vegetable dippers.
Yields ...... 1 1/2 cups.

Norita Adam
Okeene H. S., Okeene

Appetizers

VEGETABLE DIP

1 c. sour cream
1 pt. mayonnaise
1 tbsp. MSG
1 tsp. sugar
Seasoning salt and pepper to taste
1/2 to 1/3 tsp. garlic salt
1 tbsp. parsley flakes
1 tbsp. onion flakes
2 tbsp. Parmesan cheese
1 c. shredded mozzarella cheese

Blend . . . . . . first 4 ingredients and seasonings in bowl.
Stir . . . . in remaining ingredients.
Chill . . . . tightly covered, for 2 weeks or less.
Serve . . . . with fresh vegetables.
Yields . . . . . . 2 1/2 cups.

Charla Vaught
Wagoner H. S., Wagoner

LINDA'S SHRIMP DIP

1 can tomato soup
1 8-oz. package cream cheese, softened
1 env. unflavored gelatin
3/4 c. each finely chopped onion, celery
1 c. mayonnaise
1 can med. shrimp, drained

Heat . . . . soup in saucepan.
Add . . . . cream cheese, stirring until melted; cool.
Soften . . . . . . gelatin in 1/4 cup cold water.
Stir . . . . softened gelatin into hot soup until dissolved.
Mix . . . . in onion, celery, mayonnaise and shrimp.
Pour . . . . into 1-quart mold.
Chill . . . . until set.
Unmold . . . . onto serving plate.
Serve . . . . with crackers.
Yields . . . . . . 8 servings.

Linda Clinton
Eufaula H. S., Eufaula

GROUND BEEF DIP

1 lb. ground beef
1/2 c. chopped onion
1 clove of garlic
1 8-oz. can tomato sauce
1/4 c. catsup
3/4 tsp. oregano
2 tbsp. sugar
1 8-oz. package cream cheese, softened
1/3 c. Parmesan cheese

Brown . . . . . . ground beef, onion and garlic in skillet, stirring until ground beef is crumbly; drain.
Add . . . . remaining ingredients, mixing well.

Cindy Neptune
Barnsdall H. S., Barnsdall

CHIPPED BEEF DIP

1 sm. jar dried chipped beef
1 8-oz. carton sour cream
1 8-oz. package cream cheese, softened
Chopped green onions
1 green pepper, chopped

Combine . . . . all ingredients in bowl in order listed, mixing well.
Chill . . . . in refrigerator.

Wanda Baranski
Choctaw Jr. H. S., Choctaw

CHILI-CHEESE DIP

1 2-lb. package Velveeta cheese, cubed
1 16-oz. can chili
1 can Ro-Tel

Combine . . . . cheese, chili and Ro-Tel in medium saucepan, mixing well.
Heat . . . . until cheese melts, stirring constantly.
Serve . . . . with taco chips.
Yields . . . . . . 1 quart.

Andra L. Krien
Sulphur H. S., Sulphur

GUACAMOLE

2 avocados, mashed
1 med. onion, chopped
1 tbsp. lemon juice
1 tsp. salt
1/2 tsp. coarsely ground pepper
Garlic salt to taste
1 med. tomato, chopped

Combine .... avocados, onion, lemon juice and seasonings in bowl, mixing well.
Stir .... in tomato.
Chill .... covered, for 1 hour or longer.
Serve .... with tortilla chips.
Yields ...... 2 cups.

Doylene Heaton, Adviser
Leflore H. S., Leflore

JALAPENO DIP

1 lb. American cheese, grated
1 lb. Velveeta cheese, grated
1 qt. mayonnaise
1/2 c. jalapeno pepper juice
3 canned jalapeno peppers, ground

Combine .... cheeses, mayonnaise and pepper juice in mixer bowl.
Season ..... to taste with peppers.
Beat .... for 15 minutes.
Serve .... with fresh vegetables.
Yields ...... 2 1/2 quarts.

Judy Queen, Adviser
Braman H. S., Braman

EASY MEXICAN DIP

1 can bean dip
3 avocados, mashed
1 carton sour cream
1 c. grated Cheddar cheese
1 pkg. brick cheese, grated
1 c. chopped green onions
2 tomatoes, chopped
1 lg. package tortilla chips

Layer ...... first 7 ingredients in order listed in 9-inch pie plate.
Serve .... with tortilla chips

Kathy Masters
Silo H. S., Durant

HOT BEAN DIP WITH NACHOS

2 tbsp. chopped jalapeno peppers
2 cans refried beans
1 tsp. Worcestershire sauce
6 tbsp. melted margarine
Onion and garlic salt to taste

1/2 tsp. jalapeno pepper liquid
Nachos

Combine .... first 7 ingredients in saucepan.
Simmer ..... until heated through.
Serve .... with Nachos.

Nachos

Cut 10 tortillas into 4 pieces. Fry in oil in skillet until crisp; drain on paper towel. Arrange tortillas on rack in broiler pan. Top with 1/2 pound grated Cheddar cheese and 1 small can thinly sliced jalapeno peppers. Broil until cheese melts.

Tina Webb
Gould

PICANTE SAUCE

12 to 14 jalapeno peppers, finely chopped
1 lg. green pepper, finely chopped
3 lg. onions, finely chopped
2 16-oz. cans tomatoes, chopped
1 tsp. salt
1/2 c. vinegar
Garlic powder to taste

Combine .... all ingredients in saucepan.
Cook .... for 1 hour or until thick.
Pour .... into hot sterilized jars; seal.
Add .... to hot melted cheese dip, chili, tacos or burritos or serve as hot sauce over foods.
Yields ...... 3 pints.

Gary Stinebring, Sr.
Hennessey H. S., Hennessey

BLENDER SALSA

6 med. tomatoes, peeled
1/2 c. chopped green chilies
1/3 c. chopped onion
1 tsp. salt
3 jalapeno peppers
1 clove of garlic

Combine .... all ingredients in blender container.
Process ..... to desired consistency.
Freezes ..... well.
Yields ...... 2 cups.

Emily Lewis
Capitol Hill H. S., Oklahoma City

Appetizers

MEXICAN LAYERED SALAD APPETIZER

4 avocados, mashed
1 tsp. lemon juice
1 pt. sour cream
1 pkg. taco seasoning mix
1/2 c. mayonnaise
1 can bean dip
1 12-oz. can tomato wedges, drained
12 green onions, chopped
1 12-oz. can pitted black olives, drained, chopped
1 6-oz. package shredded Monterey Jack cheese
1 6-oz. package shredded Cheddar cheese

Mix . . . . avocados with lemon juice in small bowl.
Blend . . . . . . sour cream, seasoning mix and mayonnaise in bowl.
Layer . . . . . . bean dip, avocados, sour cream mixture and remaining ingredients in order listed in 9 x 13-inch casserole.
Chill . . . . for 2 hours or longer.
Serve . . . . with taco chips.

Bobbie Smith
Waynoka H. S., Waynoka

MICROWAVE BACON BREADSTICKS

10 slices bacon
Parmesan cheese
1 pkg. breadsticks

Cut . . . . bacon slices in half lengthwise.
Coat . . . . bacon with cheese then wrap around breadsticks.
Place . . . . in glass baking dish; cover with paper towel.
Microwave . . on High for 5 minutes or until bacon is crisp.

Dana Baldwin
Thomas H. S., Thomas

ALMOND-CHEESE CRISPS

1/2 c. butter, softened
1/2 tsp. dry mustard
1/8 tsp. hot pepper sauce
1 c. flour
1 tsp. baking powder
2 c. shredded sharp Cheddar cheese
1 c. crushed cornflakes
1/2 c. chopped toasted almonds
Whole blanched almonds, toasted

Cream . . . . . . butter, mustard and hot pepper sauce in bowl.
Stir . . . . in flour and baking powder.
Add . . . . cheese, cornflakes and chopped almonds, mixing well.
Shape . . . . . . into 1-inch balls.
Arrange . . . . . 2 inches apart on baking sheets; flatten with fork.
Press . . . . whole almond in center of each.
Bake . . . . at 400 degrees for 12 to 15 minutes or until lightly browned; cool.
Store . . . . in airtight containers.

Kim Bivins
Checotah H. S., Checotah

CARAMEL CORN

2 c. packed brown sugar
2 sticks butter, softened
1/2 c. light corn syrup
Salt to taste
1/2 tsp. soda
15 c. popped popcorn

Combine . . . . brown sugar, butter, corn syrup and salt in skillet.
Bring . . . . to a boil, stirring occasionally.
Cook . . . . for 5 minutes longer; remove from heat.
Stir . . . . in soda.
Pour . . . . over popcorn in two 9 x 13-inch baking pans, stirring to coat.
Bake . . . . at 200 degrees for 1 hour, stirring every 15 minutes.
Yields . . . . . . 15 cups.

Kelly Roady
Elmore City H. S., Elmore City

FAVORITE EGG ROLLS

1 can bean sprouts, drained
1/2 can bamboo shoots, drained, chopped
1/2 can water chestnuts, drained, chopped
1 c. shredded cabbage
1 sm. onion, finely chopped
1 can shrimp, drained

1 carrot, shredded
1 1/2 c. shredded pork
1 chicken, cooked, shredded
1 pkg. egg roll wrappers
Oil for deep frying

Combine .... first 9 ingredients, mixing well.
Spoon ...... mixture onto each wrapper.
Roll .... using package directions.
Deep-fry .... until golden brown.
Serve .... with sweet and sour sauce.

Crowder FHA
Crowder H. S., Crowder

SOUR CREAM ENCHILADAS

1/2 c. sour cream
2 cans cream of chicken soup
1 sm. can chopped mild green chilies
1/2 tsp. salt
1/2 green onion, chopped
2 cans chopped chicken (opt.)
12 flour tortillas
2 c. grated cheese

Combine .... first 6 ingredients in bowl, mixing well.
Spoon ...... onto tortillas; roll to enclose filling.
Arrange ..... in 9 x 13-inch baking dish.
Sprinkle .... with cheese.
Bake .... at 350 degrees for 20 to 30 minutes or until bubbly.
Yields ...... 6-8 servings.

Peggy O. Munter
Moore H. S., Moore

MICROWAVE NACHOS

16 lg. tortilla chips
6 oz. Cheddar cheese, shredded
Chopped jalapeno peppers to taste

Arrange ..... tortilla chips on waxed paper-lined paper plate.
Top .... with cheese and jalapeno peppers.
Microwave .. on High for 1 1/2 to 2 1/2 minutes or until cheese melts, turning 1 or 2 times.
Yields ...... 16 nachos.

Cindy Simmons
Elmore City H. S., Elmore City

HOT HANKY PANKIES

1 lb. ground beef
1 lb. sausage
1 lb. Velveeta cheese
1 tsp. each garlic salt, onion salt
1 tsp. oregano
1 loaf party rye bread

Brown ...... ground beef and sausage in skillet, stirring frequently; drain.
Mix .... in cheese and seasonings.
Heat .... until cheese is melted, stirring occasionally.
Spread ..... on bread slices; arrange on baking sheet.
Broil .... until bubbly.

Patricia Heck
Miami H. S., Miami

SAUSAGE-CHEESE BALLS

1 lb. hot sausage, at room temperature
8 oz. cheese, grated
3 c. baking mix

Mix .... sausage, cheese and baking mix in bowl.
Shape ...... into balls.
Place .... on baking sheet.
Bake .... at 400 degrees for 20 minutes.

Syble Ditzler, FHA Adviser
Holdenville H. S., Holdenville

SAUSAGE-CHEESE SQUARES

1 lb. Velveeta cheese, softened
1/2 lb. New York sharp cheese, cubed
1/2 lb. mild cheese, cubed
1/2 lb. sausage
3 jalapeno peppers, chopped

Heat .... cheeses in double boiler until melted, mixing well.
Brown ...... sausage in skillet, stirring occasionally; drain.
Add .... to cheese mixture, mixing well.
Stir .... in jalapeno peppers.
Spread ..... in waxed paper-lined 7 x 11-inch pan.
Chill .... until firm.
Cut .... into squares.

Amanda Gagan
Nowata H. S., Nowata

Beverages

SHRIMP SPIRALS

   1   4 1/2-oz. can shrimp, drained,
      finely chopped
   1   4-oz. carton whipped cream cheese
      with chives
   2 tbsp. finely chopped pimento
   1/2 17 1/4-oz. package frozen pastry,
      thawed

Combine . . . . first 3 ingredients in bowl, mix-
        ing well.
Roll . . . . pastry into 10 x 15-inch
        rectangle.
Spread . . . . . shrimp mixture lengthwise over
        half the pastry.
Fold . . . . in half; cut into fifteen 1-inch
        wide strips.
Twist . . . . . . into spirals.
Place . . . . on baking sheet; press ends
        down.
Bake . . . . at 450 degrees for 10 minutes;
        drain on paper towels.
Yields . . . . . . 15 servings.

Elizabeth Ann Allen
Vinita H. S., Vinita

CHOCOLATE BANANA NOG

   2 bananas, mashed
   1 qt. milk
   1/2 c. chocolate syrup
   1/8 tsp. salt

Combine . . . . all ingredients in blender
        container.
Process . . . . . until smooth.
Pour . . . . into tall glasses.
Garnish . . . . . with banana slices.
Yields . . . . . . 6 servings.

Photograph for this recipe above.

FAVORITE BANANA PUNCH

   2 to 4 c. sugar
   5 bananas, mashed
   Juice of 5 oranges
   Juice of 2 lemons
   1 lg. can pineapple juice
   3 qt. ginger ale

Boil . . . . 6 cups water and sugar in sauce-pan for 5 minutes; cool.
Combine . . . . with bananas and juices in bowl.
Pour . . . . into freezer container.
Freeze . . . . . . for 2 days.
Thaw . . . . . . until slushy.
Add . . . . ginger ale just before serving.
Yields . . . . . . 4 quarts.

Roberta Smith, Home Economics Teacher
Verden H. S., Verden

EASY BANANA PUNCH

4 bananas, sliced
1 12-oz. can frozen orange juice
   concentrate
2 c. sugar
1 lg. can pineapple juice
2 qt. ginger ale

Combine . . . . bananas and a small amount of orange juice in blender container.
Process . . . . . until smooth.
Mix . . . . with 6 cups water and remaining ingredients except ginger ale in freezer container.
Store . . . . in freezer until ready to use.
Thaw . . . . . . until slushy.
Add . . . . ginger ale just before serving time.
Yields . . . . . . 5 quarts.

Sylvia Scott
Lookeba-Sickles H. S., Lookeba

CHRISTMAS PUNCH

1 2-liter bottle of lemon-lime soda
1/2 gal. orange juice
4 oranges, thinly sliced

Combine . . . . soda and orange juice in punch bowl, mixing well.
Add . . . . orange slices before serving.

Brenda Payton
Vinita H. S., Vinita

GERRY'S PUNCH

1 20-oz. can crushed pineapple, chilled
8 drops of green food coloring (opt.)

3 6-oz. cans frozen lemonade concentrate, thawed
1 46-oz. can white grape juice, chilled
1 46-oz. can pineapple juice, chilled

Pour . . . . pineapple into large bowl.
Tint . . . . with 4 drops of food coloring.
Add . . . . remaining ingredients, mixing well.
Add . . . . remaining 4 drops of food coloring.
Serve . . . . . . over ice in punch bowl.
Yields . . . . . . 52 servings.

Gerry Marie Andzelik
Eisenhower H. S., Lawton

CHERRY PINK PUNCH

2 c. sugar
2 pkg. cherry-flavored powdered drink
   mix
1 48-oz. can pineapple juice
1/2 c. lemon juice
2 qt. ginger ale, chilled
1 qt. pineapple sherbet, softened

Combine . . . . sugar and 1 quart water in large saucepan, mixing well.
Bring . . . . to a boil; remove from heat.
Add . . . . drink mix, pineapple juice, lemon juice and 1 quart water, mixing well.
Chill . . . . in refrigerator.
Combine . . . . with ginger ale and sherbet just before serving.

Crowder FHA
Crowder H. S., Crowder

DUSTY ROSE PUNCH

1 46-oz. can pineapple juice
1 6-oz. can frozen pink lemonade concentrate, thawed
1 qt. raspberry sherbet, softened
2 qt. ginger ale, chilled

Blend . . . . . . pineapple juice and lemonade in punch bowl.
Stir . . . . in sherbet.
Add . . . . ginger ale just before serving.
Yields . . . . . . 25 servings.

Barbie Phillips
Sharon-Mutual H. S., Sharon

Beverages

BETTY'S PUNCH

1 46-oz. container unsweetened orange
   juice
1 46-oz. can pineapple juice
2 qt. 7-Up
1 c. sugar
2 pkg. cherry-flavored powdered drink
   mix

Combine .... all ingredients and 2 quarts
          water in large bowl, mixing well.
Freeze ...... until firm.
Thaw ...... until slushy to serve.

Crowder FHA
Crowder H. S., Crowder

ORANGE JULIUS

2 eggs
1 c. milk
1 6-oz. can frozen orange juice
   concentrate
2 tbsp. honey
1/2 tsp. vanilla extract
20 ice cubes

Combine .... first 5 ingredients in blender
          container.
Process ..... until smooth.
Add .... 20 ice cubes.
Process ..... until blended.
Yields ...... 4-6 servings.

Renee McHargue
Barnsdall H. S., Barnsdall

STRAWBERRY PUNCH

1 6-oz. can frozen pink lemonade
   concentrate
1 pt. vanilla ice cream
1 sm. package frozen strawberries,
   thawed

Combine .... all ingredients with 1 cup water
          in blender container.
Process ..... until smooth. May substitute
          strawberry ice cream for vanilla
          ice cream.
Yields ...... 2 servings.

Cathy James, Adviser
Crescent H. S., Guthrie

SWEETHEART PUNCH

1 3-oz. package strawberry gelatin
1 13-oz. container strawberry-flavored
   powdered drink mix
2 1/2 c. sugar
1 46-oz. can pineapple juice
1 1/4 c. ginger ale
2 pt. pineapple sherbet

Dissolve .... gelatin in 1 cup boiling water.
Dissolve .... drink mix and sugar in 2 quarts
          cold water in bowl.
Stir .... in pineapple juice and gelatin
          mixture.
Chill .... in refrigerator.
Add .... ginger ale and sherbet just before
          serving.
Yields ...... 35 servings.

Sonya Muskrat
Porum H. S., Porum

HOT APPLE CIDER PUNCH

2 tsp. whole cloves
2 oranges
1 gal. apple cider
2 3-in. cinnamon sticks
2/3 c. sugar

Insert ...... cloves in oranges.
Combine .... with cider and remaining ingre-
          dients in large saucepan.
Bring .... to a boil; reduce heat.
Simmer ..... for 20 minutes.
Yields ...... 1 gallon.

Cindy Thomas
Elgin H. S., Apache

COCOA MIX

1 11-oz. jar nondairy coffee creamer
1 16-oz. box nonfat dry milk powder
2 c. confectioners' sugar, sifted
1 24-oz. container chocolate-flavored
   instant powdered drink mix

Combine .... all ingredients in bowl, mixing
          well.
Store .... in covered container.
Mix .... with 1 cup hot water to taste.
Yields ...... 16 cups.

Robyn Greb
Okeene H. S., Okeene

Salads

MACARONI SALAD PLATTER, recipe on page 40.

Salads

WALDORF COTTAGE CHEESE SALAD

2 med. apples, chopped
1 8-oz. carton cottage cheese
1/4 c. raisins
2 tbsp. mayonnaise
1 1/4 tsp. lemon juice
1/2 tsp. salt
Cinnamon

Combine .... first 6 ingredients in bowl, mixing well.
Spoon ...... onto lettuce-lined plates; sprinkle with cinnamon.
Yields ...... 4 servings.

Kimberly D. Heinze
Okeene H. S., Okeene

BLUEBERRY GELATIN SALAD

1 6-oz. package lemon gelatin
2 c. grape juice
1 20-oz. can crushed pineapple
1 can blueberry pie filling
1 8-oz. package cream cheese, softened
1/2 c. sour cream
1/2 c. sugar
1 tsp. vanilla extract
1/2 c. chopped nuts

Dissolve .... gelatin in boiling grape juice.
Chill .... until partially set.
Combine .... with pineapple and pie filling in dish.
Chill .... until set.
Blend ...... cream cheese, sour cream, sugar and vanilla in bowl; stir in nuts.
Spread ..... evenly over congealed layer.
Garnish ..... with additional nuts.

Carol Wright
Okeene H. S., Okeene

CHERRY-COLA SALAD

1 can pitted cherries
1 can crushed pineapple
2 3-oz. packages cherry gelatin
1 c. nuts
1 12-oz. can cola

Drain ...... cherries and pineapple, reserving liquid.
Bring .... liquid to a boil in saucepan.

Stir .... in gelatin until dissolved; remove from heat.
Add .... fruit, nuts and cola, mixing well.
Pour .... into serving dish.
Chill .... until set.

Tonya Shuffield
Mustang H. S., Oklahoma City

COTTAGE CHEESE SALAD SUPREME

1 12-oz. container cottage cheese
1 3-oz. package orange gelatin
1 6-oz. container whipped topping
1 15 1/4-oz. can pineapple tidbits, drained
1 11-oz. can mandarin oranges, drained

Combine .... cottage cheese and gelatin in bowl, mixing well.
Fold .... in whipped topping and fruit.
Chill .... in refrigerator.
Yields ...... 6-8 servings.

Dawn Jantzen
Canton H. S., Canton

GRANNY'S CRANBERRY SALAD

1 lb. cranberries, ground
2 c. sugar
1 c. chopped celery
1 c. chopped apples
1 c. chopped nuts
2 c. miniature marshmallows
2 c. whipping cream, whipped

Mix .... cranberries and sugar in large bowl.
Add .... celery, apples, nuts and marshmallows, mixing well.
Fold .... into whipped cream.
Chill .... for 45 minutes.
Yields ...... 12 servings.

Angela Gregory
Beggs H. S., Beggs

CREAMY GREEN SALAD

1 sm. package lime gelatin
1 sm. package lemon gelatin
1 can sweetened condensed milk
1 8-oz. carton cottage cheese

1 c. mayonnaise
1 c. crushed pineapple, drained
1 c. chopped pecans

Dissolve .... gelatins in 1 cup boiling water in bowl.
Mix .... in condensed milk, cottage cheese and mayonnaise.
Stir .... in pineapple and pecans.
Chill .... until serving time.

Dixie Jones
Ringwood H. S., Ringwood

ORANGE FLUFF

2 eggs, beaten
1 c. sugar
1 1/2 c. orange juice
1 sm. package orange gelatin
1 lg. can Milnot, whipped
3 to 4 c. vanilla wafer crumbs

Combine .... eggs, sugar and orange juice in saucepan, mixing well.
Bring .... to a boil; remove from heat.
Stir .... in gelatin.
Beat .... with electric mixer at high speed until fluffy; cool.
Fold .... in whipped Milnot.
Place .... 3 cups crumbs in bottom of 9 x 13-inch dish.
Pour .... gelatin mixture over crumbs.
Sprinkle .... remaining crumbs over top.
Yields ...... 12-15 servings.

Jennifer Walsh
Oklahoma State FHA President 1983-84
Union City H. S., Union City

STRAWBERRY SALAD

2 pkg. strawberry gelatin
1 10-oz. package frozen strawberries, thawed
1 20-oz. can crushed pineapple
2 or 3 med. bananas, mashed
Chopped nuts (opt.)
1 carton sour cream

Dissolve .... gelatin in 1 cup boiling water in bowl.
Fold .... in fruit and nuts.
Pour .... half the gelatin mixture into 8 x 8-inch dish.
Chill .... until firm.

Spread ..... sour cream over congealed layer.
Top .... with remaining gelatin mixture.
Chill .... until set.

Shelly Yates
Stuart H. S., Haywood

SURPRISE SALAD

1 lg. container whipped topping
1 can cherry pie filling
1 can crushed pineapple
1 can sweetened condensed milk
1 can coconut
1 c. chopped pecans

Mix .... first 4 ingredients in bowl.
Stir .... in coconut and pecans.

Stephanie Myers
Byng H. S., Ada

FIVE-CUP SALAD

1 c. coconut
1 c. miniature marshmallows
1 c. manadarin oranges
1 c. pineapple tidbits
1 8-oz. carton sour cream

Combine .... all ingredients in bowl, mixing well.
Chill .... for 1 to 2 days.

Patty Harper
Okeene H. S., Okeene

FROZEN FRUIT SUMMER SALAD

1 15 1/2-oz. can apricots, drained
1 15 1/2-oz. can crushed pineapple, drained
1 12-oz. can frozen orange juice concentrate, thawed
1/4 c. lemon juice
6 bananas, sliced
2 c. sugar

Puree ...... apricots in blender container.
Combine .... with remaining ingredients in mixer bowl.
Beat .... until mixed.
Pour .... into paper-lined muffin cups.
Freeze ...... until firm.
Yields ...... 30 servings.

Michele Cohlmia
Waynoka H. S., Waynoka

Salads

REFRESHING SUMMER SALAD

12 oz. large shell macaroni, cooked,
   drained
1 1/2 c. chopped Colby cheese
1 1/2 c. chopped ham
1/2 c. chopped green onions
1/2 c. chopped ripe olives
1 c. chopped green pepper
1 c. chopped tomatoes
1 c. mayonnaise

Combine . . . . all ingredients in bowl, tossing to
   mix well.
Chill . . . . covered, for 2 hours or longer.

Gail E. Burton
Bray-Dale H. S., Bray

MACARONI SALAD PLATTER

4 c. elbow macaroni, cooked
2 c. chopped celery
1/4 c. chopped onion
1/4 c. sweet pickle relish
2 tsp. salt
3/4 tsp. dry mustard
2 tsp. vinegar
3/4 to 1 c. mayonnaise
Western iceberg lettuce
Radish roses
1 12-oz. can luncheon meat,
   chilled, cut in strips
1 12-oz. package fully cooked
   frankfurters, chilled, sliced
1 16-oz. can peas, chilled, drained

Combine . . . . first 8 ingredients in bowl, mix-
   ing well.
Chill . . . . in refrigerator.
Spoon . . . . . . onto center of lettuce-lined
   platter.
Arrange . . . . . remaining ingredients around
   salad.
Serve . . . . with assorted salad dressings.

Photograph for this recipe on page 37.

SEAFOOD CONFETTI SALAD

1 c. cooked green beans
1 c. cooked peas
1 c. chopped cooked carrots
1 c. chopped green onions
1 c. sliced radishes

1 6 1/2-oz. can tuna, drained, flaked
3 c. rice, cooked
1/4 to 1/3 c. Italian salad dressing
6 to 8 hard-boiled eggs, cut in half
1 8-oz. package cream cheese, softened
1/2 c. mayonnaise
Salt and pepper to taste
Mustard and vinegar to taste

Combine . . . . first 8 ingredients in bowl,
   mixing well.
Marinate . . . . in refrigerator for several hours.
Process . . . . . egg yolks, cream cheese and
   mayonnaise in food processor
   until smooth.
Blend . . . . . . in seasonings.
Spoon . . . . . . mixture into egg whites.
Chill . . . . in refrigerator.
Arrange . . . . . eggs on top of salad.
Garnish . . . . . eggs with radish slices and tiny
   shrimp and place parsley sprigs
   between eggs.

Velda George
Oklahoma City Schools, Oklahoma City

TACO SALAD

1 lb. ground beef
1/4 tsp. salt
Dash of pepper
1 tbsp. taco seasoning
1 can chili beans, drained
1 sm. avocado, mashed
1 tomato, chopped
1/2 c. grated cheese
1/2 c. chopped onion
1/4 c. chopped green pepper
1 sm. head lettuce, torn
1 bottle of Catalina salad dressing
1 sm. package taco chips, crushed

Brown . . . . . . ground beef with salt and pepper
   in skillet, stirring frequently;
   drain.
Stir . . . . in taco seasoning and next 6 in-
   gredients, mixing well.
Combine . . . . with lettuce in salad bowl,
   tossing lightly.
Add . . . . dressing to taste before serving.
Garnish . . . . . with taco chips.
Yields . . . . . . 6 servings.

Debbie Hart
Emerson Jr. H. S., Enid

MACARONI SALAD

1 sm. package macaroni
1 tbsp. margarine
4 hard-boiled eggs, chopped, chilled
2 tomatoes, chopped, chilled
2 cucumbers, chopped, chilled
Lettuce (opt.)
Chopped onion (opt.)
1 tbsp. mayonnaise
1/2 tbsp. vinegar
1 tbsp. sugar
1/8 tsp. mustard
1/8 tsp. salt

Cook . . . . macaroni with margarine, using package directions; drain.
Chill . . . . in refrigerator.
Combine . . . . with next 5 ingredients in bowl, mixing well.
Blend . . . . . . mayonnaise, vinegar, sugar, mustard and salt in bowl.
Add . . . . to macaroni mixture, tossing to coat. Omit lettuce if salad is not served immediately.
Yield . . . . 12 servings.

Lorean Droke
Okeene H. S., Okeene

SPAGHETTI SALAD

2 lb. spaghetti
Salt
1 cucumber, finely chopped
1 sm. onion, finely chopped
1 green pepper, finely chopped
2 med. tomatoes, finely chopped
1 tbsp. seasoned salt
1/2 sm. bottle of creamy Italian salad dressing
1/2 sm. bottle of Italian salad dressing
1 tsp. garlic-flavored red wine vinegar

Cook . . . . spaghetti in salted water in saucepan for 5 minutes, or until just tender; rinse with cool water and drain.
Combine . . . . with vegetables in bowl, mixing gently.
Sprinkle . . . . with seasoned salt.
Stir . . . . in salad dressings and salt to taste.
Sprinkle . . . . with vinegar, mixing well.

Chill . . . . in refrigerator.
Yields . . . . . . 12-18 servings.

Pat Kellner
Okeene Public Schools I-9, Okeene

COPPER PENNY SALAD

2 lb. carrots, sliced, cooked
1 med. green pepper, sliced
3 med. onions, sliced
1 can tomato soup
1/4 c. oil
1 c. sugar
3/4 c. wine vinegar
1 tsp. each salt and pepper
1 tsp. Worcestershire sauce

Combine . . . . carrots, green pepper and onions in bowl, mixing well.
Blend . . . . . . remaining ingredients in small bowl.
Pour . . . . over salad, tossing to coat.
Marinate . . . . covered, overnight.
Store . . . . in refrigerator for 3 weeks or less.

Edith Carter
Hollis

GREEN PEA SALAD

2 c. cubed longhorn cheese
1   17-oz. can young garden green peas
1/4 c. chopped green onions
2 c. elbow macaroni, cooked, drained
Tuna (opt.)
3/4 c. mayonnaise
2 tbsp. horseradish
1 tsp. mustard
3/4 c. buttermilk
1/2 tsp. each salt, celery seed
1/8 tsp. pepper
3 tbsp. sugar

Combine . . . . cheese, peas, onions, macaroni and tuna in bowl, mixing well.
Blend . . . . . . mayonnaise, horseradish, mustard and buttermilk in bowl.
Add . . . . seasonings and sugar, mixing well.
Pour . . . . over salad, tossing to coat.
Chill . . . . until serving time.
Yields . . . . . . 8-10 servings.

Delcie Barrett
Ralston H. S., Ralston

Salads

CAULIFLOWER SALAD

3/4 c. mayonnaise
3/4 c. sour cream
1 sm. package Ranch-style salad dressing
   mix
1 head cauliflower, thinly sliced
1 bunch green onions, sliced
3/4 c. ripe olives, sliced
3/4 c. green olives, sliced
1/2 c. shredded carrots

Blend ...... mayonnaise, sour cream and dressing mix in bowl.
Combine .... with remaining ingredients except carrots in serving bowl.
Chill .... covered, for 2 to 3 hours.
Top .... with shredded carrots.

Pauline Shields
Webster Middle School, Oklahoma City

CLEOPATRA'S SALAD

1 head lettuce, torn
1 head cauliflower, chopped
2 c. mayonnaise
1 lb. bacon, crisp-fried, crumbled
1/2 med. onion, chopped
1 c. grated Cheddar cheese
1/2 c. sugar

Combine .... lettuce and cauliflower in bowl.
Spread ..... mayonnaise over top, sealing to edges.
Sprinkle .... remaining ingredients over top in order listed.
Chill .... overnight.
Toss .... before serving.

Rachelle Epperson
Grove H. S., Grove

EASY COTTAGE CHEESE SALAD

1 carton cottage cheese
1/4 to 1/2 c. finely chopped onion
1/4 to 1/2 c. finely chopped green pepper
1/4 c. (about) mayonnaise
Salt and pepper to taste
1 tomato, chopped

Mix .... first 6 ingredients in bowl.
Stir .... in tomato. May substitute cauli-flowerets for tomato.

Clarabel Tepe
Fort Towson H. S., Fort Towson

SUNBURST SALAD

4 lg. Florida tomatoes
1 1/4 c. chopped seeded peeled Florida
   cucumbers
1/4 c. low-fat yogurt
1/4 tsp. curry powder
1/8 tsp. salt
1/2 c. low-fat cottage cheese
1/2 c. sliced Florida celery

Remove .... cores from tomatoes; turn stem side down.
Cut .... each into wedges nearly to but not through bottom; open wedges gently to form star.
Combine .... 1 cup cucumber, yogurt, curry powder and salt in blender container.
Process ..... until smooth.
Mix .... with 1/4 cup cucumber in bowl.
Spoon ...... mixture of cottage cheese and celery into tomatoes.
Serve .... on lettuce-lined plates with cucumber dressing.

Photograph for this recipe above.

CUCUMBER SALAD

1 1/2 c. mayonnaise
1/2 c. sugar
2 to 3 tsp. vinegar

4 med. cucumbers, thinly sliced
1 lg. onion, thinly sliced

Blend ...... mayonnaise, sugar and vinegar in bowl.
Pour .... over cucumbers and onion in bowl, tossing to coat.
Chill .... tightly covered, overnight.

Lisa Beck
Begg H. S., Begg

AUSTRIAN POTATO SALAD

1 lb. potatoes
1 sm. onion, thinly sliced
1/4 c. hot beef broth
3 tbsp. salad oil
2 tbsp. vinegar
2 tsp. Dijon mustard
1/4 tsp. each salt and pepper
1/4 c. chopped parsley

Steam ...... potatoes in 1 inch of boiling salted water in saucepan until tender; drain.
Peel .... and cut into thin slices.
Toss .... onion lightly with warm potatoes in bowl.
Mix .... remaining ingredients except parsley in small bowl.
Stir .... into potato mixture.
Add .... parsley, mixing well.
Serve .... warm on lettuce-lined plates.

Janet Damron
Elmore City H. S., Elmore City

GARDEN POTATO SALAD

6 med. potatoes, cooked, peeled
1/2 med. onion, chopped
1 stalk celery, sliced
1/4 c. sliced radishes
1/4 c. chopped green pepper
1/2 c. mayonnaise
1 tsp. mustard
4 hard-boiled eggs, chopped
Salt, pepper and paprika to taste

Cut .... potatoes into chunks.
Combine .... vegetables in large bowl.
Blend ...... mayonnaise and mustard in small bowl.
Add .... to potato mixture, tossing gently; fold in eggs.

Season ..... with salt and pepper.
Sprinkle .... with paprika.

Elizabeth Padgett
Apache H. S., Apache

CRUNCHY FRESH SPINACH SALAD

4 c. torn spinach
1 med. purple onion, sliced into rings
1 can water chestnuts, slivered
1 can bean sprouts, drained
4 hard-boiled eggs, sliced
1/2 lb. bacon, crisp-fried, crumbled
1/3 c. catsup
1 c. oil
3/4 c. sugar
1/2 c. red wine vinegar
2 tsp. salt

Layer ...... first 6 ingredients in bowl.
Blend ...... catsup, oil, sugar, vinegar and salt in small bowl.
Chill .... salad and dressing until serving time.
Pour .... dressing over salad just before serving.
Yields ...... 6 servings.

Virginia Darnell, Teacher
Apache H. S., Apache

SPINACH AND EGG SALAD

3/4 lb. spinach, torn
8 hard-boiled eggs, quartered
1/4 lb. mushrooms, sliced
4 slices crisp-fried bacon, crumbled
1/2 c. oil
1/4 c. catsup
1/4 c. minced onion
2 tbsp. sugar
2 tbsp. lemon juice
1 1/2 tsp. Worcestershire sauce
1/4 tsp. salt
1/8 tsp. pepper

Layer ...... first 4 ingredients in bowl in order listed.
Combine .... remaining ingredients, mixing well.
Pour .... over salad, tossing lightly.
Yields ...... 4 servings.

Kristi Kelley
Barnsdall H. S., Barnsdall

Salads

SUMMERTIME SALAD

1 can white corn, drained
1 can French-style green beans, drained
2 cans early June peas, drained
1 onion, chopped
1 green pepper, chopped
1/2 c. chopped celery
2/3 c. vinegar
1/2 tsp. salt
1/2 c. oil
1/2 c. sugar

Combine .... first 6 ingredients in bowl, mixing well.
Blend ...... vinegar, salt, oil and sugar in small bowl.
Pour .... over salad, tossing to coat.
Let .... stand overnight before serving.

Ronda Karbs
Okeene H. S., Okeene

SEVEN-LAYER SALAD

1 med. head lettuce, shredded
1 c. coarsely chopped celery
1 c. coarsely chopped green peppers
3/4 c. coarsely chopped onion
1 c. frozen peas
1 c. mayonnaise
2 tbsp. sugar
2 1/2 c. shredded Cheddar cheese
8 slices crisp-fried bacon, crumbled

Layer ...... first 5 ingredients in order listed in salad bowl.
Spread ..... mayonnaise evenly over top.
Sprinkle .... with sugar and cheese.
Chill .... covered, for 4 hours or longer.
Top .... with bacon before serving.
Yields ...... 15-20 servings.

Linda Smith
Vinita H. S., Vinita

LAYERED LETTUCE SALAD

1 sm. head lettuce, finely chopped
1/2 c. chopped green onions
1/2 c. each chopped celery, green pepper
2 pkg. frozen green peas
3/4 c. sour cream
3/4 c. mayonnaise
1/2 lb. Cheddar cheese, grated
Bacon bits

Combine .... first 4 ingredients in loaf pan.
Layer ...... peas over top.
Blend ...... sour cream and mayonnaise in bowl.
Spread ..... over peas.
Sprinkle .... with cheese and bacon bits.
Chill .... covered, for 25 hours to 1 week.

Lorrie Reeves
Barnsdall H. S., Barnsdall

OVERNIGHT SALAD

1 head lettuce, torn
1 green pepper, chopped
1 bunch green onions, chopped
1/2 pkg. frozen peas
6 to 8 slices crisp-fried bacon, crumbled
2 c. salad dressing
2 tbsp. sugar
2 c. shredded Cheddar cheese

Layer ...... first 5 ingredients in bowl in order listed.
Blend ...... salad dressing and sugar in bowl.
Spread ..... over layers, sealing to edges.
Top .... with cheese.
Chill .... for 4 hours or longer.

Patriece Winters
Geary H. S., Geary

ORIENTAL SALAD DRESSING

1/3 c. vinegar
1/3 c. soy sauce
3 tbsp. sesame oil
2/3 c. oil
1/2 tsp. Worcestershire sauce
3 tbsp. sugar
3/4 tsp. minced garlic
1 tsp. ginger
1 tsp. dry mustard
Salt to taste
1/3 c. sesame seed
1 1/2 tbsp. sliced scallions

Blend ...... first 5 ingredients in bowl.
Stir .... in sugar, seasonings, sesame seed and scallions.
Serve .... over mixture of salad greens, diced chicken, water chestnuts, mushrooms and bean sprouts.

Micki Jeffery
Highland West Middle School, Moore

Fruits

SPICY APPLE PRESERVES, recipe on page 46. CLOVE APPLES, recipe on page 47. BRANDIED PEARS, recipe on page 48. PLUM RELISH, recipe on page 49. TIPSY MINCEMEAT, recipe on page 53.

Fruits

APPLE DUMPLINGS

8 c. flour
Salt
3 c. shortening
Chopped apples
3 c. sugar
1 stick margarine
1 tsp. each cinnamon, nutmeg

Combine . . . . flour and 2 teaspoons salt in bowl.
Cut . . . . in shortening until crumbly.
Add . . . . 1 1/2 cups water, mixing to form soft dough.
Roll . . . . a small amount at a time into circles on floured surface.
Spoon . . . . . . apples onto pastry circles.
Fold . . . . to enclose filling, sealing edges.
Place . . . . in baking dish.
Combine . . . . remaining ingredients, 5 cups water and pinch of salt in saucepan.
Boil . . . . for 20 minutes.
Pour . . . . over dumplings.
Bake . . . . at 350 degrees until brown.
Yields . . . . . . 50 servings.

Troy Lynn Roberts
FHA Secretary 1983-84, Westville H. S.

FALL HARVEST APPLE PIE

1 c. shortening
Salt
Sugar
Flour
1/2 tsp. each cinnamon, nutmeg
6 c. thinly sliced apples
2 tbsp. butter

Pour . . . . 1/2 cup boiling water over shortening in bowl, stirring until melted.
Mix . . . . in 1 teaspoon salt, 1 tablespoon sugar and enough flour to make easily handled dough.
Roll . . . . into 2 large circles on floured surface.
Line . . . . 9-inch pie plate with half the pastry.
Mix . . . . 1/4 cup flour, 3/4 cup sugar, spices and dash of salt in bowl.
Add . . . . apples.

Spoon . . . . . . into pie shell; dot with butter.
Cover . . . . . . with remaining pastry; flute edge.
Cut . . . . steam vents; cover edge with 3-inch foil rim.
Bake . . . . at 425 degrees for 25 minutes; remove foil.
Bake . . . . for 15 to 25 minutes longer or until brown.

Randy Barrett
Waynoka H. S., Waynoka

DEEP-DISH APPLE CRISP

1 c. sugar
2 tsp. butter, melted
2 eggs, beaten
1 c. flour
1 tsp. baking powder
1/2 tsp. salt
1 tsp. vanilla extract
6 med. tart apples, peeled, sliced

Beat . . . . sugar and butter into eggs in bowl.
Sift . . . . in flour, baking powder and salt.
Stir . . . . in vanilla.
Arrange . . . . . apples in greased 9-inch pie plate.
Spread . . . . . egg mixture over apples.
Bake . . . . at 350 degrees for 45 minutes.
Serve . . . . with whipped cream.
Yields . . . . . . 8 servings.

Anita Orsburn
Wagoner H. S., Wagoner

SPICY APPLE PRESERVES

2 lb. apples, peeled, cored
4 c. sugar
1 tbsp. crushed gingerroot
12 cloves
Peelings of 2 apples

Cut . . . . large apples into halves or quarters.
Mix . . . . sugar with 2 1/2 cups water in large saucepan.
Boil . . . . for 3 minutes.
Cook . . . . apples several at a time until tender.
Remove . . . . with slotted spoon; pack into hot sterilized Ball jars.

Add .... gingerroot, cloves and peelings to syrup.
Bring .... to a boil; remove and discard gingerroot, cloves and peelings.
Pour .... over apples leaving 1/4-inch headspace; seal.
Process ..... in water bath for 15 minutes. May substitute whole peeled crab apples for apples.
Yields ...... 2 pints.

Photograph for this recipe on page 45.

CLOVE APPLES

4 c. sugar
2 lb. apples, peeled, quartered
12 cloves
Peelings of 3 apples
Red food coloring (opt.)

Boil .... sugar dissolved in 2 1/2 cups water in saucepan for 3 minutes.
Add .... apples.
Cook .... until tender.
Remove .... apples with slotted spoon; pack into hot sterilized Ball jars.
Add .... cloves and peelings.
Boil .... until syrup sheets from spoon.
Remove .... cloves and peelings; stir in food coloring.
Pour .... over apples; seal.
Process ..... in hot water bath for 15 minutes.

Photograph for this recipe on page 45.

APPLE GOODIE

10 c. sliced apples
1 1/2 c. (about) sugar
1 tsp. cinnamon
1 c. oats
1 c. flour
1/4 tsp. salt
1/2 c. butter
1 c. packed brown sugar
1 tsp. each soda, baking powder

Mix .... apples, 1 1/2 cups plus 1 teaspoon sugar and cinnamon in bowl.
Spoon ...... into 9 x 13-inch baking dish.

Mix .... remaining ingredients in bowl.
Spread ..... over apple mixture.
Bake .... at 350 degrees for 45 minutes or until golden brown and apples are tender.

Edith Carr
Vinita H. S., Vinita

BLACKBERRY ICE CREAM

2 c. blackberry pulp
16 lg. marshmallows
1 tbsp. lemon juice
1 c. sugar
1/8 tsp. salt
1 1/2 c. whipping cream, whipped

Heat .... blackberry pulp in double boiler.
Add .... marshmallows, lemon juice, sugar and salt.
Cook .... until marshmallows are melted, stirring constantly.
Chill .... in refrigerator.
Fold .... in whipped cream.
Spoon ...... into mold.
Freeze ...... until firm.
Yields ...... 6-8 servings.

Teresa Allen
Geary H. S., Geary

MELON ANGEL CAKE

1 10-in. angel food cake
2 c. whipping cream, whipped
1 1/2 c. finely chopped cantaloupe
2 tbsp. sugar
1/2 tsp. vanilla extract
1 tsp. grated lemon rind
1/4 c. flaked coconut

Cut .... cake into 3 layers.
Mix .... whipped cream, cantaloupe, sugar, vanilla and lemon rind in bowl.
Spread ..... between layers and over top of cake.
Sprinkle .... with coconut.
Chill .... for several hours.
Yields ...... 8 servings.

Pat Romine
Byng H. S., Ada

Fruits

FRESH BLUEBERRY COBBLER

Sugar
1 tbsp. cornstarch
4 c. blueberries
1 tsp. lemon juice
1 c. flour
1 1/2 tsp. baking powder
1/2 tsp. salt
3 tbsp. shortening
1/2 c. milk

Combine .... 1/2 cup sugar and cornstarch in saucepan.
Stir .... in blueberries and lemon juice.
Boil .... for 1 minute or until thickened, stirring constantly.
Pour .... into 2-quart casserole.
Bake .... at 400 degrees for several minutes.
Mix .... flour, 1 tablespoon sugar, baking powder and salt in bowl.
Add .... shortening and milk.
Cut .... through shortening 6 times until dough forms ball.
Drop .... by spoonfuls into hot blueberry mixture.
Bake .... for 25 to 30 minutes or until browned.
Yields ...... 6 servings.

Robin Mason
Eisenhower Sr. H. S., Lawton

CHAMPAGNE SALAD

1   15-oz. can crushed pineapple, drained
2 bananas, chopped
1   10-oz. package frozen strawberries
1 c. chopped nuts
1   8-oz. package cream cheese, softened
3/4 c. sugar
1   10-oz. carton whipped topping

Mix .... fruits, nuts, cream cheese and sugar in bowl.
Fold .... in whipped topping.
Spread ..... in 9 x 13-inch pan.
Freeze ...... until firm.
Yields ...... 15 servings.

Cheryl Hathaway
Boise City H. S., Boise City

PEACH CREAM PIE

1 egg
2 tbsp. cream
1/2 c. sugar
4 c. sliced peaches
Nutmeg to taste
1/4 c. butter, softened
1/4 c. packed brown sugar
1/2 c. flour

Beat .... egg and cream in bowl.
Mix .... in sugar, peaches and nutmeg.
Pour .... into 8 1/2-inch square baking dish.
Blend ...... butter and brown sugar in bowl.
Mix .... in flour.
Sprinkle .... over peaches.
Bake .... at 425 degrees for 20 minutes.
Yields ...... 6 servings.

Martha Pearce
Muskogee H. S., Muskogee

PEACH SHERBET DELIGHT

2/3 c. sweetened condensed milk
2 tbsp. lemon juice
2 tbsp. melted butter
1 c. mashed fresh peaches
2 egg whites, stiffly beaten

Blend ...... condensed milk, lemon juice, butter and 1/2 cup water in bowl.
Stir .... in peaches.
Chill .... in refrigerator.
Fold .... in egg whites.
Pour .... into freezer tray.
Freeze ...... until partially frozen.
Turn .... into mixer bowl; beat until smooth.
Freeze ...... in freezer tray until firm.
Yields ...... 6 servings.

Donna Kaye Holub
Ringwood H. S., Ringwood

BRANDIED PEARS

5 lb. ripe unblemished pears
3 lb. sugar
2 c. white Brandy

Peel . . . . pears; cut in half and remove cores.

Mix . . . . sugar with 4 cups water in large saucepan.

Bring . . . . to a boil.

Cook . . . . pears several at a time in syrup for 5 minutes or until just tender; remove pears with slotted spoon.

Cool . . . . slightly and pack into hot sterilized Ball jars.

Cook . . . . syrup for 15 minutes longer or until thickened.

Stir . . . . in Brandy.

Pour . . . . over pears leaving 1/4-inch headspace; seal.

Process . . . . . in water bath for 15 minutes.

Yields . . . . . . 4 quarts.

Photograph for this recipe on page 45.

RASPBERRY BOMBE

3 pt. raspberry sherbet, softened
2 pt. pink peppermint ice cream, softened
1 c. whipping cream
3 tbsp. sugar
Dash of salt
1/4 c. chopped mixed candied fruits and rinds
1/4 c. chopped almonds, toasted
Rum flavoring to taste

Spread . . . . . sherbet over bottom and sides of chilled 2 1/2-quart mold.

Freeze . . . . . . until firm.

Spread . . . . . ice cream over sherbet layer.

Freeze . . . . . . until firm.

Whip . . . . cream, sugar and salt in bowl.

Fold . . . . in fruit, almonds and flavoring.

Spoon . . . . . . into center of mold.

Freeze . . . . . . covered, for 6 hours or overnight.

Unmold . . . . onto chilled serving plate.

Yields . . . . . . 12-16 servings.

Georgia Penner
Ringwood H. S., Ringwood

RASPBERRY FROST

2 tbsp. sweetened crushed raspberries
1/4 c. milk (opt.)
1 tbsp. lemon juice

1 scoop lemon ice cream
Sparkling water, chilled

Mix . . . . raspberries, milk and lemon juice in tall glass.

Add . . . . ice cream.

Stir . . . . in sparkling water.

Yields . . . . . . 1 serving.

Tammy Jeffcoat
Ft. Towson H. S., Ft. Towson

BUTTERMILK-RASPBERRY FREEZE

1 10-oz. package frozen raspberries
2 c. buttermilk
1 tsp. grated lemon rind
1/2 tsp. vanilla extract

Combine . . . . raspberries, buttermilk, lemon rind and vanilla in blender container.

Process . . . . . until fluffy.

Pour . . . . into 9-inch square pan.

Freeze . . . . . . until firm.

Spoon . . . . . . into chilled mixer bowl.

Beat . . . . until fluffy; pour into pan.

Freeze . . . . . . for 2 hours.

Yields . . . . . . 6 servings.

Tammy Webber
Ringwood School, Ringwood

PLUM RELISH

2 qt. coarsely ground pitted ripe plums
1 orange, ground
4 c. sugar
Dash each of cinnamon, nutmeg
1/2 c. vinegar
1 c. chopped nuts (opt.)

Combine . . . . all ingredients except nuts in large saucepan.

Cook . . . . until thick, stirring occasionally.

Stir . . . . in nuts.

Spoon . . . . . . into hot sterilized jars leaving 1/4-inch headspace; adjust lids.

Process . . . . . in water bath canner for 15 minutes.

Yields . . . . . . 4 p. graph for this recipe on page 45.

Fruits

FROSTY STRAWBERRY SQUARES

1 c. flour
1/4 c. packed brown sugar
1/2 c. chopped nuts
1/2 c. margarine
2 egg whites
2/3 c. sugar
2 c. strawberries
2 tbsp. lemon juice
2 c. whipping cream, whipped

Mix . . . . flour, brown sugar, nuts and margarine in bowl.
Spread . . . . . evenly in baking dish.
Bake . . . . at 350 degrees until golden, stirring occasionally.
Sprinkle . . . . 2/3 of crumb mixture in 9 x 13-inch pan; cool.
Combine . . . . egg whites, sugar, strawberries and lemon juice in mixer bowl.
Beat . . . . on high speed for 10 minutes or until stiff peaks form.
Fold . . . . in whipped cream.
Spoon . . . . . . into prepared pan.
Sprinkle . . . . with remaining crumbs.
Freeze . . . . . . for 6 hours to overnight.
Garnish . . . . . with whole strawberries.
Yields . . . . . . 10-12 servings.

Crystal Scott
Moore H. S., Moore

CHEESECAKE SUPREME WITH STRAWBERRY GLAZE

1 recipe crumb crust mixture
5 8-oz. packages cream cheese, softened
1/4 tsp. vanilla extract
3/4 tsp. grated lemon rind
2 1/4 c. sugar
3 tbsp. flour
1/4 tsp. salt
1 c. whole eggs
2 egg yolks
1/4 c. heavy cream
1 c. strawberries, crushed
2 tbsp. cornstarch
Several drops of red food coloring (opt.)
1 c. whole strawberries

Press . . . . crumb crust mixture into bottom of just mixture into bottom of springform pan.
Beat . . . . cream cheese in bowl; add vanilla and lemon.

Mix . . . . in 1 3/4 cups sugar, flour and salt.
Beat . . . . in eggs and egg yolks 1 at a time.
Stir . . . . in cream; pour into prepared pan.
Bake . . . . at 450 degrees for 12 minutes; reduce temperature to 300 degrees.
Bake . . . . for 55 minutes longer.
Cool . . . . for 30 minutes in pan; remove side to cool completely.
Cook . . . . crushed strawberries in 3/4 cup water in saucepan for 2 minutes.
Put . . . . through sieve.
Mix . . . . in cornstarch, 1/2 cup sugar and several drops of food coloring.
Cook . . . . until thickened, stirring constantly; cool.
Arrange . . . . . whole strawberries over cheesecake.
Pour . . . . glaze over strawberries.
Chill . . . . for 2 hours.
Yields . . . . . . 12 servings.

Kelli Doll
Ringwood H. S., Ringwood

MICROWAVE STRAWBERRY TRIFLE

1/2 c. sugar
3 tbsp. flour
1/4 tsp. salt
3 c. milk
4 eggs, beaten
1 tsp. vanilla extract
8 to 10 slices pound cake, cut into strips
1 1/2 c. sliced strawberries

Mix . . . . sugar, flour and salt in glass bowl.
Stir . . . . in milk gradually.
Microwave . . on High for 7 to 9 minutes or until thick, stirring every 2 minutes.
Stir . . . . 1/2 cup hot mixture into beaten eggs; stir eggs into hot custard.
Microwave . . on Medium for 5 to 6 minutes, stirring 2 or 3 times.
Add . . . . vanilla; cool.
Layer . . . . . . 1/3 of the custard, half the cake and half the strawberries in bowl.

Repeat ..... layers, ending with custard.
Chill .... in refrigerator.
Garnish ..... with whole strawberries and whipped topping.
Yields ...... 10 servings.

Lori Worthington
Chattanooga H. S., Chattanooga

FRESH STRAWBERRY CAKE

1 pkg. white cake mix
1 sm. package strawberry gelatin
1 c. oil
3 eggs
1 1/2 c. strawberries
1 stick butter, melted
1 16-oz. package confectioners' sugar

Combine .... cake mix, gelatin, oil, eggs, 1/2 cup hot water and 1/2 cup strawberries in bowl, mixing well.
Pour .... into greased and floured 9 x 13-inch baking pan.
Bake .... at 350 degrees for 30 to 35 minutes or until cake tests done.
Mix .... butter, confectioners' sugar and 1 cup strawberries in bowl.
Spread ..... over cooled cake.

Allenia Lester
Choctaw Jr. H. S., Newalla

GLAZED STRAWBERRY PIE

1 stick margarine, softened
1 c. flour
1/2 c. chopped nuts
2 tbsp. cornstarch
1 c. sugar
1 sm. package strawberry gelatin
2 c. sliced strawberries

Cut .... margarine into flour and nuts in bowl until crumbly.
Press .... in bottom and side of 9-inch pie plate.
Bake .... at 350 degrees for 20 minutes.
Combine .... cornstarch, sugar and 1 3/4 cups water in saucepan.
Cook .... until clear and thickened, stirring constantly.

Stir .... in gelatin; cool to room temperature.
Spoon ...... strawberries into pie shell.
Pour .... gelatin mixture over strawberries.
Chill .... until set.
Serve .... with whipped topping.

Dorothy Stanton
Tomlinson Jr. H. S., Lawton

STRAWBERRY THICK SHAKES

2 pt. fresh strawberries
1 qt. vanilla ice cream, softened

Puree ...... strawberries in blender container.
Strain ...... through double thickness of cheesecloth to remove seeds.
Puree ...... with ice cream in blender container.
Freeze ...... in blender container for 1 hour.
Process ..... for several seconds or until smooth.
Pour .... into tall glasses; garnish with whole strawberries.
Yields ...... 4 servings.

Lisa Anne Rullinson
Geary H. S., Geary

EASY STRAWBERRY PIE

3 tbsp. cornstarch
1 c. sugar
7 oz. 7-Up
Red food coloring
2 to 3 pt. fresh strawberries
1 baked pie shell
Whipping cream, whipped

Mix .... cornstarch and sugar.
Stir .... into 7-Up in saucepan.
Cook .... until thickened, stirring constantly; stir in food coloring.
Fold .... in strawberries.
Pour .... into pie shell.
Chill .... until firm.
Top .... with whipped cream.

Tracy Ragen
Granite H. S., Granite

51

FROZEN FRUIT SLUSH

1 6-oz. can frozen lemonade concentrate
1 6-oz. can frozen orange juice
   concentrate
1 10-oz. package frozen strawberries
1 can juice-pack crushed pineapple
1 can juice-pack pineapple chunks
1/2 to 3/4 c. sugar (opt.)
3 bananas, sliced

Reconstitute . lemonade and orange juice con-
centrates using package
directions.
Mix . . . . with remaining ingredients in
freezer container.
Freeze . . . . . . until firm.
Thaw . . . . . . for 2 hours or until slushy.
Yields . . . . . . 12-14 servings.

Crowder FHA, Crowder

DANISH COLD FRUIT SOUP

1 1/2 c. dried California apricots
1 c. pitted prunes
1 c. sugar
1/4 c. dark seedless raisins
1/2 lemon, sliced
1 cinnamon stick
1/2 tsp. whole cloves
3 tbsp. cornstarch
1 c. Chablis

Combine . . . . first 7 ingredients with 5 cups
water in saucepan.
Simmer . . . . . for 5 minutes, stirring
occasionally.
Blend . . . . . . cornstarch with Chablis.
Stir . . . . into fruit mixture gradually.
Cook . . . . until thick, stirring constantly.
Remove . . . . and discard cloves, cinnamon
and lemon slices.
Chill . . . . in refrigerator.
Garnish . . . . . with lemon wedges.

Photograph for this recipe on opposite page.

TIPSY MINCEMEAT

5 c. ground cooked beef
1 qt. ground suet
3 qt. chopped peeled tart apples
1 1/2 c. chopped oranges
1/4 c. lemon juice
3 11-oz. packages currants
1 c. Brandy
3 c. sweet cider
1/3 c. finely chopped orange rind
3 lb. mixed light and dark raisins
1 8-oz. package chopped candied citron
2 1-lb. packages brown sugar
1 tbsp. each salt, cinnamon, allspice
2 tsp. nutmeg
1 tsp. cloves
1/3 tsp. ginger

Combine . . . . all ingredients in large kettle.
Simmer . . . . . for 1 hour, stirring frequently.
Spoon . . . . . . into hot sterilized Ball jars, leav-
ing 1-inch headspace; adjust lids.
Process . . . . . at 10 pounds pressure for 20
minutes.
Yields . . . . . . 6 quarts.

Photograph for this recipe on page 45.

SIMPLE FRUIT SALAD

1 can fruit for salads
1 can pineapple chunks
1 can mandarin oranges, drained
2 bananas, sliced
1 lg. package vanilla instant pudding mix

Combine . . . . fruits and pudding mix in bowl,
mixing well.
Chill . . . . in refrigerator.
Yields . . . . . . 8 servings.

Dawn Lawson
Lindsay Jr. H. S., Lindsay

EASY FRUIT SALAD

1 can apricots
1 pkg. vanilla instant pudding mix
1 can pineapple chunks, drained
2 bananas, sliced

Drain . . . . . . apricots, reserving juice.
Stir . . . . apricot juice into pudding mix in
bowl.
Mix . . . . in pineapple, apricots and
bananas.

Jamiesue Sanders
Elgin H. S., Elgin

Fruits

REFRESHING FRUIT PIZZA

1 15-oz. can pineapple chunks
3 bananas, sliced
1 15-oz. package sugar cookie mix
1 8-oz. carton whipped topping
2 c. sliced strawberries
1/2 c. cherry pie filling
1 10 1/2-oz. can mandarin oranges, drained
1 kiwi fruit, sliced

Drain .... pineapple, reserving juice.
Combine ..... reserved juice and bananas; set aside.
Prepare ...... cookie mix according to package directions.
Press .... to 1/8-inch thickness in greased 12-inch pizza pan.
Bake .... at 375 degrees for 12 to 15 minutes or until edges are brown; cool.
Spread ...... whipped topping over cookie crust.
Arrange ..... strawberries, drained bananas, pie filling, pineapple, mandarin oranges and kiwi in concentric circles in order listed from outer edge.
Place .... 1 whole strawberry in center.
Chill .... until serving time.
Yields ...... 8 servings.

Vicki McCloud
Barnsdall H. S., Barnsdall

GOOD AND FRUITY

1 17-oz. package refrigerator sugar cookie dough
1 8-oz. package cream cheese, softened
1/4 c. sour cream
2 tbsp. sugar
1/2 tsp. almond extract
Assorted fresh fruit
Apricot jam, melted

Slice .... cookie dough 1/8 inch thick.
Arrange ..... over bottom and side of greased 14-inch pizza pan, overlapping slightly.
Bake .... at 375 degrees for 12 to 14 minutes or until brown; cool.

Beat .... cream cheese, sour cream, sugar and flavoring in bowl.
Spread ..... over cookie crust.
Arrange ..... overlapping slices of fruit over top.
Brush .... with jam.
Chill .... in refrigerator.
Yields ...... 12 servings.

Lori Savage
Rush Springs H. S., Rush Springs

FRUIT SALAD SUPREME

1 can pineapple tidbits, drained
1 can fruit cocktail
1 can mandarin oranges, drained
Bananas (opt.)
Green grapes (opt.)
Strawberries (opt.)
1/2 pkg. miniature marshmallows
Nuts (opt.)
2 pkg. vanilla instant pudding mix
1 8-oz. carton whipped topping

Mix .... fruits, marshmallows, nuts and pudding mix in bowl.
Fold .... in whipped topping.
Yields ...... 10-12 servings.

Angie Sankey
Canton H. S., Canton

FRUIT COBBLER

2 c. frozen fruit
1 c. flour
1 c. sugar
3/4 c. milk
2 tsp. baking powder
1 stick margarine, melted

Bring .... fruit to a boil in saucepan.
Mix .... flour, sugar, milk and baking powder in bowl.
Pour .... into melted margarine in baking dish.
Spoon .... fruit over top.
Bake .... at 350 degrees for 30 to 40 minutes or until browned.

Karenda Griffith
Bray-Doyle H. S., Marlow

Meats

AROMATIC BEEF STEW, recipe on page 57.

Meats

BEEF PARMIGIANA

1 1/2 lb. round steak
2 eggs, beaten
2/3 c. Parmesan cheese
2/3 c. fine dry bread crumbs
1/3 c. oil
1 med. onion, minced
1 tsp. salt
1/4 tsp. pepper
1/2 tsp. marjoram
1/2 tsp. sugar
1 6-oz. can tomato paste
1/2 lb. mozzarella cheese, sliced

Pound ...... steak to 1/4-inch thickness; cut into serving pieces.
Dip .... in eggs and coat with mixture of Parmesan cheese and bread crumbs; repeat.
Brown ...... in oil in skillet.
Place .... in shallow baking dish.
Saute ...... onion in pan drippings.
Stir .... in remaining ingredients except cheese and 2 cups hot water.
Cook .... for 5 minutes.
Pour .... 2/3 of the sauce over steak.
Top .... with cheese slices and remaining sauce.
Bake .... at 350 degrees for 1 hour or until steak is tender, adding a small amount of water if necessary.
Serve .... with spaghetti and green salad.

Cathy Shadid
Weatherford H. S., Weatherford

BEEF STROGANOFF

2 lb. sirloin steak, cut into serving-sized pieces
Flour
1/2 tsp. salt
1/4 c. melted butter
1 c. thinly sliced mushrooms
1/2 c. chopped onion
1 tbsp. tomato paste
1 1/4 c. beef stock
1 8-oz. carton sour cream
2 tbsp. cooking Sherry

Coat .... steak with mixture of 1/2 cup flour and salt.
Brown ...... in 2 tablespoons butter in skillet; remove steak.

Saute ...... mushrooms and onion in pan drippings for 3 to 4 minutes or until onion is just tender; remove.
Blend ...... 3 tablespoons flour into remaining 2 tablespoons butter and pan drippings.
Stir .... in tomato paste and beef stock gradually.
Cook .... until thick, stirring constantly.
Add .... steak, mushrooms and onion.
Simmer ..... for 1 hour.
Add .... sour cream and Sherry just before serving.
Heat .... to serving temperature.
Serve .... over buttered rice or noodles.
Yields ...... 6-8 servings.

Emberly Taylor
Meeker H. S., Meeker

SWISS STEAK

Flour
Salt and pepper
3 lb. round steak, cut into serving pieces
3 tbsp. oil
1 onion, chopped
1 c. chopped celery
1 green pepper, chopped
1 can tomatoes
1 sm. can mushrooms

Pound ...... flour, salt and pepper into steak with meat mallet.
Brown ...... in oil in electric skillet.
Add .... remaining ingredients and 1/2 cup water.
Simmer ..... at 300 degrees for 1 hour or until steak and vegetables are tender.

Kindra Doll
Ringwood H. S., Ringwood

ENGLISH PUB STEW WITH YORKSHIRE PUDDING

2 lb. bottom round steak, cubed, trimmed
1 or 2 veal kidneys, cubed, trimmed
1/4 c. flour
3 or 4 tbsp. oil
1 med. onion, thinly sliced

Meats

1/4 lb. mushrooms, sliced
1/2 c. beef broth
1/2 c. dry red wine
1 tbsp. tomato paste
1 tsp. Worcestershire sauce
1/2 tsp. salt
1/4 tsp. each pepper, tarragon
Rosemary to taste
3 carrots, cut into 1-in. pieces
Yorkshire Pudding

Coat .... steak and kidneys with flour.
Brown ...... several pieces at a time in oil in stock pot; remove.
Saute ...... onion in pan drippings until tender.
Add .... mushrooms.
Cook .... for several minutes longer.
Stir .... in broth, wine, tomato paste and next 5 seasonings.
Simmer ..... covered, for 1 hour.
Add .... carrots.
Cook .... for 1 hour longer.
Chill .... for several hours to overnight.
Skim .... reserving 2 tablespoons drippings.
Heat .... to serving temperature.
Prepare ..... Yorkshire Pudding.

Yorkshire Pudding

Beat 2 eggs in bowl. Mix in 1 cup milk. Sift in 1 cup flour and 1/2 teaspoon salt; beat until smooth. Heat reserved drippings in 6-cup casserole. Pour batter into hot casserole. Spoon stew over batter to within 1 inch of edge. Bake at 400 degrees for 30 minutes or until puffed and brown. Yield: 6 servings.

Dolores Coale
Drumright H. S., Drumright

AROMATIC BEEF STEW

2 lb. chuck roast
Prepared mustard
1 med. onion, chopped
2 tsp. salt
1 tsp. pepper
1/2 c. chopped celery
1 c. canned tomatoes
6 potatoes, peeled
6 carrots, peeled, cut into chunks
1 tbsp. angostura bitters
1 recipe biscuits, baked

Cut .... roast into cubes.
Coat .... cubes with mustard.
Brown ...... on all sides in a small amount of shortening in cast iron skillet over low heat.
Add .... onion, salt, pepper and 2 cups water.
Simmer ..... covered, for 1 1/2 hours.
Add .... remaining vegetables and bitters.
Simmer ..... covered, for 1 hour longer.
Top .... with hot biscuits just before serving.

Photograph for this recipe on page 55.

OLD-FASHIONED BEEF STEW

2 lb. beef chuck, cubed
2 tbsp. shortening
1 clove of garlic
1 med. onion, sliced
1 tsp. Worcestershire sauce
1 or 2 bay leaves
1 tsp. salt
Dash of allspice
1 tsp. sugar
1/2 tsp. each pepper, paprika
6 carrots, quartered
1 lb. small white onions
4 potatoes, peeled, quartered
2 tbsp. flour

Brown ...... beef in shortening in stock pot, stirring frequently.
Add .... 2 cups hot water, garlic, sliced onion and next 7 seasonings.
Simmer ..... covered, for 1 1/2 hours, stirring occasionally; remove garlic and bay leaves.
Add .... carrots, whole onions and potatoes.
Simmer ..... covered, for 30 to 45 minutes or until vegetables are tender; skim.
Remove .... 1 3/4 cups hot pan juices to saucepan.
Blend ...... flour with 1/4 cup cold water.
Stir .... into hot juices gradually.
Cook .... for 3 minutes, stirring constantly.
Stir .... into stew.
Yields ...... 6-8 servings.

Mary Moreland
Byng H. S., Ada

57

Meats

PEPPERED STEAK

2 or 3 cloves of garlic, crushed
3 1/2 tbsp. oil
1 1/2 to 2 lb. steak, thinly sliced
1/4 c. soy sauce
1 1/2 onions, sliced
1 green pepper, sliced

Brown . . . . . . garlic in oil in wok.
Add . . . . steak.
Stir-fry . . . . . steak until tender.
Sprinkle . . . . with soy sauce.
Cook . . . . for 5 minutes longer.
Add . . . . onions and green pepper.
Stir-fry . . . . . until vegetables are tender-crisp.
Serve . . . . over rice. May thicken pan juices using a small amount of flour blended with a small amount of water and sugar to taste.

Barbara Carl
Chickasha H. S., Chickasha

SAVORY STEAK MOZZARELLA

2 lb. top round steak
1/2 c. flour
1/4 c. oil
1/4 tsp. each savory, pepper
1 15-oz. can tomatoes
1 8-oz. can tomato sauce
1 c. each chopped celery, green pepper
1/2 lb. mozzarella cheese, thinly sliced

Cut . . . . steak into 6 portions; pound with mallet.
Coat . . . . with 1/4 cup flour.
Brown . . . . . . in oil in skillet; place in baking dish.
Blend . . . . . . remaining 1/4 cup flour into pan drippings.
Stir . . . . in 1 cup water, seasonings, tomatoes, tomato sauce, celery and green pepper.
Bring . . . . to a boil, stirring constantly.
Pour . . . . over steak.
Bake . . . . at 325 degrees for 2 to 2 1/2 hours.
Top . . . . with cheese slices.
Bake . . . . for 5 minutes longer.
Yields . . . . . . 4-6 servings.

Jamie Rush
Union City H. S., Union City

STEAK-IN-A-BAG

1/4 c. butter, softened
1/4 c. oil
1 tsp. crushed garlic
2 tsp. seasoned salt
2 1/2 tsp. seasoned pepper
1 2 to 3-lb. 2 1/2-in. thick sirloin steak, trimmed
1 c. bread crumbs
1 c. shredded sharp Cheddar cheese
1 Oven Cooking Bag

Combine . . . . butter, oil, garlic, seasoned salt and seasoned pepper in bowl, mixing well.
Spread . . . . . over both sides of steak.
Coat . . . . steak with mixture of bread crumbs and cheese.
Place . . . . steak in Oven Cooking Bag; fasten, using manufacturer's directions.
Bake . . . . on baking sheet at 375 degrees for 30 minutes for rare; at 425 degrees for 45 minutes for medium-rare; or at 425 degrees for 45 minutes and 375 degrees for 5 minutes for medium-well done.
Remove . . . . from bag to serving plate.
Let . . . . stand for 5 minutes before carving into thin slices.
Yields . . . . . . 4-6 servings.

Waurika FHA, Waurika

TACO STEAK

1 2 to 4-lb. 1-inch thick center cut round steak
1 tsp. tenderizer
1 tsp. each pepper, garlic powder
2 tsp. seasoned salt
1 8-oz. package mushrooms, sliced
1 med. green pepper, chopped
1 med. onion, chopped
1 tsp. mustard seed
1 8-oz. jar medium taco sauce

Place . . . . steak in 9 x 13-inch baking dish; pierce with fork and sprinkle with tenderizer.
Let . . . . stand for 15 minutes.

Sprinkle .... with mixture of pepper, garlic powder and seasoned salt.
Layer ...... remaining ingredients in order listed over steak.
Bake .... at 350 degrees for 3 hours.
Yields ...... 6 servings.

Christy Nelson
Midwest City H. S., Midwest City

WESTERN ROUND STEAK

1 round steak
1/4 c. mustard
Flour
1 clove of garlic, finely chopped
1/2 c. each chopped onion, green pepper
1 6-oz. can tomato paste
1/4 c. packed brown sugar
1/2 tsp. Worcestershire sauce

Cut .... steak into serving portions.
Brush ...... with mustard; coat with flour.
Brown ...... steak in a small amount of oil in skillet; drain.
Mix .... remaining ingredients with 1/4 cup water in bowl.
Pour .... over steak.
Cook .... covered, over low heat for 1 to 1 1/2 hours or until tender.

Vicki Rothell
Elgin H. S., Lawton

MEXICAN ROAST

1 lg. beef roast
2 beef bouillon cubes
1 can green chilies, drained
1/2 pkg. taco seasoning mix
1 c. chopped tomatoes
1 tbsp. sugar

Sear .... beef on both sides in Dutch oven.
Dissolve .... bouillon cubes in 1/4 cup hot water in bowl.
Mix .... in remaining ingredients.
Pour .... over roast.
Bake .... at 225 degrees for 1 hour; turn.
Bake .... for 1 to 2 hours longer or to desired degree of doneness.
Yields ...... 6-8 servings.

Angel Todd
Rush Springs H. S., Rush Springs

ROULADEN

1 sm. jar mustard
8 veal cutlets
1 pkg. bacon, chopped
1 jar pickles, chopped
2 med. onions, chopped
Salt and pepper to taste

Spread ..... mustard over 1 side of cutlets.
Layer ...... bacon, pickles, onions and seasonings over mustard.
Roll .... veal to enclose filling; secure with thread and toothpicks.
Cook .... in skillet over low heat for 20 minutes or until brown.
Cook ...... over medium heat for 1 hour.
Remove .... thread before serving.
Yields ...... 8 servings.

Cathy Tysdal
Eisenhower H. S., Lawton

COMPANY LASAGNA

1 1/2 lb. ground beef
2 cloves of garlic, crushed
2 tsp. seasoned salt
1/2 tsp. pepper
1 29-oz. can tomatoes
2 sm. cans tomato sauce
1 pkg. spaghetti sauce mix
1 8-oz. package lasagna noodles, cooked
1/2 lb. mozzarella cheese, shredded
1 16-oz. carton cottage cheese
1/2 c. Parmesan cheese

Brown ...... ground beef in skillet, stirring frequently.
Add .... garlic and seasonings.
Simmer ..... for 10 minutes.
Add ...... tomatoes, tomato sauce and spaghetti sauce mix.
Simmer ..... for 30 minutes.
Layer ...... sauce, noodles, mozzarella and cottage cheeses alternately in baking dish until all ingredients are used, ending with sauce.
Sprinkle .... with Parmesan cheese.
Bake .... at 350 degrees for 30 minutes.
Yields ...... 6-8 servings.

Pam Wallace
Choctaw Jr. H. S., Choctaw

Meats

CHEESY LASAGNA

1 lb. ground beef
1 sm. onion, chopped
1 sm. carton cottage cheese
2 eggs
6 lasagna noodles, cooked
1 sm. jar spaghetti sauce
1 lb. mozzarella cheese, shredded
1 lb. Velveeta cheese, shredded
Parmesan cheese

Brown . . . . . . ground beef and onion in skillet, stirring frequently; drain.
Mix . . . . cottage cheese and eggs in small bowl.
Layer . . . . . . half the ground beef mixture, noodles, sauce, cottage cheese mixture, mozzarella and Velveeta cheeses in casserole.
Repeat . . . . . layers.
Sprinkle . . . . with Parmesan cheese.
Bake . . . . at 350 degrees for 30 minutes.

Tami Chance
Ringwood H. S., Ringwood

TRACY'S BEEF-SAUSAGE CASSEROLE

1 lb. ground beef
1 lb. hot sausage
1 med. onion, chopped
2 green peppers, chopped
5 stalks celery, chopped
1 c. rice
3 env. dry chicken noodle soup mix

Brown . . . . . . ground beef and sausage in skillet, stirring frequently; drain, reserving pan drippings.
Saute . . . . . . vegetables in pan drippings.
Combine . . . . all ingredients with 5 cups water in large casserole, mixing well.
Bake . . . . at 350 degrees for 1 1/2 hours, stirring occasionally.

Tracy Boone
Hennessey H. S., Hennessey

DONNA'S A-OK CASSEROLE

1 lb. ground beef
1 tsp. salt
1/4 tsp. pepper
1 c. chopped onion
1 c. each canned tomatoes, corn, peas
1 c. cooked rice
1 c. grated Cheddar cheese
Paprika

Brown . . . . . . ground beef at 350 degrees in electric skillet, stirring frequently.
Add . . . . seasonings; drain.
Add . . . . onion.
Saute . . . . . . until tender.
Stir . . . . in vegetables and rice.
Cook . . . . for 10 minutes, stirring frequently.
Sprinkle . . . . with cheese and paprika.
Let . . . . stand, covered, until cheese melts.
Yields . . . . . . 6 servings.

Donna Workman
Caney H. S., Caney

BEEF-CHILI CASSEROLE

1 lb. ground beef
1 med. onion, chopped
3 tbsp. chili seasoning mix
4 tbsp. picante sauce
1 can cream-style corn
1 can chopped green chilies
1 can tomato paste
1 can mushrooms
3 c. cooked noodles
2 c. grated cheese

Brown . . . . . . ground beef and onion in skillet, stirring frequently.
Add . . . . next 6 ingredients, mixing well.
Cook . . . . for 15 minutes.
Spoon . . . . . . into large casserole.
Top . . . . with noodles.
Sprinkle . . . . with cheese.
Bake . . . . at 350 degrees until cheese melts.

Linda Ensminger
Okeene H. S., Okeene

HEARTY GROUND BEEF CASSEROLE

2 lb. ground beef
1 can cream of chicken soup
1 can cream of mushroom soup
1 can jalapeno pinto beans

1 soup can grated Cheddar cheese
1 pkg. tortilla chips, crushed

Brown . . . . . . ground beef in skillet, stirring
frequently; drain.
Mix . . . . in soups, beans, cheese and tor-
tilla chips.
Spoon . . . . . . into casserole.
Sprinkle . . . . with additional cheese.
Bake . . . . at 350 degrees for 45 minutes.

Deana Rene Sullivan
Chickasha H. S., Chickasha

GROUND BEEF-TATER TOT CASSEROLE

1 1/2 lb. ground beef
1/4 c. chopped onion
1 pkg. frozen Tater Tots
1 can cream of mushroom soup

Press . . . . ground beef into 8-inch square
pan.
Layer . . . . . . onion, Tater Tots and soup over
top.
Bake . . . . at 325 degrees for 1 1/2 hours.

Sherry McClain
Barnsdall H. S., Skiatook

KIM'S CASSEROLE

2 lb. ground beef
1 15-oz. can ranch-style beans
1 14-oz. can Spaghetti-O's
1 14-oz. can Spanish rice
1 8-oz. can tomato sauce
1 tsp. Worcestershire sauce
1/4 tsp. oregano
1 clove of garlic, minced

Brown . . . . . . ground beef in skillet, stirring
frequently; drain.
Stir . . . . in remaining ingredients.
Spoon . . . . . . into 9 x 13-inch baking dish.
Bake . . . . at 350 degrees for 30 minutes.

Kim Griffith
Frederick H. S., Frederick

MEZETTI

1 lb. ground beef
1/4 c. chopped green pepper
1 c. chopped onion
2 tbsp. shortening

1 tbsp. chili powder
1 tsp. garlic salt
1 8-oz. package noodles
1 can tomato soup
1 can mushroom soup
1 c. grated cheese

Brown . . . . . . ground beef, green pepper and
onion in shortening in skillet,
stirring frequently.
Stir . . . . in chili powder and garlic salt.
Top . . . . with noodles.
Add . . . . 1 cup water.
Blend . . . . . . soups in bowl.
Pour . . . . over noodles.
Simmer . . . . . covered, for 25 minutes.
Sprinkle . . . . cheese over top.
Simmer . . . . . for 5 minutes longer.
Yields . . . . . . 8 servings.

Janice Simon
Elgin H. S., Elgin

MICROWAVE GROUND BEEF AND CORN CASSEROLE

1 lb. ground beef, crumbled
1/4 c. chopped onion
Chopped green pepper
1 16-oz. can tomatoes
1 12-oz. can whole kernel corn, drained
1 8-oz. can tomato sauce
1/2 c. sliced stuffed olives
1 to 2 tsp. chili powder
1 c. coarsely crumbled corn chips
1/2 c. shredded Cheddar cheese

Combine . . . . ground beef, onion and green
pepper in 2-quart glass casserole.
Microwave . . on High for 6 minutes, stirring
after 3 minutes; drain.
Stir . . . . in chopped tomatoes and 1/4
cup tomato liquid.
Add . . . . corn, tomato sauce, olives and
chili powder.
Microwave . . covered, on High for 6 to 8 minutes or until heated through;
stir.
Sprinkle . . . . with corn chips and cheese.
Microwave . . uncovered, on High for 2 minutes or until cheese melts.
Yields . . . . . . 4-6 servings.

Missy Wilcox
Apache H. S., Apache

Meats

FAVORITE ENCHILADA CASSEROLE

1 lb. ground beef
3/4 tsp. garlic salt
1 med. onion, chopped
2 tsp. chili powder
1 can tomato sauce
1 sm. package tortilla chips
1 can cream of chicken soup
1/2 soup can milk
2 c. grated American cheese

Brown . . . . . . ground beef with garlic salt and onion in skillet, stirring frequently.
Add . . . . chili powder, tomato sauce and 1 sauce can water.
Simmer . . . . . for several minutes.
Layer . . . . . . half the tortilla chips and all the ground beef mixture in casserole.
Top . . . . with remaining tortilla chips.
Pour . . . . soup blended with milk over top.
Sprinkle . . . . with cheese.
Bake . . . . at 350 degrees for 1 hour.

Cheryl Alexander
Byng H. S., Ada

ENCHILADA PIE

1 1/2 lb. ground beef
1/2 c. chopped onions
1 can chili
1 can cream of mushroom soup
1/4 tsp. each salt and pepper
1/2 tsp. garlic powder
Corn tortillas, quartered
1 1/2 c. grated cheese

Brown . . . . . . ground beef and onions in skillet, stirring frequently.
Stir . . . . in chili, soup and seasonings.
Layer . . . . . . tortillas and ground beef mixture alternately in pie plate.
Sprinkle . . . . with cheese.
Bake . . . . at 350 degrees until heated through.
Yields . . . . . . 8 servings.

Angela Gwen Lott
Waurika H. S., Waurika

EASY ENCHILADA CASSEROLE

1 lb. ground beef
1 onion, chopped
1 clove of garlic, crushed
1 can chili without beans
1 tsp. pepper
1/4 tsp. salt
1 8-oz. can tomato sauce
6 corn tortillas
2 c. shredded sharp Cheddar cheese

Brown . . . . . . ground beef with onion and garlic in skillet, stirring frequently.
Stir . . . . in chili, 2/3 cup water, seasonings and tomato sauce.
Cook . . . . until heated through.
Layer . . . . . . tortillas, sauce and cheese alternately in 1 1/2-quart glass casserole.
Bake . . . . at 400 degrees until heated through and cheese has melted.

Tonia Tucker
Bray-Doyle H. S., Marlow

COMPANY ENCHILADA CASSEROLE

2 lb. ground beef
Chopped onions
1 c. enchilada sauce
1 c. chopped green chilies
2 c. cream of mushroom soup
1 c. Milnot
1 pkg. tortilla chips, crushed
Grated cheese

Brown . . . . . . ground beef with onions in skillet, stirring frequently.
Mix . . . . in enchilada sauce, green chilies, soup and Milnot.
Layer . . . . . . tortillas, sauce and cheese in casserole.
Bake . . . . at 350 degrees for 15 minutes or until heated through.

La Ronda Bates
Copan H. S., Pawhuska

JALAPENO CASSEROLE

3 lb. ground beef
1 sm. onion, finely chopped
2 cans mushroom soup
1 soup can milk
1 pkg. flour tortillas

1 pkg. shredded Cheddar cheese
Jalapeno peppers, chopped
Salt and pepper to taste

Brown . . . . . . ground beef and onion in skillet, stirring frequently.
Stir . . . . in soup and milk.
Layer . . . . . . tortillas and ground beef mixture in 9 x 13-inch baking dish.
Top . . . . with cheese, jalapeno peppers, salt and pepper.
Bake . . . . at 250 degrees for 20 minutes.
Yields . . . . . . 6 servings.

Duane London
Apache H. S., Apache

QUICK MEXICAN CASSEROLE

1 lb. ground beef
1 green pepper, chopped
1 onion, chopped
1 can Spanish rice
1 can ranch-style beans
1 med. package corn chips
6 slices cheese

Brown . . . . . . ground beef, green pepper and onion in skillet, stirring frequently; drain.
Add . . . . rice and beans, mixing well.
Spoon . . . . . . into casserole.
Top . . . . with corn chips and cheese.
Bake . . . . at 350 degrees for 10 minutes.
Yields . . . . . . 5 servings.

LaDonna Boggess
Chickasha H. S., Chickasha

MEXICAN BEEF AND RICE

2 lb. ground beef
1 sm. onion, chopped
2 c. cooked rice
1 can cream of chicken soup
1 can cream of mushroom soup
1 sm. can tomato paste
2 sm. cans taco sauce
1 sm. can chopped green chilies
1 sm. package tortilla chips, crushed
8 oz. cheese, shredded

Brown . . . . . . ground beef and onion in skillet, stirring frequently; drain.
Add . . . . next 7 ingredients and one-half the cheese, mixing well.

Cook . . . . until heated through.
Spoon . . . . . . into large baking dish; sprinkle with remaining cheese.
Bake . . . . at 350 degrees for 30 minutes or until bubbly.

Lorean Droke
Okeene H. S., Okeene

MEXICAN-OKIE HASH

1 lb. ground beef
1/3 c. chopped onion
Salt and pepper to taste
1 1/2 c. finely chopped potatoes
1 16-oz. can stewed tomatoes, chopped
1 12-oz. can whole kernel corn, drained
1 can tomato soup
1 1/2 tsp. chili powder
8 oz. Cheddar cheese, grated

Brown . . . . . . ground beef and onion in skillet, stirring frequently.
Mix . . . . in salt and pepper, potatoes, tomatoes, corn, soup and chili powder.
Pour . . . . into 1 1/2-quart casserole.
Bake . . . . covered, at 350 degrees for 20 to 25 minutes or until bubbly.
Sprinkle . . . . with cheese.
Yields . . . . . . 6 servings.

Michelle Nelms
Apache H. S., Apache

TINA'S MEXICAN CASSEROLE

1 lb. ground beef
1 med. package tortilla chips, crushed
1 can ranch-style beans
1 can cream of chicken soup
1 can Ro-Tel
1 c. grated cheese

Brown . . . . . . ground beef in skillet, stirring frequently.
Layer . . . . . . tortilla chips, ground beef and remaining ingredients except cheese in order listed in casserole.
Bake . . . . at 350 degrees for 30 minutes.
Top . . . . with cheese.
Bake . . . . until cheese melts.

Tina Furr
Hugo H. S., Hugo

Meats

SPECIAL MEXICAN CASSEROLE

2 lb. ground beef
1/4 c. chopped onions
1 sm. can taco sauce
1 can cream of celery soup
1 can cream of chicken soup
1 sm. can evaporated milk
1 pkg. taco-flavored corn chips
2 c. shredded Cheddar cheese

Brown . . . . . . ground beef and onions in skillet, stirring frequently; drain.
Stir . . . . in taco sauce.
Blend . . . . . . soups, evaporated milk and 1 cup water in bowl.
Layer . . . . . . corn chips, ground beef and soup mixtures alternately in 9 x 13-inch baking dish until all ingredients are used.
Sprinkle . . . . with cheese.
Bake . . . . at 350 degrees for 30 to 35 minutes or until heated through.
Yields . . . . . . 12 servings.

Gayla Carrier
Crescent H. S., Crescent

EASY MEXICAN CASSEROLE

1 lb. ground beef
1 can cream of chicken soup
1 can cream of mushroom soup
1 10-oz. can enchilada sauce
1 3 1/2-oz. can chopped green chilies
1 12-oz. bag nacho-flavored tortilla chips
12 oz. Cheddar cheese, grated

Brown . . . . . . ground beef in skillet, stirring frequently; drain.
Blend . . . . . . soups and sauce in bowl; add chilies.
Stir . . . . into ground beef mixture.
Crumble . . . . tortilla chips in bottom of 9 x 13-inch pan.
Spoon . . . . . . ground beef mixture over chips.
Sprinkle . . . . with cheese.
Bake . . . . at 350 degrees for 30 minutes.
Yields . . . . . . 4 servings.

Donna Edwards
Checotah H. S., Checotah

TACO CASSEROLE

1 lb. ground beef
1 env. taco seasoning mix
1 16-oz. package tortilla chips, crushed
1 16-oz. can Mexican beans, drained
1 16-oz. can tomatoes, drained, chopped
1 4-oz. can chopped green chilies
2 c. grated Cheddar cheese

Brown . . . . . . ground beef in skillet, stirring frequently; drain.
Stir . . . . in seasoning mix.
Layer . . . . . . half the tortilla chips and ground beef mixture, all the beans, tomatoes and green chilies, remaining ground beef mixture, cheese and remaining chips in 9 x 13-inch baking dish.
Bake . . . . at 350 degrees for 25 to 30 minutes.

Debbie Reding
Geary H. S., Geary

GREEN CHILI BURRITOS

2 lb. ground beef
1 med. onion, chopped
1 chili pepper, chopped
Salt and pepper to taste
1 pkg. flour tortillas
1/4 lb. Velveeta cheese, cubed
1 can cream of chicken soup
1/2 c. evaporated milk
1 can chopped green chilies

Brown . . . . . . ground beef with onion, chili pepper and seasonings in skillet, stirring frequently.
Warm . . . . . . each tortilla in heavy skillet, turning once.
Spoon . . . . . . ground beef mixture into centers of tortillas; roll to enclose filling.
Place . . . . in 9 x 13-inch casserole.
Mix . . . . cheese, soup, evaporated milk and chilies in saucepan.
Heat . . . . until cheese melts, stirring constantly.
Pour . . . . over burritos.
Bake . . . . at 350 degrees for 30 minutes or until bubbly.
Yields . . . . . . 6 servings.

Judy Lee Nichols
Vinita H. S., Vinita

MICROWAVE CHILI

2 lb. ground beef
1/2 c. chopped onion
1 8-oz. jar picante sauce
1 14 1/2-oz. can stewed tomatoes
1 beef bouillon cube
1 can cream of mushroom soup
Chili powder, oregano, salt and pepper
    to taste

Crumble .... ground beef into 2-quart casserole.
Microwave .. covered, on High for 5 minutes; drain.
Mix .... in onion.
Microwave .. on High for 3 minutes; drain.
Stir .... in picante sauce, tomatoes, bouillon cube, soup blended with 1/2 soup can water and seasonings.
Microwave .. on High for 10 minutes.
Yields ...... 8 servings.

Charity Caywood
Canton H. S., Canton

TEXAS HASH

1 c. chopped onion
2 tbsp. shortening
1 lb. ground beef
1 c. chopped green pepper
2 tsp. salt
1/4 tsp. each pepper, chili powder
1/2 c. rice
1 29-oz. can tomatoes

Saute ...... onion in shortening in 10-inch skillet until brown.
Add .... ground beef, green pepper, seasonings and rice, mixing well.
Spoon ...... into 2-quart casserole.
Pour .... tomatoes over top.
Bake .... covered, at 350 degrees for 30 minutes.
Yields ...... 6 servings.

Betty Burnes
Stigler H. S., Stigler

BAKED CABBAGE ROLLS

3 8-oz. cans tomato sauce
Juice of 1 lg. lemon
1/3 c. packed brown sugar

3/4 lb. ground beef
1/2 c. finely chopped onion
1/2 c. chopped tomato
3/4 c. rice
1 egg
Salt and pepper to taste
1/2 tsp. nutmeg
Pinch of thyme
1 lg. head cabbage

Blend ...... tomato sauce, lemon juice and brown sugar in bowl.
Mix .... 1/2 cup tomato sauce mixture with next 5 ingredients and seasonings in large bowl.
Parboil ..... cabbage leaves for 4 to 5 minutes.
Spoon ...... ground beef mixture onto cabbage leaves; roll to enclose filling.
Place .... in 8 x 10-inch baking pan.
Pour .... tomato sauce mixture over cabbage rolls.
Bake .... covered, at 350 degrees for 1 3/4 hours.
Yields ...... 12 servings.

Debbie Jacoway
Central Jr. H. S., Oklahoma City

SAUCY CABBAGE ROLLS

8 lg. cabbage leaves
1 lb. ground beef
1 1/2 c. soft bread crumbs
1/2 c. chopped onion
2 eggs
1 1/2 tsp. salt
1/4 tsp. pepper
1 16-oz. can tomato sauce

Cook .... cabbage leaves in boiling water for 5 minutes; drain.
Combine .... remaining ingredients except tomato sauce in bowl, mixing well.
Spoon ...... ground beef mixture onto cabbage leaves; roll to enclose filling.
Place .... in electric skillet.
Pour .... tomato sauce over rolls.
Cook .... at 375 degrees for 35 minutes.

Tanja Jenceleski
Eisenhower Jr. H. S., Lawton

Meats

MICROWAVE CABBAGE ROLLS

1 med. head cabbage, cored
3/4 c. chopped celery
3/4 c. shredded carrots
1/2 c. chopped onion
1 tbsp. butter
1 lb. ground beef
1/2 tsp. salt
1/8 tsp. pepper
1 egg
1 can Cheddar cheese soup

Microwave .. cabbage on High in loosely covered glass bowl in 1 cup water for 10 to 12 minutes or until tender; drain.
Microwave .. next 4 ingredients on High in loosely covered glass bowl for 5 to 6 minutes or until tender-crisp.
Mix .... in ground beef, seasonings, egg and 1/2 cup soup.
Spoon ...... 1/3 cup ground beef mixture onto base of each of 10 cabbage leaves; fold in side and roll to enclose filling.
Place .... in glass casserole.
Spread ..... soup over top.
Microwave .. on High for 14 to 16 minutes or until cooked through, turning once.

Evie Herndon
Tonkawa H. S., Tonkawa

SPANISH DUMPLINGS

2 heads cabbage
2 lb. ground beef
1 c. cooked rice
1/2 lb. sausage
1 tbsp. chili powder
1 16-oz. can tomato soup
1 tsp. onion salt
Salt and pepper to taste

Peel .... 20 large whole leaves from cabbage; remove heavy ribs.
Combine .... next 4 ingredients in bowl, mixing well.
Place .... spoonful of ground beef mixture on each cabbage leaf; roll to enclose filling and secure with toothpicks.

Place .... dumplings in large skillet.
Add .... tomato soup and enough water to cover.
Simmer ..... for 2 to 3 hours or until cooked through.
Season ..... with onion salt, salt and pepper to taste.

Michelle L. Kammerzell
Okeene Public Schools, Okeene

CHEESE ENCHILADAS

1 1/2 lb. ground beef
1/4 tsp. garlic salt
1 tsp. salt
1 c. chopped onion
3/4 lb. longhorn cheese, grated
24 tortillas
Oil
1 can cream of chicken soup
1 lg. package Velveeta cheese
Milk
1 pkg. dry onion dip mix
1 sm. jar chopped pimento
1 sm. can chopped green chilies

Brown ...... ground beef with garlic salt, salt and onion in skillet, stirring frequently; drain.
Stir .... in longhorn cheese.
Dip .... tortillas in hot oil to soften.
Spoon ...... ground beef mixture onto tortillas.
Roll .... to enclose filling; place in baking dish.
Heat .... soup, Velveeta cheese and enough milk to make of desired consistency in saucepan until cheese melts.
Stir .... in remaining ingredients.
Pour .... over enchiladas.
Bake .... at 350 degrees for 30 minutes.

Vetagene Roe
Checotah H. S., Checotah

DELICIOUS ENCHILADAS

1 1/2 to 2 lb. ground beef
1 or 2 pkg. enchilada sauce mix
2 cans tomato paste
1 or 2 pkg. flour tortillas
1 onion, chopped
1 green pepper, chopped

Shredded Cheddar cheese
Shredded Monterey Jack cheese
Salt and pepper to taste
Mild taco sauce

Brown . . . . . . ground beef in skillet, stirring frequently; drain.
Prepare . . . . . enchilada sauce with tomato paste, using package directions.
Dip . . . . tortillas in enchilada sauce.
Top . . . . each tortilla with onion, green pepper, ground beef, cheeses, seasonings and taco sauce; roll to enclose filling.
Arrange . . . . . in 9 x 12-inch baking dish.
Pour . . . . additional sauce over top.
Sprinkle . . . . with additional cheeses.
Bake . . . . at 350 degrees for 30 minutes.

Debbie D. Cooper
Eisenhower Jr. H. S., Lawton

MEXICAN ENCHILADAS

1 can cream of chicken soup
1 can cream of mushroom soup
1 sm. can tomato sauce
1/2 c. jalapeno sauce
2 lb. ground beef
2 med. onions, chopped
2 pkg. frozen tortillas, thawed
2 c. grated cheese
1 carton sour cream

Heat . . . . soups and sauces in saucepan, stirring frequently.
Brown . . . . . . ground beef and onions in skillet, stirring frequently; drain.
Soften . . . . . . tortillas in hot shortening in skillet.
Spoon . . . . . . ground beef mixture onto tortillas; sprinkle with cheese.
Top . . . . each with 1 tablespoon sauce; roll to enclose filling.
Place . . . . in 9 x 13-inch baking dish.
Top . . . . with sour cream, remaining sauce and cheese.
Bake . . . . at 350 degrees for 20 minutes.

Carol Taylor
Rush Springs H. S., Rush Springs

GREEN CHILI ENCHILADAS

1 lb. ground beef
1 onion, chopped

1 pkg. enchilada seasoning
12 flour tortillas
1/2 lb. grated Cheddar cheese
1/2 lb. Velveeta cheese, cubed
1 can cream of chicken soup
1 sm. can Milnot
1 4-oz. can chopped green chilies

Brown . . . . . . ground beef and onion in skillet, stirring frequently.
Stir . . . . in enchilada seasoning.
Spoon . . . . . . onto tortillas; sprinkle with Cheddar cheese.
Roll . . . . to enclose filling; place in 9 x 13-inch baking dish.
Heat . . . . Velveeta cheese, soup and Milnot in saucepan over low heat until Velveeta melts, stirring constantly.
Stir . . . . in green chilies.
Pour . . . . sauce over enchiladas.
Bake . . . . covered, at 350 degrees for 30 minutes.
Yields . . . . . . 12 servings.

Linda Schwarz
North Intermediate H. S., Broken Arrow

SOUR CREAM ENCHILADAS

1 lb. ground beef
1 bunch green onions, chopped
4 or 5 jalapeno peppers, chopped
1 lg. carton sour cream
1 can cream of mushroom soup
1 pkg. corn tortillas
1 8-oz. package grated cheese

Brown . . . . . . ground beef in skillet, stirring frequently; drain.
Combine . . . . with next 4 ingredients in bowl, mixing well.
Soften . . . . . . tortillas in hot oil in skillet.
Spoon . . . . . . half the ground beef mixture onto tortillas; roll to enclose filling.
Place . . . . in 9 x 13-inch baking dish.
Spoon . . . . . . remaining ground beef mixture over top.
Sprinkle . . . . with cheese.
Bake . . . . at 350 degrees for 25 to 30 minutes or until heated through.

Teresa Garnett
Eisenhower H. S., Lawton

Meats

MEATBALLS ORIENTAL

1 1/2 lb. lean ground beef
2 eggs, lightly beaten
1/2 c. fine dry bread crumbs
1 tsp. onion powder
1/8 tsp. pepper
2 1/4 tsp. salt
1/4 c. oil
1/4 c. instant minced onion
1/4 tsp. instant minced garlic
1 1/2 c. minute rice
1 1-lb. can tomatoes
1 8-oz. can pineapple chunks
1 10-oz. package frozen peas, thawed
1 tbsp. brown sugar
1/4 tsp. ginger
1 tbsp. lemon juice

Combine . . . . first 5 ingredients, 1 1/2 teaspoons salt and 1/2 cup water in
bowl, mixing well.
Shape . . . . . . into 18 meatballs.
Brown . . . . . . in oil in skillet; remove
meatballs.
Mix . . . . onion and garlic with 1/4 cup
water.
Let . . . . stand for 10 minutes.
Saute . . . . . . rice, onion and garlic in pan
drippings until golden.
Stir . . . . in 1/2 cup water, 3/4 teaspoon
salt and remaining ingredients.

Arrange . . . . . meatballs in skillet; spoon rice
mixture over top.
Simmer . . . . . covered, for 7 minutes or until
rice is tender.
Yields . . . . . . 6 servings.

Photograph for this recipe on this page.

FAMILY-STYLE MEAT LOAF

2 lb. ground beef
1 c. baby oat cereal
1/2 c. each chopped onion, green pepper
2 eggs, slightly beaten
1 1/2 tsp. salt
1/4 tsp. each rosemary, oregano, basil
1 8-oz. can tomato sauce

Combine . . . . all ingredients in bowl, mixing
well.
Shape . . . . . . into loaf in loaf pan.
Bake . . . . at 400 degrees for 50 minutes or
until brown; drain.
Let . . . . stand in pan for 5 minutes.
Place . . . . on serving platter.
Garnish . . . . . with parsley or watercress.

Somnuck Ward
Eisenhower H. S., Lawton

QUICK MEAT LOAF

1 lb. ground beef
1 c. oats
1 egg, beaten
1 c. tomato sauce
Salt and pepper to taste

Mix . . . . all ingredients in bowl.
Shape . . . . . . into loaf in loaf pan.
Bake . . . . at 350 degrees for 1 hour.

Leann Miller
Geary H. S., Geary

MICHELLE'S OWN MEAT LOAF

1 1/2 lb. ground beef
1/2 c. milk
1/2 c. finely chopped onion
1/2 c. finely chopped green pepper
2 eggs
1 8-oz. can tomato sauce
6 slices bread, trimmed, diced
Pinch of MSG
1 tsp. seasoned salt

Pinch each of salt and pepper
1 can cream of mushroom soup
1 2 1/2-oz. jar sliced mushrooms

Combine . . . . all ingredients except soup and mushrooms in bowl, mixing well with hands.
Shape . . . . . . into loaf in 7 x 11-inch baking dish.
Bake . . . . at 375 degrees for 30 minutes; drain.
Pour . . . . mixture of soup and mushrooms over loaf.
Bake . . . . for 40 minutes longer.

Michelle Morphew
Maysville H. S., Maysville

POT ROAST MEAT LOAF

1 lb. lean ground beef
2/3 c. evaporated milk
1/3 c. fine bread crumbs
1/4 c. chili sauce
2 tsp. Worcestershire sauce
2 tsp. salt
Pepper
3 med. potatoes, peeled, cut into
   1/4-in. slices
3 med. onions, sliced
3 med. carrots, quartered
2 tsp. parsley flakes

Mix . . . . first 5 ingredients, 1 teaspoon salt and 1/4 teaspoon pepper in bowl.
Shape . . . . . . into loaf in center of 9 x 13-inch baking dish.
Arrange . . . . . vegetables around loaf.
Sprinkle . . . . with 1 teaspoon salt, dash of pepper and parsley.
Bake . . . . covered, at 375 degrees for 1 hour.
Bake . . . . uncovered, for 10 minutes longer or until brown.

Robbie Keene
Copan H. S., Copan

PEPPER PATTIES

2 lb. ground beef
1 c. chopped green pepper
1/2 c. chopped onion
1/2 c. bread crumbs

2 eggs
2 tbsp. oil

Combine . . . . first 5 ingredients in bowl, mixing well.
Shape . . . . . . into patties.
Brown . . . . . . in oil in skillet; drain.
Yields . . . . . . 6 servings.

Lis Shaw
Drumright H. S., Drumright

RICE ITALIAN

1 lg. onion, finely chopped
2 green peppers, cut into 1-in. pieces
1 clove of garlic, minced
1 tbsp. oil
1 1/2 lb. ground chuck
1 tsp. oregano
1 can sliced mushrooms (opt.)
2 16-oz. cans tomato sauce
1 1/2 c. rice
Salt and pepper to taste

Saute . . . . . . onion, green peppers and garlic in oil in skillet until tender.
Add . . . . ground chuck.
Cook . . . . until brown and crumbly.
Stir . . . . in remaining ingredients.
Simmer . . . . . covered, for 45 minutes, adding small amounts of water as necessary.
Yields . . . . . . 8 servings.

Sherry Dawn Coffey
Beggs H. S., Tulsa

STUFFED GREEN PEPPERS

1/2 lb. ground beef
1 c. chopped onion
3 c. cooked rice
1 lg. can Ro-Tel
4 lg. green pepper shells

Brown . . . . . . ground beef and onion in skillet, stirring frequently.
Stir . . . . in rice and Ro-Tel.
Spoon . . . . . . into green pepper shells.
Place . . . . in 8-inch square baking dish.
Cover . . . . . . with remaining rice mixture.
Bake . . . . at 350 degrees for 30 minutes.
Yields . . . . . . 4 servings.

Robin Taylor
Bray-Doyle H. S., Marlow

Meats

CHEESEBURGER PIE

1 lb. ground beef
1 tbsp. minced onion
1 tsp. salt
1/4 tsp. pepper
3/4 tsp. Italian seasoning
2 6-oz. cans tomato paste
1 can refrigerator crescent rolls
4 slices mozzarella cheese
1/4 c. butter

Brown . . . . . . ground beef in skillet, stirring frequently; drain.

Stir . . . . in onion, seasonings and 1 can tomato paste.

Separate . . . . rolls into 8 triangles; press into 9-inch pie plate to form crust.

Layer . . . . . . ground beef mixture and cheese over crust.

Bake . . . . at 375 degrees for 25 to 30 minutes or until bubbly.

Blend . . . . . . remaining can tomato paste, butter and 3/4 cup water in saucepan.

Cook . . . . until heated through.

Serve . . . . with pie.

Yields . . . . . . 7-8 servings.

Sandy Devine
Waynoka H. S., Waynoka

SPANISH STEAK

Onion
2 lb. ground beef
4 slices crisp-fried bacon, crumbled
1 egg
1 tsp. salt
1 tsp. paprika
1/4 tsp. pepper
1 16-oz. can tomatoes, drained, cut into wedges
12 stuffed olives, sliced
1/2 c. grated cheese
1 green pepper, cut into rings

Mix . . . . 1/2 cup finely chopped onion, next 3 ingredients and seasonings in bowl.

Shape . . . . . . into 2-inch thick oval on greased foil in shallow baking dish.

Layer . . . . . . with tomatoes, olives and cheese.

Arrange . . . . . green pepper rings and onion slices on top.

Bake . . . . at 400 degrees for 1 hour.

Yields . . . . . . 5-6 servings.

Lora May Pembrook
Ringwood H. S., Ringwood

BREAKFAST PIZZA SUPREME

1/2 lb. ground beef
1/2 lb. sausage
2 pkg. refrigerator crescent rolls
1 c. grated potatoes
1/4 c. chopped onion
1/4 c. chopped green pepper
1 c. shredded sharp Cheddar cheese
1 c. shredded mozzarella cheese
5 eggs
1 c. milk
1/2 tsp. each salt, pepper
1 c. chopped ham
1/4 c. Parmesan cheese

Brown . . . . . . ground beef and sausage in skillet, stirring until crumbly; drain.

Separate . . . . rolls into 16 triangles.

Press . . . . over bottom and sides of 12-inch pizza pan.

Layer . . . . . . meat mixture, potatoes, onion, green pepper, Cheddar and mozzarella cheeses over crust.

Beat . . . . eggs, milk and seasonings in bowl.

Pour . . . . over layers.

Sprinkle . . . . with chopped ham and Parmesan cheese.

Bake . . . . at 375 degrees for 25 to 30 minutes or until set.

Yields . . . . . . 8-10 servings.

Lori Ann Kalka
Chandler H. S., Chandler

INDIVIDUAL PIZZAS

1 c. tomato sauce
1/2 tsp. each salt, garlic salt
1/2 tsp. Worcestershire sauce
1/4 tsp. thyme

3 or 4 drops of Tabasco sauce
1 can refrigerator biscuits
1/2 lb. ground beef
1 c. grated sharp cheese
Oregano to taste

Blend ...... tomato sauce and next 5 ingredients in bowl.
Roll .... each biscuit into 4-inch circle.
Cover ..... with uncooked ground beef and sauce.
Sprinkle .... with cheese and oregano.
Place .... on baking sheet.
Bake .... at 425 degrees for 10 minutes.
Yields ...... 10 servings.

Gladys Cassell
Eisenhower Jr. H. S., Lawton

1 c. buttermilk
Oil for deep frying

Brown ...... ground beef with onion, salt and pepper in skillet, stirring frequently; drain.
Stir .... in next 4 ingredients.
Cook .... until thickened.
Mix .... flour and buttermilk in bowl.
Pat .... into small circles.
Fry .... in 400-degree oil, turning once; drain.
Serve .... with prepared chili, shredded cheese and lettuce and chopped tomatoes.

Darla Mathis
Oney Sch., Albert

SUMMER SAUSAGE

2 lb. lean ground beef
2 tbsp. Tender-Quick
1/4 tsp. garlic powder
1 tbsp. pepper
2 tbsp. liquid smoke
Pinch of salt
1 1/2 tsp. mustard seed

Mix .... all ingredients with 1 cup water in bowl.
Chill .... in refrigerator for 1 to 3 days.
Shape ...... into 4 or 5 rolls; wrap in foil.
Chill .... for 8 hours; remove foil.
Bake .... on rack in broiler pan at 300 degrees for 45 to 60 minutes or until cooked through.
Yields ...... 4-5 rolls.

Kristy Grimm
Union City H. S., El Reno

INDIAN TACOS

2 lb. ground beef
1/4 onion, chopped
Salt and pepper to taste
1/2 pkg. chili seasoning mix
1 can ranch-style beans
1 can green chilies and tomatoes
1 can tomatoes
2 c. self-rising flour

TACO QUICHE

2 lb. ground beef
1 lg. purple onion, chopped
1 clove of garlic
1 tsp. chili powder
1/4 tsp. cumin
1/4 tsp. thyme
1/4 tsp. salt
1/2 tsp. oregano
8 corn tortillas
1 lb. Monterey Jack cheese, grated
6 eggs
2 c. milk
1   8-oz. carton sour cream

Brown ...... ground beef in skillet, stirring frequently; add onion, garlic and seasonings.
Layer ...... tortillas, ground beef mixture and cheese in greased 9 x 13-inch baking dish.
Beat .... eggs and milk in bowl.
Pour .... over layers.
Bake .... at 350 degrees for 1 hour or until set.
Spread ..... sour cream over top.
Garnish ..... with avocado, tomato slices and shredded lettuce.
Serve .... with salsa.
Yields ...... 8 servings.

Tina McKnight
South Intermediate Sch., Broken Arrow

Meats

TAMALE PIE

1 onion, chopped
2 tbsp. bacon drippings
1 lb. coarsely ground beef
1 lb. ground pork
1 sm. can tomatoes
2 tbsp. chili powder
Salt and pepper to taste
2 c. cornmeal

Saute ...... onion in bacon drippings in skillet.
Add .... ground beef and pork.
Cook .... until brown and crumbly.
Stir .... in tomatoes and seasonings.
Simmer ..... for 10 minutes.
Stir .... cornmeal gradually into 5 cups boiling water in saucepan.
Cook .... until thick, stirring constantly.
Spread ..... cornmeal mixture 3/4 inch thick over bottom of pie plate and thinly up sides; reserve remaining mush for topping.
Spoon ...... ground beef mixture into pie plate.
Cover ...... with remaining cornmeal mixture.
Bake .... at 350 degrees for 2 hours.
Let .... stand for several minutes to set before serving.

Crowder FHA, Crowder

IMPOSSIBLE HAM AND SWISS PIE

2 c. chopped cooked smoked ham
1 c. shredded Swiss cheese
1/3 c. chopped green onions
4 eggs
2 c. milk
1 c. baking mix
1/4 tsp. salt (opt.)
1/8 tsp. pepper

Sprinkle .... ham, cheese and onions in greased 10-inch pie plate.
Process ..... remaining ingredients in blender container for 15 seconds or until smooth.
Pour .... into pie plate.
Bake .... at 400 degrees for 35 to 40 minutes or until set.

Cool .... for 5 minutes.
Yields ...... 8 servings.

Laura Meek
Tuttle H. S., Tuttle

BREAKFAST CASSEROLE

3 slices bread, buttered, cubed
2 1/4 c. milk
10 eggs
1 1/2 tsp. dry mustard
1/2 tsp. salt
1 1/2 c. shredded Cheddar cheese
1 lb. bacon, crisp-fried, crumbled

Spread ..... buttered bread cubes in greased 9 x 13-inch baking pan.
Combine .... milk, eggs, mustard and salt in mixer bowl.
Beat .... at medium speed for 1 minute.
Stir .... in cheese and bacon.
Pour .... over bread cubes.
Bake .... at 350 degrees for 30 to 40 minutes or until set.

Willene Walsh
Union City H. S., Union City

BRUNCH CASSEROLE

4 eggs, beaten
Milk
8 lg. slices bread, cubed
3/4 pkg. sliced ham
3/4 tsp. dry mustard
1 1/2 c. shredded Cheddar cheese
1 can cream of mushroom soup

Beat .... eggs with 2 cups milk in bowl.
Stir .... in bread, ham and mustard.
Spoon ...... into buttered casserole.
Sprinkle .... with cheese.
Chill .... covered, overnight.
Blend ...... soup with 1/4 soup can milk.
Pour .... over cheese.
Bake .... covered, at 325 degrees for 1 hour.
Bake .... uncovered, for 40 to 45 minutes longer or until brown.
Yields ...... 8 servings.

Charolette Hacker
Tuttle H. S., Tuttle

BREADED PORK CHOPS WITH APPLE RINGS

1 egg
1 tsp. salt
1/4 tsp. pepper
4 1/2-in. thick pork chops
1/2 c. fine bread crumbs
1/4 c. shortening
3 or 4 apples

Mix .... egg, seasonings and 2 table-spoons water in bowl.
Dip .... pork chops in egg mixture; coat with bread crumbs.
Let .... stand for several minutes.
Brown ...... pork chops on both sides in shortening in 10-inch skillet.
Cook .... covered, over low heat for 30 minutes.
Core .... apples; slice into 1/2-inch rings.
Remove .... chops to serving plate.
Saute ...... apple rings in pan drippings until lightly browned.
Serve .... apple rings with chops.
Yields ...... 4 servings.

Melisa Matthews
Elmore City H. S., Elmore City

PORK CHOPS WITH MUSHROOM SOUP

4 pork chops
3 c. soft bread cubes
2 tbsp. chopped onions
1/4 c. butter, melted
1/4 tsp. poultry seasoning
1 can mushroom soup

Brown ...... pork chops in skillet; drain.
Mix .... next 4 ingredients and 1/4 cup water in bowl.
Shape ...... into 4 balls.
Place .... on pork chops in casserole.
Blend ...... soup and 1/3 soup can water in bowl.
Pour .... over pork chops.
Bake .... covered, at 350 degrees for 1 hour.
Yields ...... 4 servings.

Billie Robinson
Silo H. S., Durant

SAUCY APPLE PORK CHOPS

6 1-in. thick pork chops
2 tbsp. shortening
1 1/2 tsp. salt
1/8 tsp. pepper
1 14-oz. jar spiced apple rings
2/3 c. applesauce
1 tsp. lemon juice
1/3 c. golden raisins
1 tbsp. cornstarch

Brown ...... pork chops in shortening in Dutch oven.
Sprinkle .... with salt and pepper.
Drain ...... apple rings reserving juice.
Mix .... applesauce, reserved juice, lemon juice and raisins in bowl.
Spoon ...... around chops.
Bake .... covered, at 350 degrees for 1 hour or until tender.
Remove .... chops to serving platter.
Stir .... cornstarch blended with 1/3 cup water into applesauce mixture.
Cook .... until thick, stirring constantly.
Add .... apple rings.
Cook .... for 1 minute longer.
Spoon ...... over chops.

Photograph for this recipe above.

Meats

PORK CHOPS AND RICE

1/4 c. butter
Salt
3 c. minute rice
8 to 10 center cut pork chops
1 can cream of mushroom soup
1 c. milk

Bring .... butter, 1 teaspoon salt and 3 cups water to a boil in saucepan.
Stir .... in rice; remove from heat.
Let .... stand, covered, for 5 minutes.
Season ..... pork chops generously with salt.
Heat .... soup with milk in saucepan.
Layer ...... rice, pork chops and soup in greased 9 x 13-inch baking dish.
Bake .... at 325 degrees for 1 hour or until tender.
Yields ...... 10 servings.

Darla Lacy
Canton H. S., Canton

PORK CHOP SUPPER FOR TWO

2 3/4-in. thick pork chops
2 tbsp. chopped onion
1/3 c. rice
1 tbsp. instant chicken bouillon
Apples
1 tbsp. butter, melted
1 tbsp. brown sugar
1/4 tsp. cinnamon

Cook .... fat trimmed from pork chops in skillet to produce 2 tablespoons drippings; discard trimmings.
Brown ...... pork chops in drippings.
Add .... onions and rice.
Cook .... until rice is golden, stirring constantly.
Add .... 1 cup water and bouillon.
Bring .... to a boil; stir in 1/2 cup chopped apples.
Spoon ...... into baking dish.
Bake .... covered, at 350 degrees for 30 minutes.
Brush ...... 1/2 cup sliced apples with mixture of butter, brown sugar and cinnamon.
Arrange ..... around pork chops.

Bake .... uncovered, for 20 minutes longer or until pork and apples are tender.
Yields ...... 2 servings.

Wendy Sue Smith
Ringwood H. S., Ringwood

SWEET AND SOUR PORK

2 tbsp. Sherry
5 tbsp. soy sauce
2 tbsp. cornstarch
1 egg, beaten
3 tbsp. flour
1 lb. lean pork, cubed
Oil for deep frying
1 sm. onion, chopped
3 green peppers, chopped
1 clove of garlic, minced
3 tbsp. oil
1 sm. can pineapple chunks
3 sm. tomatoes, quartered
2 tbsp. vinegar
1/3 c. sugar
1/4 c. catsup

Blend ...... 1 tablespoon Sherry, 1 tablespoon soy sauce, 1 tablespoon cornstarch, egg and flour in bowl.
Coat .... pork with batter.
Deep-fry .... in hot oil; drain.
Saute ...... onion, green peppers and garlic in 3 tablespoons oil in skillet; drain.
Stir .... in pineapple and tomatoes.
Blend ...... 1 tablespoon cornstarch, 1/3 cup water, vinegar, sugar, catsup, 1 tablespoon Sherry and 1/4 cup soy sauce in saucepan.
Bring .... to a boil, stirring constantly.
Mix .... vegetables, pork and sauce.
Serve .... over rice. May substitute chicken breast for pork.
Yields ...... 4-6 servings.

Julie Stearman
Meeker H. S., Meeker

CALZONE

1 1/2 pkg. dry yeast
Salt
2 tsp. sugar

2 tbsp. oil
4 c. flour
12 oz. Italian sausage
16 oz. mozzarella cheese, grated
8 to 15 oz. ricotta cheese
2 oz. Romano cheese
6 oz. pepperoni, sliced
1 8-oz. can tomato sauce
Oregano, garlic and pepper to taste
Melted butter

Combine .... yeast dissolved in 1 1/4 cups warm water, 2 teaspoons salt, sugar and oil in bowl.
Knead ...... in flour until smooth.
Divide ...... into 2 portions.
Let .... rise until doubled in bulk.
Roll .... each portion into thin rectangle.
Cook .... sausage in skillet until brown and crumbly; drain.
Mix .... with next 5 ingredients and seasonings to taste.
Spread ..... over dough; fold as for turnover and pinch edges to seal.
Brush ...... with butter; cut steam vent.
Place .... on baking sheet.
Bake .... at 400 degrees until brown.

Crowder FHA

EASY BREAKFAST OMELET

1 lb. pork sausage
8 eggs
3 c. milk
8 slices bread, cubed
1 4-oz. can mushroom pieces
2 c. shredded Cheddar cheese
1/2 c. chopped onion

Brown ...... sausage in skillet, stirring frequently; drain.
Beat .... eggs and milk in bowl.
Layer ...... bread cubes, sausage, mushrooms and cheese in greased 9 x 13-inch baking dish.
Pour .... egg mixture over layers.
Top .... with onion.
Chill .... in refrigerator overnight.
Bake .... at 350 degrees for 45 to 60 minutes or until set.
Yields ...... 8 servings.

Cindy Jackson
Elmore City H. S., Elmore City

ITALIAN LASAGNA

1 lb. Italian sausage
1 clove of garlic, minced
1 tbsp. salt
1 16-oz. can tomatoes
1/2 tsp. pepper
3 c. cottage cheese
1/2 c. grated Romano cheese
2 tbsp. parsley flakes
2 eggs, beaten
10 oz. lasagna noodles, cooked
1 lb. mozzarella cheese, shredded

Brown ...... sausage in skillet, stirring frequently; drain.
Mix .... in garlic, salt, tomatoes and pepper.
Simmer ..... for 30 minutes, stirring occasionally.
Mix .... cottage cheese with next 3 ingredients in bowl.
Layer ...... half the noodles, cottage cheese mixture, mozzarella cheese and sauce in 9 x 13-inch baking dish; repeat layers.
Bake .... at 375 degrees for 30 minutes.
Let .... stand for 10 minutes before serving.
Yields ...... 12 servings.

Kristin Veldhuizen
Eisenhower H. S., Lawton

SAUSAGE AND EGG CASSEROLE

1 lb. sausage
8 eggs
1 c. grated sharp Cheddar cheese
6 slices whole wheat bread, cubed
2 c. milk
1 tsp. salt
1 tsp. dry mustard

Brown ...... sausage in skillet, stirring frequently; drain.
Mix .... remaining ingredients in bowl.
Stir .... into sausage.
Spoon ...... into 7 x 10-inch casserole.
Chill .... in refrigerator for 12 hours.
Bake .... covered, at 350 degrees for 35 minutes.
Yields ...... 10 servings.

Tammy Funburg
Oilton H. S., Oilton

Meats

PIZZA TURNOVERS

1 pkg. pizza crust mix
1/2 lb. mild pork sausage
1 c. chopped onion
1/2 c. chopped green pepper
2 med. tomatoes, chopped
1/3 c. tomato paste
1 tsp. basil
1/2 tsp. salt
1/2 tsp. thyme
1 1/2 c. shredded mozzarella cheese
1 egg, slightly beaten

Mix .... pizza crust using package directions.
Let .... rise, covered, in warm place for 1 hour or until doubled in bulk.
Saute ...... sausage, onion and green pepper in skillet; drain.
Mix .... tomatoes with next 4 ingredients and 3 tablespoons water in bowl.
Stir .... into sausage mixture.
Divide ...... dough into 6 equal portions.
Let .... rest, covered, for 10 minutes.
Roll .... each portion into 8-inch circle on floured surface.
Spoon ...... 2/3 cup sausage mixture and 1/4 cup cheese into half of each circle.
Moisten ..... edges with mixture of egg and 1 teaspoon water; fold over to enclose filling, sealing edges.
Place .... on greased baking sheet.
Prick .... tops; brush with remaining egg mixture.
Bake .... at 375 degrees for 30 to 35 minutes or until brown.
Yields ...... 6 servings.

Shelly Hines
Elmore H. S., Elmore City

FAVORITE CORN DOGS

3/4 c. self-rising flour
1/4 c. self-rising cornmeal
2 tbsp. minced onion
1 tbsp. sugar
1 tsp. dry mustard
1/2 c. milk
1 egg, beaten
1 lb. frankfurters
Oil for deep frying

Combine .... first 5 ingredients in bowl.
Mix .... milk and egg in small bowl.
Stir .... into cornmeal mixture.
Pat .... frankfurters dry; insert Popsicle stick in each.
Dip .... into batter.
Deep-fry .... in 350 to 400-degree oil for 2 to 3 minutes or until brown, turning once; drain on paper towels.

Judy Streumph
Vinita H. S., Vinita

MICROWAVE TAMALE CASSEROLE

1 16-oz. can tamales, chopped
1 16-oz. can chili
1 can bean with bacon soup
1 16-oz. can tomato sauce
1 c. grated Cheddar cheese

Place .... tamales in 8-inch square glass casserole.
Mix .... in remaining ingredients except cheese.
Sprinkle .... with cheese.
Microwave .. on High for 6 to 8 minutes, turning after 4 minutes.
Serve .... with tortilla chips or salad.
Yields ...... 6 servings.

Melinda Combs
Cleveland H. S., Cleveland

CAROL'S VENISON CHILI

2 lb. ground venison
1 pkg. chili seasoning mix
1 15-oz. can tomato sauce
1 tsp. each cayenne pepper, chili powder, dry red pepper
1 can ranch-style beans
1 can ranch-style beans with jalapeno peppers

Cook .... venison in skillet, stirring frequently; drain.
Stir .... in chili seasoning mix, tomato sauce, seasonings and beans.
Cook .... over low heat for 1 1/2 hours.
Serve .... with crackers.

Carol Vandeslunt
Sperry H. S., Sperry

Poultry & Seafood

CHICKEN MEDITERRANEAN, recipe on page 81.

Poultry

BAKED CHICKEN AND DRESSING

1 lg. chicken
Salt and pepper to taste
3 1/2 c. corn bread crumbs
3 1/2 c. mixed biscuit, cracker and
  bread crumbs
1 med. onion, chopped
1 stalk celery, chopped
3 eggs, beaten
1 tbsp. each sage, poultry seasoning

Combine .... chicken, 2 quarts water, salt and pepper in pressure cooker.
Cook .... at 10 pounds pressure for 35 to 40 minutes, using pressure cooker directions.
Remove .... chicken; reserve stock.
Mix .... remaining ingredients in bowl.
Add .... enough chicken stock to make of cake batter consistency, mixing well.
Place .... chicken in baking pan.
Pour .... dressing around and into chicken.
Bake .... at 350 degrees for 15 to 20 minutes, or until brown.
Yields ...... 8-10 servings.

Doris Gailean Greenhaw
Porum H. S., Porum

CALICO CHICKEN

1 2 1/2 to 3-lb. fryer, cut up
1/4 c. seasoned flour
1/2 c. oil
1 8-oz. can tomato sauce
1/2 c. chicken broth
1 12-oz. can whole kernel corn with
  sweet peppers
2 tbsp. chopped parsley

Coat .... chicken with flour.
Brown ...... in oil in skillet; pour off drippings.
Add .... tomato sauce and broth.
Simmer ..... covered, for 40 minutes.
Stir .... in corn and parsley.
Simmer ..... covered, for 10 minutes longer.
Yields ...... 4 servings.

Patty Jane Hardaman
Lawton H. S., Lawton

EASY FRIED CHICKEN

1 fryer, cut up
1/4 c. flour
1/2 tsp. salt
1/8 tsp. pepper
1/4 c. shortening

Rinse ...... chicken under running water; pat dry.
Coat .... with mixture of flour, salt and pepper.
Brown ...... on both sides in shortening in skillet; reduce heat.
Cook .... covered, for 50 to 60 minutes or until tender, turning occasionally.
Serve .... with cream gravy.
Yields ...... 4-6 servings.

Donna Winn
E H. S., Lawton

ITALIAN CHICKEN AND SAUSAGE

1/2 lb. sweet Italian sausage
3 tbsp. oil
1 1/4 lb. boned skinned chicken breasts
2 c. chopped green pepper
1 c. sliced onion
2 c. sliced mushrooms
1 clove of garlic, minced
1 16-oz. can crushed tomatoes
1/4 tsp. oregano
1/8 tsp. each salt, pepper

Brown ...... sausage in 2 tablespoons oil in skillet over medium-high heat for 5 minutes, stirring frequently; add chicken.
Cook .... until chicken is lightly browned; remove.
Saute ...... green pepper and onion in pan drippings and 1 tablespoon oil for 5 minutes.
Add .... mushrooms and garlic.
Cook .... over medium heat for 5 minutes.
Add .... sausage, chicken and remaining ingredients.
Simmer ..... covered, for 20 minutes.
Boil .... uncovered, for 5 to 7 minutes.
Yields ...... 5 servings.

Chris Crow
Ringwood H. S., Meno

HOT CHINESE CHICKEN

8 chicken thighs, skinned, cut into
    1-in. pieces
1/4 c. cornstarch
1/4 tsp. corn oil
1/8 tsp. garlic powder
1 lg. tomato, chopped
1 4-oz. can sliced water chestnuts,
    drained
1 bunch green onions, sliced
1 can sliced mushrooms
1 c. sliced celery
1 tsp. MSG
1/4 c. soy sauce
2 c. finely shredded lettuce

Coat . . . . chicken with cornstarch.
Stir-fry . . . . . in hot oil in wok.
Sprinkle . . . . with garlic powder.
Stir . . . . in tomato, water chestnuts, green onions, mushrooms and celery.
Sprinkle . . . . with MSG and soy sauce.
Simmer . . . . . covered, for 5 minutes.
Stir . . . . in lettuce.
Serve . . . . over rice.

Crowder FHA

ISLAND CHICKEN

1 clove of garlic, minced
1/3 c. oil
2 tbsp. lemon juice
1 tbsp. soy sauce
1/2 tsp. oregano
1/4 tsp. salt
1/8 tsp. pepper
1 broiler-fryer, quartered

Combine . . . . first 7 ingredients in bowl, mixing well.
Pour . . . . over chicken in glass bowl.
Marinate . . . . tightly covered, in refrigerator for several hours, turning once.
Place . . . . skin side down on rack in broiler pan.
Broil . . . . 5 to 7 inches from heat for 25 minutes; turn.
Broil . . . . for 15 minutes longer.
Yields . . . . . . 4 servings.

Darlene Caddell
Central Jr. H. S., Lawton

HUNTER-STYLE CHICKEN

4 slices bacon, cut into 1-in. pieces
1 med. onion, sliced
2 to 2 1/2 lb. chicken pieces
Salt and pepper to taste
1 16-oz. can tomatoes
1/3 to 1/2 c. steak sauce
1 tbsp. sugar
Flour (opt.)

Saute . . . . . . bacon in skillet until partially cooked.
Add . . . . onion.
Cook . . . . until onion is tender; remove.
Drain . . . . . . reserving 2 tablespoon drippings.
Brown . . . . . . chicken in reserved drippings; drain.
Sprinkle . . . . with salt and pepper.
Mix . . . . tomatoes, steak sauce, sugar and bacon mixture.
Pour . . . . over chicken.
Simmer . . . . . covered, for 40 to 45 minutes or until chicken is tender, basting occasionally.
Remove . . . . chicken.
Stir . . . . a small amount of flour blended with a small amount of water into pan drippings.
Cook . . . . until thick, stirring constantly.
Serve . . . . . . with hot buttered rice.
Yields . . . . . . 4-5 servings.

Melanie Byrd
Ringwood H. S., Ringwood

MARINATED CHICKEN BREASTS

4 chicken breasts, skinned, boned
1/2 c. Italian salad dressing
1 tbsp. seasoned salt
4 pineapple slices

Rinse . . . . . . and drain chicken; arrange in shallow dish.
Sprinkle . . . . with salad dressing and seasoned salt.
Let . . . . stand for 1 hour or longer.
Broil . . . . until medium brown on both sides.
Brown . . . . . . pineapple rings on both sides.
Place . . . . on chicken breasts.
Serve . . . . . . with rice.

Marsha Manar
Apache H. S., Apache

Poultry

MICROWAVE CHICKEN NUGGETS

2 c. cornflake crumbs
3/4 c. Parmesan cheese
1/4 c. basil
Salt and pepper to taste
2 lb. chicken breasts, skinned, boned,
    cut into 2-in. pieces
1 c. melted margarine

Combine .... crumbs, cheese and seasonings in bowl, mixing well.
Dip .... chicken in margarine; coat with cornflake mixture.
Arrange ..... in 9 x 12-inch glass baking dish.
Microwave .. on High for 6 to 8 minutes or until chicken is tender.
Yields ...... 4-6 servings.

Sarah Wheatley
Dewar H. S., Dewar

SPANISH CHICKEN

1   2 1/2-lb. chicken, cut up
1/2 c. each chopped onion, green pepper
1   4-oz. can mushrooms
2 c. stewed tomatoes
1 c. tomato sauce
2 carrots, thinly sliced
2 stalks celery, thinly sliced
1 tsp. each oregano, salt
1/2 tsp. pepper
1 bay leaf
1 chicken bouillon cube, crumbled

Arrange ..... chicken in stock pot.
Layer ...... remaining ingredients over chicken, stirring lightly.
Simmer ..... covered, for 1 hour.
Stir .... to blend flavors; discard bay leaf.
Serve .... over rice.
Yields ...... 4 servings.

Carol Hudson
Western Oklahoma AVTS, Burns Flat

SPECIAL STUFFED CHICKEN

4 chicken breasts
Flour
1/4 tsp. paprika
1 1/2 tsp. salt
Pepper
2 c. dry bread crumbs
1 tbsp. chopped onion
1/4 tsp. poultry seasoning
3/4 c. melted butter
Parsley
1/2 lb. fresh mushrooms, cut into halves
1/4 c. minced onion
1/2 c. heavy cream
1/2 c. sour cream

Split .... chicken breasts enough to fold.
Coat .... chicken with mixture of 1/4 cup flour, paprika, 1/2 teaspoon salt and dash of pepper.
Mix .... bread crumbs, onion, poultry seasoning, dash of pepper and 1/2 teaspoon salt in bowl.
Add .... 2 tablespoons butter and 1/4 cup hot water, tossing to moisten.
Stuff .... chicken with dressing; fasten with toothpicks.
Dip .... in 1/2 cup butter; place in baking dish.
Bake .... at 325 degrees for 45 minutes or until tender.
Sprinkle .... with parsley.
Saute ...... mushrooms and onion in 2 tablespoons butter in skillet. Do not brown.
Cook .... covered, over low heat for 10 minutes.
Blend ...... in 1 to 2 tablespoons flour.
Stir .... in cream, sour cream, 1/2 teaspoon salt and 1/4 teaspoon pepper gradually.
Cook .... until thickened, stirring constantly. Do not boil.
Serve .... sauce over chicken.
Yields ...... 4 servings.

Debbie Helm
Geary H. S., Geary

CHICKEN-CHILIES CASSEROLE

4 to 6 chicken breasts
1 can cream of celery soup
1 can cream of mushroom soup
1 soup can milk
12 tortillas, torn
1 lg. onion, chopped
1 sm. can green chilies, chopped
1 lb. Cheddar cheese, grated

Bake . . . . chicken, wrapped in foil, at 400 degrees for 1 hour.
Cut . . . . into bite-sized pieces.
Blend . . . . . . soups and milk in bowl.
Layer . . . . . . 1/3 of the soup mixture, half the tortillas, chicken, onion, green chilies and cheese in 9 x 13-inch baking dish.
Repeat . . . . . with half the remaining soup mixture, remaining tortillas, chicken, onion, green chilies, remaining soup mixture and cheese.
Bake . . . . 350 degrees for 1 hour.

Sylvia Bayless
Carl Albert H. S., Midwest City

CHICKEN MEDITERRANEAN

3 lb. chicken pieces
2 tbsp. oil
1 c. chopped onion
1 clove of garlic, crushed
1 c. orange juice
1 tsp. salt
1 tsp. grated orange rind
1/4 tsp. rosemary
Dash of pepper
4 med. Florida tomatoes, chopped

Brown . . . . . . chicken in oil in skillet; remove chicken.
Saute . . . . . . onion and garlic in pan drippings until tender.
Stir . . . . in remaining ingredients except tomatoes with 1/2 cup water.
Bring . . . . to a boil.
Add . . . . chicken and tomatoes.
Simmer . . . . . covered, for 50 minutes or until chicken is tender, stirring occasionally.

Photograph for this recipe on page 77.

QUICK CHICKEN AND RICE

2 c. minute rice
1 env. dry onion soup mix
1 can cream of celery soup
1 can cream of mushroom soup
1 can evaporated milk
1 chicken, cut up

Spread . . . . . rice and soup mix in 9 x 13-inch baking pan.
Pour . . . . mixture of soups and milk over rice.
Arrange . . . . . chicken over rice.
Bake . . . . covered, at 350 degrees for 1 hour.
Yields . . . . . . 6 servings.

Denna Suit
Ringwood H. S., Ringwood

CREAMY CHICKEN CASSEROLE

1 c. elbow macaroni, cooked
3/4 c. milk
1 can cream of chicken soup
2 c. chopped cooked chicken
1 c. shredded sharp American cheese
1 4-oz. can mushrooms
1/4 c. chopped pimento

Mix . . . . macaroni and remaining ingredients in bowl.
Spoon . . . . . . into casserole.
Bake . . . . at 350 degrees for 30 minutes.
Yields . . . . . . 4 servings.

Glynis Bryant
Barnsdall H. S., Barnsdall

QUICK CHICKEN CASSEROLE

2 10-oz. packages frozen corn, carrots and pearl onions with cream sauce, cooked
2 5-oz. cans boned chicken, chopped
1/4 c. chopped parsley
1 pkg. refrigerator butter flake rolls
Sesame seed

Combine . . . . vegetables, chicken and parsley in bowl, mixing well.
Spoon . . . . . . into 1 1/2-quart baking dish.
Separate . . . . rolls into 24 pieces.
Arrange . . . . . buttered side up on chicken mixture.
Sprinkle . . . . with sesame seed.
Bake . . . . at 375 degrees for 15 minutes or until biscuits are golden brown.
Yields . . . . . . 4 servings.

Lori Snare
Elgin H. S., Elgin

Poultry

SESAME-BAKED CHICKEN

1/4 c. sesame seed
2/3 c. fine cracker crumbs
1 2 1/2 to 3-lb. broiler-fryer, cut up
1/3 c. evaporated milk
1/2 c. melted butter

Toast ...... sesame seed in baking pan at 350 degrees for 10 minutes, stirring 1 or 2 times.
Mix .... with cracker crumbs in bowl.
Dip .... chicken in evaporated milk and coat with crumb mixture.
Place .... skin side down in butter in 7 x 11-inch baking pan; turn skin side up.
Bake .... at 350 degrees for 1 1/2 hours.
Garnish ..... with parsley.
Yields ...... 3-4 servings.

Linda Carter, Adviser
Stilwell Sr. H. S., Stilwell

TURKEY-SPAGHETTI CASSEROLE

1 8-oz. jar Cheez Whiz, softened
1/2 c. milk
2 tbsp. melted butter
7 oz. spaghetti, cooked
1 10-oz. package frozen broccoli, cooked, drained
1 4-oz. can mushrooms, drained
1/4 tsp. each poultry seasoning, onion salt
2 tbsp. chopped pimento
Chopped cooked turkey

Blend ...... Cheez Whiz and milk in bowl.
Pour .... butter over spaghetti, tossing to coat.
Combine .... Cheez Whiz mixture, spaghetti and remaining ingredients in bowl, mixing well.
Spoon ...... into 2-quart casserole.
Bake .... covered, at 350 degrees for 30 to 35 minutes or until heated through.
Stir .... before serving.
Yields ...... 6 servings.

La Dawna McMillian
Vinita H. S., Vinita

TURKEY DUMPLINGS

1 3-oz. package cream cheese, softened
3 tbsp. margarine
2 c. chopped cooked turkey
1/4 tsp. salt
1/8 tsp. pepper
1 tbsp. chopped chives
2 tbsp. milk
1 tbsp. chopped pimento
2 8-oz. cans refrigerator crescent dinner rolls
3/4 c. crushed seasoned croutons

Blend ...... cream cheese and 2 tablespoons margarine in bowl.
Add .... next 6 ingredients, mixing well.
Separate .... rolls into 8 rectangles, sealing perforations.
Spoon ...... 1/4 cup turkey mixture onto each rectangle.
Pull .... 4 corners of dough to center to enclose filling.
Arrange ..... on baking sheet.
Brush ...... with remaining tablespoon margarine; sprinkle with croutons.
Bake .... at 350 degrees for 20 to 25 minutes or until golden brown.
Yields ...... 8 servings.

Theresa Gullett
Konawa H. S., Konawa

TUNA-BROCCOLI-RICE CASSEROLE

1 can cream of mushroom soup
1 6-oz. can tuna, drained
1 10-oz. package frozen broccoli, cooked
1 c. rice, cooked
1 16-oz. jar Cheez Whiz, melted
10 crackers, crushed

Blend ...... soup with 1/2 soup can water in bowl.
Add .... tuna, broccoli, rice and Cheez Whiz, mixing well.
Pour .... into 9 x 13-inch baking dish.
Sprinkle .... with cracker crumbs.
Bake .... at 350 degrees for 20 minutes.
Yields ...... 5 servings.

Susan Bowles
Lawton Sr. H. S., Lawton

CREAMY TUNA DELUXE

1   7 1/4-oz. package macaroni and
    cheese dinner
3/4 c. milk
1/2 c. chopped onion
1/4 c. chopped green pepper
1 tbsp. margarine
1 can cream of celery soup
1   4-oz. can mushrooms, drained
1/4 c. chopped pimento
1   6 1/2-oz. can tuna, drained

Prepare ..... macaroni and cheese according to package directions using 3/4 cup milk.

Saute ...... onion and green pepper in margarine in skillet.

Stir .... in macaroni and remaining ingredients.

Cook .... until heated through, stirring occasionally.

Yields ...... 6-8 servings.

Lorrie Hixson
Macomb H. S., Macomb

TUNA-POTATO SKILLET MEAL

1   1-lb. package frozen shredded
    potatoes
3 tbsp. shortening
1 1/2 c. milk
3 tbsp. flour
2 tbsp. chopped pimento
1 1/2 tsp. salt
1 tbsp. dried onion flakes
2   7-oz. cans oil-pack tuna
1   10-oz. package frozen lima beans,
    cooked, drained

Cook .... potatoes in shortening in large skillet for 5 minutes.

Combine .... milk, flour, pimento, salt and onion flakes in bowl; mix well.

Add .... to potatoes with tuna.

Cook .... for about 5 minutes until sauce thickens, stirring occasionally.

Stir .... in lima beans.

Heat .... to serving temperature.

Photograph for this recipe on this page.

FAVORITE TUNA-NOODLE CASSEROLE

3 c. noodles, cooked
1   7-oz. can tuna, drained
1/2 c. mayonnaise
1 c. sliced celery
1/3 c. chopped onion
1/2 c. pimento
1/2 tsp. salt
3/4 c. chopped green pepper
1 c. evaporated milk
1 c. shredded sharp process cheese

Combine .... first 7 ingredients with 1/4 cup green pepper in bowl, mixing well.

Heat .... milk and cheese in saucepan until cheese is melted, stirring constantly.

Stir .... into noodle mixture.

Pour .... into 9 x 13-inch baking dish.

Bake .... at 425 degrees for 20 minutes.

Add .... 1/2 cup green pepper before serving.

Yields ...... 6 servings.

Tayna F. Fraley
Ringwood H. S., Ringwood

Seafood

SALMON LOAF

    2 cans salmon
    1 tbsp. Season-All salt
    Salt and pepper to taste
    2 tbsp. mustard
    1 tsp. Worcestershire sauce
    Chopped onion
    Catsup
    1 med. tomato, sliced
    1 tbsp. lemon juice

Mix . . . . salmon, seasonings, mustard, Worcestershire sauce, 1/2 cup onion and 2 tablespoons catsup in bowl.
Shape . . . . . . into loaf in loaf pan.
Top . . . . with 1 cup catsup and tomato slices.
Sprinkle . . . . with lemon juice and onion.
Bake . . . . at 350 degrees for 45 minutes.
Yields . . . . . . 6 servings.

Karen Jane Nagel
Tomlinson Jr. H. S., Lawton

CREAMY SALMON

    2 tbsp. flour
    1/2 tsp. dry mustard
    3 tbsp. melted butter
    1 lg. can evaporated milk
    1 pkg. frozen mixed vegetables, thawed,
        drained
    3 c. wide noodles, cooked
    1 1/2 c. shredded Cheddar cheese
    1 can salmon, drained

Blend . . . . . . flour, mustard and butter in skillet.
Stir . . . . in evaporated milk gradually.
Cook . . . . until slightly thickened, stirring constantly.
Add . . . . vegetables, noodles and 1 cup cheese, mixing well.
Fold . . . . in salmon.
Pour . . . . into greased 2-quart baking dish.
Bake . . . . covered, at 350 degrees for 25 minutes.
Sprinkle . . . . with remaining 1/2 cup cheese.
Bake . . . . uncovered, for 5 minutes or until cheese melts.

Leslie Christian
N I H. S., Broken Arrow

QUICK-FRIED CRYSTAL PRAWNS

    1 egg white
    1 tbsp. cornstarch
    1 lb. prawns, shelled
    6 tbsp. oil
    1 tsp. chopped gingerroot
    2 tsp. chopped onion
    1/2 tsp. salt
    1 tbsp. Sherry
    2 tbsp. broth
    1/2 tbsp. vinegar

Blend . . . . . . egg white and cornstarch.
Add . . . . prawns, tossing to coat.
Stir-fry . . . . . in hot oil in wok for 2 to 3 minutes or until pink.
Remove . . . . prawns and drain excess oil.
Stir . . . . in gingerroot, onion, salt, Sherry and broth.
Bring . . . . to a boil; add prawns.
Cook . . . . for several seconds, stirring constantly.
Sprinkle . . . . with vinegar.

Cherry A. Caro
Vinita H. S., Vinita

TROUT AMANDINE

    2 lb. trout fillets, cut into 6 portions
    1/4 c. flour
    1 tsp. each seasoned salt, paprika
    1/4 c. melted butter
    1/2 c. sliced almonds
    2 tbsp. lemon juice
    4 or 5 drops of hot pepper sauce
    1 tbsp. chopped parsley

Coat . . . . trout with mixture of flour, seasoned salt and paprika.
Arrange . . . . . skin side down in single layer in greased 2-quart casserole.
Drizzle . . . . . with 2 tablespoons butter.
Broil . . . . 4 inches from heat source for 10 to 15 minutes or until trout flakes easily.
Saute . . . . . . almonds in 2 tablespoons butter in skillet until golden brown; remove from heat.
Mix . . . . in lemon juice, hot pepper sauce and parsley.
Pour . . . . over trout.

Glenda Geis
Ringwood H. S., Ringwood

Vegetables & Side Dishes

VEGETABLES A LA ESPANA, recipe on page 90.

Vegetables

CREAMY ASPARAGUS CASSEROLE

2 cans asparagus
2 c. milk
Butter
Salt and pepper to taste
1/2 c. flour
4 hard-boiled eggs, sliced
1 sm. jar sliced pimentos
1 1/2 c. shredded Cheddar cheese
2 c. bread crumbs

Drain ...... asparagus, reserving juice.
Heat .... reserved juice, milk, 2 table-
spoons butter and salt and pep-
per in saucepan.
Stir .... in mixture of flour and 2 table-
spoons water.
Cook .... until thickened, stirring
constantly.
Add .... asparagus, eggs, pimentos, cheese
and 3 to 4 tablespoons butter.
Pour .... into casserole.
Top .... with crumbs.
Bake .... at 300 degrees for 10 minutes or
until bubbly.

Etta Hasenbeck
Tomlinson Jr. H. S., Lawton

EASY GREEN BEANS

1 tbsp. finely chopped onion
5 slices bacon
2 cans cut Italian green beans, drained
1 can tomato soup
1/2 c. packed brown sugar

Brown ...... onion and bacon in skillet; drain
and crumble bacon.
Combine .... with remaining ingredients in
1-quart casserole.
Bake .... covered, at 300 degrees for 2
hours.

Karrie Thompson
Harding Middle H. S., Oklahoma City

PEPPERONI NAVY BEANS

1 lb. navy beans
1 ham hock
2 bay leaves
1 onion, chopped
1 green pepper, chopped
1 tbsp. oil
1 lg. potato, chopped
1 lb. pepperoni, sliced

Cook .... beans with ham hock and bay
leaves in water in saucepan until
beans are tender.
Drain ...... beans; remove ham hock and
bay leaves.
Saute ...... onion and green pepper in oil in
skillet.
Add .... to beans.
Simmer ..... for 15 to 20 minutes or until
vegetables are tender.
Add .... potato and pepperoni.
Simmer ..... for 45 minutes longer.
Yields ...... 6-8 servings.

Sandra Whitman, Teacher
Porum H. S., Porum

BROCCOLI-POTATO BAKE

3 c. mashed potatoes
1/2 c. sour cream
1/4 tsp. seasoned salt
1   10-oz. package frozen chopped
broccoli, cooked, drained
1/4 c. butter, melted
4 c. Corn Chex, crushed
1 c. shredded cheese

Mix .... potatoes, sour cream, seasoned
salt and broccoli in bowl.
Stir .... butter into cereal crumbs in
small bowl until moistened.
Layer ...... half the potato mixture, cheese
and Corn Chex mixture in
casserole.
Repeat ..... layers with remaining ingredients.
Bake .... at 350 degrees for 20 to 25
minutes.
Yields ...... 8 servings.

Latrenda Cooper
Pryor Jr. H. S., Pryor

PARTY BROCCOLI-RICE CASSEROLE

1/2 c. chopped onions
1/2 c. chopped celery
3 tbsp. butter
2 c. cooked rice
2 pkg. frozen chopped broccoli, cooked,
drained

1 can cream of mushroom soup
1 can cream of chicken soup
1/2 lb. Velveeta cheese

Saute . . . . . . onions and celery in butter in saucepan.
Add . . . . remaining ingredients.
Simmer . . . . . until cheese is melted, stirring frequently.
Spoon . . . . . . into baking dish.
Bake . . . . at 375 degrees for 10 minutes or until bubbly.

Missy McKiddy
Noble Jr. H. S., Noble

FAVORITE RICE AND BROCCOLI CASSEROLE

1 sm. onion, chopped
1 8-oz. package frozen chopped broccoli, thawed
1 stick margarine
1 can cream of chicken soup
1/2 c. milk
1 12-oz. jar Cheez Whiz
1 1/2 c. rice, cooked

Saute . . . . . . onion and broccoli in margarine in saucepan.
Add . . . . soup, milk, cheese and rice.
Simmer . . . . . for 1 minute.
Spoon . . . . . . into 2-quart casserole.
Bake . . . . at 350 degrees for 30 minutes.
Yields . . . . . . 8 servings.

Michelle Bobo
Apache H. S., Apache

CARROTS LYONNAISE

6 med. carrots, cut into julienne strips
1 chicken bouillon cube
1 med. onion, sliced
1/4 c. margarine
1 tbsp. flour
1/4 tsp. salt
Dash of pepper
Pinch of sugar

Cook . . . . carrots in 1/2 cup boiling water with bouillon cube in covered saucepan for 10 minutes.
Saute . . . . . . onion in margarine in covered skillet for 15 minutes, stirring occasionally.

Stir . . . . in flour, seasonings and 3/4 cup water.
Bring . . . . to a boil.
Add . . . . carrots and cooking liquid.
Simmer . . . . . for 10 minutes.
Yields . . . . . . 6 servings.

Sabrina Keener
Noble Jr. H. S., Noble

CHILES RELLENOS

1 8-oz. can green chilies, cut in half, seeded
1/2 lb. Monterey Jack cheese, grated
2 eggs
2 tbsp. flour
1 13-oz. can evaporated milk
1/2 lb. Cheddar cheese, grated

Rinse . . . . . . chilies in cold water.
Arrange . . . . . half the chilies in 9 x 9-inch baking dish.
Layer . . . . . . Monterey Jack cheese and remaining chilies on top.
Pour . . . . mixture of eggs, flour and evaporated milk over chilies.
Sprinkle . . . . with Cheddar cheese.
Bake . . . . at 350 degrees for 30 minutes.
Let . . . . stand for 10 minutes before serving.
Yields . . . . . . 6 servings.

Christine Cagle
Lindsay H. S., Lindsay

SHOE PEG CORN CASSEROLE

1 16-oz. can Shoe Peg corn, drained
1 3-oz. package cream cheese, softened
1/3 c. butter, melted
1 c. crushed saltines

Mix . . . . corn, cream cheese and 1/4 cup boiling water in 1 1/2-quart casserole.
Sprinkle . . . . with mixture of butter and cracker crumbs.
Bake . . . . at 350 degrees for 30 minutes or until bubbly.
Yields . . . . . . 4 servings.

Deanne Hardesty, Teacher
Tuttle H. S., Tuttle

Vegetables

BEER-BATTERED ONION RINGS

1 c. flour
Pinch of salt
1 c. beer
1 onion, sliced
Oil for deep frying

Mix .... flour, salt and beer in bowl.
Dip .... onion in batter.
Deep-fry .... until browned.
Drain ...... on paper towels.
Yields ...... 4 servings.

Karen Cary
Barnsdall H. S., Bartlesville

EVERYDAY POTATO SOUP

6 lg. potatoes, peeled, cubed
1 tsp. salt
2 carrots, grated
1 lg. onion, grated
2 to 4 stalks celery, chopped
1 qt. milk
1 c. cream (opt.)
1/4 tsp. pepper
Dash of nutmeg
1/4 c. butter

Cook .... potatoes in salted water in saucepan until tender; drain.
Simmer ..... carrots, onion and celery in a small amount of water in saucepan until carrots are tender; drain.
Add ...... potatoes and remaining ingredients.
Cook .... until heated through. Do not boil.
Yields ...... 4-5 servings.

Jamie R. Stoughton
Northeastern State University, Shady Point

CREAMY CHEESE POTATOES

1 1/4 c. milk
1 8-oz. package cream cheese, softened
1 tbsp. chopped chives
1/2 tsp. instant minced onion
1/4 tsp. salt
4 c. chopped cooked potatoes
Paprika

Blend ...... milk and cream cheese in saucepan over low heat.
Stir .... in chives, onion and salt.
Pour .... over potatoes in 2-cup casserole; sprinkle with paprika.
Bake .... at 350 degrees for 30 minutes.
Yields ...... 8 servings.

Yolanda Turner
Howe H. S., Howe

PARMESAN POTATOES

6 to 8 potatoes, peeled, cut into chunks
1/4 c. flour
1/4 c. Parmesan cheese
1/8 tsp. each salt, pepper
1 stick margarine, melted

Coat .... potatoes with mixture of flour, Parmesan cheese and seasonings.
Melt .... margarine in 9 x 12-inch baking dish.
Arrange ..... potatoes in prepared dish.
Bake .... at 350 degrees for 30 minutes; turn potatoes.
Bake .... for 30 minutes longer.

Arlene Hicks
Coyle H. S., Coyle

SHAKE AND BAKE POTATOES

6 med. potatoes, peeled, quartered
1 pkg. Shake and Bake pork seasoning mix
1 stick margarine, sliced

Shake ...... potatoes in seasoning mix in bag.
Arrange ..... in 1 1/2-quart casserole.
Dot .... with margarine.
Bake .... at 350 degrees for 45 minutes.
Yields ...... 6 servings.

Tonia Colwell
Cache H. S., Cache

SPINACH WITH CARAMELIZED ONIONS

1 lg. red onion, thinly sliced
3 tbsp. olive oil
1 lb. spinach leaves, stems removed
1 tbsp. lemon juice
Freshly ground pepper

Saute . . . . . . onion in olive oil in skillet for 15 minutes or until caramelized, stirring constantly.
Cook . . . . for 3 minutes longer.
Stir . . . . in spinach.
Cook . . . . until wilted; remove from heat.
Add . . . . lemon juice and pepper, tossing gently.

Kim Lippard
Ringwood H. S., Ringwood

SQUASH-CHILIES CASSEROLE

6 med. zucchini, sliced, cooked
1/2 c. shredded Cheddar cheese
1   4-oz. can green chilies
Salt to taste
Bread crumbs
Margarine

Layer . . . . . . zucchini, cheese and green chilies in casserole.
Season . . . . . with salt.
Sprinkle . . . . with bread crumbs.
Dot . . . . with margarine.
Bake . . . . at 350 degrees for 10 minutes or until bubbly.
Yields . . . . . . 6 servings.

Elouise Scheirman
Tonkawa H. S., Tonkawa

SPAGHETTI SQUASH CASSEROLE

1 lg. spaghetti squash, cut in half
Garlic salt
1/2 stick butter
2 1/2 c. barbecue sauce
1 med. onion, chopped
1 lg. green pepper, chopped
1 lb. ground beef
1/2 c. grated cheese

Cook . . . . squash with garlic salt in 2-quart saucepan half filled with water until tender; drain.
Scoop . . . . . . out pulp with fork; combine with butter in bowl.
Let . . . . stand for 10 minutes.
Add . . . . mixture of barbecue sauce, onion and green pepper.
Let . . . . stand for 15 minutes.

Brown . . . . . . ground beef in skillet, stirring frequently.
Stir . . . . into squash mixture.
Spoon . . . . . . into casserole.
Sprinkle . . . . with cheese.
Bake . . . . in warm oven until cheese melts.
Yields . . . . . . 8-10 servings.

Reesa La Gail King
Beggs H. S., Mounds

NUTTY SWEET POTATO CASSEROLE

3 lg. sweet potatoes, cooked, mashed
1 c. sugar
1/2 tsp. salt
1/2 c. milk
2 eggs, beaten
1/2 tsp. vanilla extract
3/4 c. butter
1 c. packed brown sugar
1/2 c. flour
1 c. chopped nuts

Mix . . . . first 6 ingredients and 1/4 cup melted butter in bowl.
Spoon . . . . . . into 1-quart casserole.
Mix . . . . brown sugar, flour, nuts and remaining 1/2 cup melted butter in bowl.
Sprinkle . . . . over sweet potato mixture.
Bake . . . . at 350 degrees for 35 minutes.
Yields . . . . . . 10 servings.

Peggy O. Munter
Moore H. S., Moore

LAYERED VEGETABLE CASSEROLE

5 green tomatoes, sliced
4 white onions, sliced
1 1/2 lb. sharp Cheddar cheese, grated

Layer . . . . . . tomatoes, onions and cheese alternately in buttered casserole until all ingredients are used, ending with cheese.
Bake . . . . at 350 degrees for 45 minutes to 1 hour or until vegetables are tender.
Broil . . . . for several minutes until browned.
Yields . . . . . . 6-8 servings.

Diane Smith
Verden H. S., Verden

Side Dishes

VEGETABLES A LA ESPANA

1 can chicken broth
2 tbsp. lemon juice
1/3 c. olive oil
1/4 tsp. pepper
1 clove of garlic, crushed
1 tsp. oregano
4 med. carrots, thickly sliced
1 c. thickly sliced celery
1 lg. green pepper, coarsely chopped
2 10-oz. packages frozen cauliflower
1 lb. zucchini, thickly sliced
1 c. sliced pimento-stuffed olives

Combine .... first 6 ingredients in large saucepan.
Bring .... to a boil.
Add .... vegetables.
Simmer ..... covered, for 10 minutes or until tender; drain.
Stir .... in olives.
Serve .... hot or cold.

Photograph for this recipe on page 85.

EASY DUMPLINGS

1 c. flour
1/2 tsp. salt
1 1/2 tsp. baking powder
2 tbsp. oil
1/2 c. milk
3 c. chicken or beef broth

Sift .... flour, salt and baking powder in bowl.
Add .... mixture of oil and milk.
Drop .... mixture by spoonfuls into boiling broth in saucepan.
Steam ...... covered, for 12 to 15 minutes or until dumplings are cooked through. Vegetable soup may be substituted for broth, if desired.
Yields ...... 4 servings.

Lisa Hill
1983, 1984 State Secretary
Crescent H. S., Crescent

SOUR CREAM ENCHILADAS

1 10-oz. can enchilada sauce
1 can whole tomatoes
1/3 c. chopped onion
1/2 tsp. salt
12 corn tortillas
Oil
1 c. grated Cheddar cheese
1 8-oz. carton sour cream

Bring .... first 4 ingredients to a boil in saucepan.
Dip .... tortillas in hot oil in skillet; drain on paper towels.
Spoon ...... 1 tablespoon sauce onto each tortilla.
Sprinkle .... with cheese; roll up.
Place .... in baking dish.
Pour .... remaining sauce over top.
Bake .... at 450 degrees for 5 minutes.
Spoon ...... sour cream over enchiladas.

Kristi Robinson
Gould FHA, Gould

GREEN CHILIES GRITS

3 eggs
1 tbsp. salt
1 tsp. paprika
1 1/2 c. quick-cooking grits
1 lb. Cheddar cheese, grated
3/4 c. butter
2 3-oz. cans chopped green chilies

Beat .... eggs, salt and paprika in bowl.
Cook .... grits in 5 1/2 cups boiling water using package directions.
Mix .... in cheese, butter, chilies and egg mixture.
Spoon ...... into buttered 2-quart casserole.
Bake .... at 350 degrees for 1 hour or until set.
Yields ...... 24 servings.

Phyllis K. Sams
Muskogee H. S., Muskogee

HOMINY CASSEROLE

3 cans hominy, drained
1 can green chilies
1 8-oz. carton sour cream
1 jar Cheez Whiz
Grated Cheddar cheese

Mix .... hominy, green chilies, sour cream and Cheez Whiz in bowl.
Spoon ...... into casserole.

Sprinkle .... with Cheddar cheese.
Bake .... at 300 degrees until cheese melts.

Randa McGee
Gould H. S., Gould

NOODLE-MUSHROOM CARBONARA

1/4 lb. bacon
1/2 lb. sliced fresh mushrooms
1 12-oz. package curly egg noodles, cooked
1/4 c. butter, softened
1/4 c. milk, at room temperature
1/2 c. Parmesan cheese
2 eggs, slightly beaten
2 tbsp. chopped parsley
Salt and pepper to taste

Saute ...... bacon in skillet until crisp.
Drain ...... and crumble; reserve drippings.
Saute ...... mushrooms in reserved bacon drippings until tender; set aside.
Place .... hot noodles in large warm serving dish.
Add .... bacon, mushrooms, butter, milk, cheese, eggs and parsley; toss until noodles are well coated.
Season ..... to taste.
Yields ...... 6-8 servings.

Photograph for this recipe on this page.

CHEESY NOODLE RING

1 lb. noodles
1 tsp. salt
3 tbsp. butter
2 c. shredded Cheddar cheese
1 1/2 tsp. Worcestershire sauce

Cook .... noodles in boiling salted water in saucepan until tender; drain.
Add .... butter; toss to mix.
Spoon ...... into greased ring mold.
Place .... in pan of hot water.
Bake .... at 350 degrees for 25 minutes.
Unmold .... onto serving plate.
Melt .... cheese in saucepan.
Stir .... in Worcestershire sauce.
Pour .... over noodle ring.

Connie Alsobrook
Bray-Doyle H. S., Marlow

EIGHT-TREASURES RICE

3/4 c. short grain rice
2/3 c. packed brown sugar
1/2 c. each dates, raisins
1/3 c. each glace cherries, pineapple
1/2 c. mixed grated lemon and orange rind
1/2 c. blanched almonds
1/2 c. walnuts

Cook .... rice in boiling water in saucepan for 15 minutes or until tender; drain.
Stir .... in brown sugar.
Place .... layer of rice in oiled 1 1/2-pint bowl.
Press .... layer of fruits, rind and nuts into rice in decorative pattern.
Layer ...... remaining rice, fruits, rinds and nuts into bowl until all ingredients are used.
Cover ...... bowl with greased foil.
Place .... on rack in saucepan filled with a small amount of water.
Steam ...... for 30 to 40 minutes or until set.
Unmold .... on serving plate. Serve hot.
Yields ...... 6-8 servings.

Melissa Teepe
Carrier H. S., Enid

Side Dishes

BAKED RICE CASSEROLE

1 c. rice
1 onion, finely chopped
1 stick margarine
1 can beef consomme
1 can mushrooms
1/2 to 1 c. grated Cheddar cheese

Brown . . . . . . rice and onion in margarine in skillet.
Pour . . . . into deep 2 1/2-quart casserole.
Stir . . . . in consomme.
Drain . . . . . . mushroom liquid into consomme can. Add enough water to fill 1/2 full.
Add . . . . with mushrooms to rice.
Sprinkle . . . . with cheese.
Bake . . . . covered, at 350 degrees for 45 minutes.

Pat Ulmer
Taft Middle H. S., Oklahoma City

BROWN RICE

1 6-oz. can sliced mushrooms
1 onion, chopped
1 c. chopped celery
1/4 c. margarine, melted
1 c. rice
1 tsp. salt
2 chicken bouillon cubes
1/2 tsp. marjoram

Drain . . . . . . mushrooms, reserving liquid.
Saute . . . . . . onion, celery and mushrooms in margarine in saucepan.
Mix . . . . in remaining ingredients.
Combine . . . . reserved liquid with enough water to measure 2 cups.
Add . . . . to rice mixture.
Bring . . . . to a boil, covered.
Simmer . . . . . for 20 minutes.

Virginia Searles
Westville H. S., Westville

AUNT MARY'S RICE DISH

3 eggs
1 1/2 c. cubed ham
1/2 c. chopped celery
1/4 c. sliced green onions
1 tbsp. oil
6 c. cooked rice
2 tbsp. soy sauce

Scramble . . . . eggs in skillet.
Saute . . . . . . ham, celery and onions in oil in skillet.
Stir . . . . in eggs, rice and soy sauce.

Diane Ford
Empire H. S., Duncan

ORIENTAL RICE

1 sm. package minute rice
1 green pepper, chopped
1 onion, chopped
1 can mushrooms, drained
1/4 c. margarine
1/2 c. soy sauce
1 sm. can chopped pimentos
1 can blanched almonds

Prepare . . . . . rice using package directions.
Saute . . . . . . green pepper, onion and mushrooms in margarine in skillet. Do not brown.
Stir . . . . in rice.
Add . . . . soy sauce, pimentos and almonds.
Heat . . . . to serving temperature.

Shelly Dillahunty
Granite H. S., Granite

SPANISH RICE

8 slices bacon
1 c. chopped onion
1/4 c. chopped green pepper
1 can tomatoes
1/2 c. chili sauce
3/4 c. rice
1 tsp. salt
Dash of pepper
1/2 tsp. Worcestershire sauce
1 tsp. brown sugar

Fry . . . . bacon in skillet until crisp; remove and crumble bacon.
Saute . . . . . . onion, green pepper and half the bacon in half the bacon drippings.
Add . . . . tomatoes, chili sauce, rice and seasonings.
Cook . . . . covered, until rice is tender.
Sprinkle . . . . remaining bacon over top.

Danelle Lureen DeWitt
Silo H. S., Mead

Breads

CHEDDAR-APPLE BREAD, recipe on page 96.

Breads

BEER BREAD

3 c. self-rising flour
3 tbsp. sugar
1 can warm beer

Combine .... all ingredients in bowl, mixing well.
Pour .... into greased loaf pan.
Bake .... at 350 degrees for 45 minutes or until bread tests done.

Ruth Knight
Panama H. S., Panama

EASY CHEESE BREAD

1/4 c. butter, melted
1/2 c. grated cheese
6 1-in. slices French bread
1 tbsp. poppy seed

Combine .... butter and cheese in bowl, mixing well.
Spread ..... mixture on both sides of bread.
Sprinkle .... with poppy seed.
Place .... on baking sheet.
Bake .... at 350 degrees for 12 minutes or until cheese melts.

Connie Hagan
Moore Sr. H. S., Moore

CHEESE-BISCUIT LOAF

1 10-count can refrigerator biscuits
2 tbsp. butter, melted
1/4 c. grated Parmesan cheese

Dip .... biscuits in melted butter and Parmesan cheese.
Arrange ..... in 2 overlapping rows on baking sheet.
Bake .... at 475 degrees for 8 to 10 minutes or until lightly browned.
Yields ...... 5-6 servings.

Stacey Welty
Ringwood H. S., Ringwood

SPECIAL HUSH PUPPIES

1/2 c. flour
1/2 c. white cornmeal
1 tsp. salt
Dash of pepper
1 tsp. baking powder
1 sm. onion, chopped
1/2 c. white corn, drained
1 egg
Milk (opt.)
Oil for deep frying

Sift .... dry ingredients into bowl, mixing well.
Stir .... in onion, corn and egg.
Add .... a small amount of milk if necessary.
Drop .... by spoonfuls into hot oil.
Deep-fry .... for 2 minutes or until golden brown.
Drain ...... on paper towels.

Becky McGlothlin
Barnsdall H. S., Barnsdall

FAVORITE HUSH PUPPIES

1 1/2 c. cornmeal
1/3 c. milk
1 tbsp. oil
2 tsp. grated onion
2 eggs, beaten
1 c. flour
1 tbsp. baking powder
2 tsp. salt
1 tsp. sugar
Oil for deep frying

Combine .... cornmeal and 1 1/2 cups water in saucepan.
Cook .... for 6 minutes or until thickened, stirring constantly; remove from heat.
Stir .... in milk, oil and onion.
Add .... to eggs gradually, mixing well.
Sift .... in dry ingredients, mixing well.
Deep-fry .... by teaspoonfuls in 375-degree oil for 6 to 7 minutes or until golden brown.
Drain ...... on paper towels.
Yields ...... 2-2 1/2 dozen.

Laverne Earls
Gould FHA, Gould

MEXICAN CORN BREAD

1 lb. ground beef
1 lg. onion, finely chopped

94

2 pkg. corn bread mix
1/2 c. oil
2 tbsp. sugar
2 eggs, slightly beaten
1 can cream-style corn
1   4-oz. can chopped green chilies
3/4 c. milk
1 c. grated cheese

Brown ...... ground beef with onion in skillet, stirring frequently; drain.
Combine .... remaining ingredients except cheese in bowl, mixing well.
Pour .... half the batter into greased 9 x 13-inch baking pan; top with ground beef mixture.
Pour .... remaining batter on top.
Bake .... at 375 degrees for 20 to 25 minutes.
Sprinkle .... with cheese.
Bake .... for 10 minutes longer until cheese melts and bread tests done.
Yields ...... 24 servings.

Annys Brantley, Adviser
Rush Springs H. S., Rush Springs

BANANA-WALNUT BREAD

1/3 c. shortening
1/2 c. sugar
2 eggs
1 3/4 c. sifted flour
1 tsp. baking powder
1/2 tsp. each soda, salt
1 c. mashed ripe bananas
1/2 c. chopped walnuts

Cream ...... shortening and sugar in bowl.
Beat .... in eggs.
Add .... sifted dry ingredients alternately with bananas, mixing well after each addition.
Stir .... in walnuts.
Pour .... into greased 5 x 9-inch loaf pan.
Bake .... at 350 degrees for 45 to 50 minutes or until bread tests done.
Cool .... on wire rack.

Vickie DeHerrera
Ringwood H. S., Meno

SOUR CREAM-BANANA-NUT BREAD

1 stick butter, softened
1 1/2 c. sugar
2 eggs
1/2 c. sour cream
1 tsp. vanilla extract
1 tsp. soda
2 c. flour
2 lg. bananas, mashed
1/2 c. chopped nuts

Cream ...... butter and sugar in mixer bowl.
Beat .... in eggs, sour cream, vanilla and soda until creamy.
Add .... flour gradually, mixing well after each addition.
Stir .... in bananas and nuts.
Spoon ...... into greased 5 x 9-inch loaf pan.
Bake .... at 350 degrees for 45 minutes to 1 hour or until bread tests done.

Beth Burgess
Choctaw Jr. H. S., Choctaw

CHERRY-PECAN BREAD

2 c. flour
1 tsp. soda
1/2 tsp. salt
3/4 c. sugar
1 stick butter, softened
2 eggs
1 tsp. vanilla extract
1 c. buttermilk
1 c. chopped pecans
1 c. chopped maraschino cherries

Combine .... flour, soda and salt in small bowl, mixing well.
Cream ...... sugar, butter, eggs and vanilla in bowl.
Add .... flour mixture and buttermilk alternately, blending well after each addition.
Fold .... in pecans and cherries.
Pour .... into greased 5 x 9-inch loaf pan.
Bake .... at 350 degrees for 55 to 65 minutes or until bread tests done.
Cool .... in pan for 10 minutes.
Glaze ...... with confectioners' sugar icing if desired.

Rosie Nixon
Chickasha H. S., Chickasha

Breads

CHEDDAR-APPLE BREAD

1/2 c. shortening
1/2 c. sugar
1 egg
1 can apple pie filling
2 1/2 c. sifted flour
1 tsp. each salt, soda, baking powder
1 c. shredded Cheddar cheese
1/2 c. chopped pecans

Cream . . . . . . shortening and sugar in bowl.
Add . . . . egg; mix well.
Beat . . . . in pie filling.
Add . . . . sifted dry ingredients, cheese and pecans, mixing well.
Pour . . . . into greased loaf pan.
Bake . . . . at 350 degrees for 1 1/2 hours.

Photograph for this recipe on page 93.

GRAPE NUTS BREAD

2 eggs, beaten
1 c. sugar
1 8-oz. carton sour cream
1 c. sour milk
1 tsp. salt
1 tsp. each baking powder, soda
3 c. flour
1 c. Grape Nuts

Cream . . . . . . eggs and sugar in mixer bowl.
Blend . . . . . . in sour cream and sour milk.
Add . . . . combined dry ingredients, mixing well.
Pour . . . . into greased loaf pan.
Bake . . . . at 350 degrees for 1 hour.
Serve . . . . . . with butter or cream cheese spread.
Yields . . . . . . 12 servings.

Jeanne Shirley, Adviser
Wynnewood H. S., Wynnewood

ORANGE-WALNUT SHORTBREAD

1 3/4 c. sifted cake flour
1/2 c. sugar
1/8 tsp. salt
2 1/2 tsp. grated orange rind
1/2 c. firm butter
3/4 c. California walnuts, finely chopped
3 tbsp. orange juice

1 c. sifted confectioners' sugar
Walnut halves

Combine . . . . flour, sugar, salt and 2 teaspoons orange rind in bowl.
Cut . . . . in butter until crumbly.
Stir . . . . in chopped walnuts and 1 tablespoon orange juice.
Pour . . . . into greased foil-lined 8-inch round cake pan.
Press . . . . foil edge with fingertips to flute.
Bake . . . . at 350 degrees for 30 minutes.
Cool . . . . in pan; remove foil liner.
Combine . . . . 2 tablespoons juice, 1/2 teaspoon rind and confectioners' sugar in bowl.
Spread . . . . . over shortbread; mark into 12 wedges.
Decorate . . . . each wedge with walnut half.

Photograph for this recipe above.

HOLIDAY BUNNY BREAD

1 stick margarine, softened
1 c. sugar
2 eggs
3 tbsp. buttermilk
1 tsp. soda
1/2 tsp. salt
2 c. flour
1 c. finely grated carrots
1 c. walnuts, chopped
1 c. raisins

Cream ...... margarine and sugar in bowl.
Add .... eggs and buttermilk, mixing well.
Beat .... in remaining ingredients in order listed.
Spoon ..... into greased and floured 4 x 8-inch loaf pan.
Bake .... at 350 degrees for 1 hour.

Lisa McKinney
Maysville H. S., Maysville

PUMPKIN BREAD

3 c. sugar
1 c. oil
4 eggs, beaten
1 can pumpkin
3 1/2 c. flour
2 tsp. each soda, salt
1 tsp. baking powder
1 tsp. each nutmeg, allspice, cinnamon
1/2 tsp. cloves

Combine .... sugar and oil in bowl, mixing well.
Stir .... in eggs and pumpkin.
Add .... sifted dry ingredients alternately with 2/3 cup water.
Pour .... into 2 greased and floured 5 x 9-inch loaf pans.
Bake .... at 350 degrees for 1 1/2 hours or until bread tests done.
Cool .... in pans for 10 minutes.

Teresa Tillery
Porum Jr. H. S., Porum

STRAWBERRY-NUT BREAD

3 c. flour
2 c. sugar
1 tbsp. cinnamon
1 tsp. each soda, salt
1 1/4 c. oil
4 eggs, beaten
2 10-oz. packages frozen strawberries, thawed
1 1/4 c. chopped nuts

Combine .... dry ingredients in large bowl, mixing well.
Stir .... in oil and eggs.
Fold .... in strawberries and nuts.

Pour .... into 2 greased and floured 5 x 9-inch loaf pans.
Bake .... at 350 degrees for 1 1/4 hours.
Let .... stand, tightly wrapped, over-night to improve flavor.

Charla Stehr
Clinton Jr. H. S., Clinton

BRAN MUFFINS

2 1/3 c. 40% bran flakes
1 c. milk
1 egg
1/3 c. oil
1 c. flour
1/3 c. packed brown sugar
1 tbsp. baking powder

Mix .... bran flakes and milk in large bowl.
Let .... stand for 3 minutes; mix well.
Stir .... in egg and oil.
Add .... combined dry ingredients, mixing well.
Spoon ..... into muffin cups.
Bake .... at 400 degrees for 25 minutes.

Lorrie Reed
Noble Jr. H. S., Noble

RAISIN-OATMEAL MUFFINS

3/4 c. sifted flour
2 tsp. baking powder
3/4 tsp. salt
1/3 c. sugar
1 c. oats
1 c. raisins
2 eggs, slightly beaten
1/2 c. milk
1/4 c. oil

Sift .... flour, baking powder, salt and sugar into bowl.
Stir .... in oats and raisins.
Combine .... eggs, milk and oil in small bowl, mixing well.
Add .... to flour mixture, stirring until just moistened.
Fill .... greased muffin cups 2/3 full.
Bake .... at 400 degrees for 20 minutes or until muffins test done.

Kayrone Long
Eisenhower H. S., Lawton

Breads

FAVORITE PANCAKES

2 eggs
2 tbsp. butter, melted
2 c. buttermilk
2 c. flour
1 tsp. baking powder
1/2 tsp. soda
1/4 c. sugar
1/2 tsp. salt

Combine .... eggs, butter and buttermilk in bowl, mixing well.
Add .... combined dry ingredients, stirring until just blended.
Cook .... on hot greased griddle until golden brown on both sides.

Bud and Alicia Osborne
FHA Advisory Committee
Pryor Public Schools, Pryor

POPOVERS

1 1/4 c. sifted flour
1/2 tsp. salt
1 1/4 c. milk
3 jumbo eggs

Sift .... flour and salt together in bowl; add milk.
Beat .... with wire whisk until just blended.
Add .... eggs, 1 at a time, beating well after each addition.
Fill .... greased popover cups 1/2 full.
Bake .... at 425 degrees for 20 minutes.
Reduce ..... temperature to 325 degrees; bake for 15 to 20 minutes longer or until golden brown. May add 1/2 cup finely grated Cheddar cheese or 1 teaspoon sugar and 1/2 teaspoon grated orange rind to batter.

Kristy Ensminger
Okeene Public Schools, Isabella

MAGIC MARSHMALLOW CRESCENT PUFFS

2 8-oz. cans refrigerator crescent dinner rolls
16 lg. marshmallows
1/4 c. butter, melted
1/4 c. sugar
1 tsp. cinnamon
1/2 c. confectioners' sugar
1/2 tsp. vanilla extract
2 or 3 tsp. milk

Separate .... dough into 16 triangles.
Dip .... marshmallows in butter.
Roll .... in mixture of sugar and cinnamon.
Wrap .... dough around marshmallows, sealing edges.
Dip .... in butter.
Place .... in muffin cups; place muffin cups on baking sheet.
Bake .... at 375 degrees for 10 to 15 minutes or until golden brown.
Blend ...... confectioners' sugar, vanilla and milk in bowl.
Drizzle ..... over rolls.

Hope Koester
Barnsdall H. S., Barnsdall

SPANISH CRULLERS

1 stick margarine
1/4 tsp. salt
1 c. flour
3 eggs
Oil for deep frying
1/4 c. sugar
1/4 tsp. cinnamon

Combine .... margarine, salt and 1 cup water in saucepan.
Bring .... to a boil.
Add .... flour.
Cook .... until mixture forms ball, stirring constantly; remove from heat.
Beat .... in eggs until smooth.
Spoon ...... into pastry tube with large star tip.
Press .... into 4-inch strips into 360-degree oil.
Deep-fry .... for 4 minutes, turning once.
Drain .... on paper towels.
Coat .... with mixture of sugar and cinnamon.

Donna McGivern
Deer Creek Public School, Edmond

ANGEL BISCUITS

1 pkg. dry yeast
3 tbsp. sugar

3/4 c. shortening
5 c. flour
1/2 tsp. salt
1 tsp. soda
1 tbsp. baking powder
2 c. buttermilk

Dissolve .... yeast and sugar in 1/2 cup warm water in small bowl.
Cut .... shortening into dry ingredients in bowl until crumbly.
Stir .... in mixture of yeast and buttermilk.
Chill .... in refrigerator.
Roll .... on floured surface; cut with biscuit cutter.
Place .... on greased baking sheet.
Let .... rise for 30 minutes.
Bake .... at 400 degrees until golden brown.

Nadine Carpenter
Leflore H. S., Leflore

COWBOY BISCUITS

2 pkg. yeast
11 c. flour
1/2 c. sugar
8 tsp. baking powder
1/4 c. oil
4 c. milk

Dissolve .... yeast in 1 cup warm water in large bowl.
Add .... dry ingredients to mixture alternately with oil and milk, mixing well after each addition.
Let .... rise in warm place for 1 hour or until doubled in bulk.
Shape ...... into rolls; place in baking pan.
Let .... rise in warm place for 30 minutes to 1 hour before baking.
Bake .... at 350 degrees for 30 minutes.
May .... store dough in refrigerator 1 week or less.
Yields ...... 5 dozen.

Cheryl Pierce
Macomb H. S., Macomb

SOURDOUGH BISCUITS

1 pkg. yeast
2 c. buttermilk

3/4 c. oil
4 tsp. baking powder
1/4 tsp. soda
6 c. flour
1/4 c. sugar
2 tsp. salt

Dissolve .... yeast in 1 cup warm water in bowl.
Mix .... in remaining ingredients.
Chill .... covered, in refrigerator.
Roll .... on floured surface; cut with biscuit cutter.
Bake .... at 425 degrees for 12 to 15 minutes or until golden brown.

Michelle Holmes
Beggs H. S., Beggs

YEAST PULL BREAD

1 pkg. yeast
Sugar
Butter
1 1/2 tsp. salt
1 c. milk, scalded
3 eggs, beaten
4 c. flour
Sesame seed

Dissolve .... yeast and 1 teaspoon sugar in 1/4 cup warm water in bowl.
Let .... stand for 10 minutes or until bubbly.
Mix .... 3/4 cup butter, salt, 1/2 cup sugar and milk in bowl; cool to lukewarm.
Stir .... in yeast mixture.
Mix .... in eggs and flour. Dough will be very sticky.
Let .... rise until doubled in bulk.
Punch ...... dough down.
Chill .... in refrigerator overnight.
Roll .... dough into 3 rectangles 6 inches wide and 1/2 inch thick.
Cut .... into 6 x 1/2-inch strips.
Dip .... in 1 cup melted butter.
Shape ...... into loose spiral from center of 8-inch baking pans.
Sprinkle .... with sesame seed; pat down.
Let .... rise until doubled in bulk.
Bake .... at 350 degrees for 15 minutes.
Drizzle ..... with melted butter.

Pam Sparks
Tuttle H. S., Tuttle

Breads

PULL APARTS

1/4 c. packed brown sugar
2 tbsp. corn syrup
1 pkg. frozen dinner roll dough, thawed
1 stick butter, melted
1 c. sugar
2 tsp. cinnamon

Combine . . . . brown sugar and corn syrup in bowl, mixing well.
Pour . . . . into tube pan.
Dip . . . . rolls in melted butter; coat with mixture of sugar and cinnamon.
Arrange . . . . . in pan.
Let . . . . rise, covered, overnight.
Bake . . . . at 350 degrees for 30 to 40 minutes or until brown.
Invert . . . . . . on serving plate.
Yields . . . . . . 6 servings.

Deana Jantz
Ringwood Public School, Meno

OVERNIGHT COFFEE CAKE

1 pkg. frozen cloverleaf roll dough
1 stick butter, melted
1/2 c. packed brown sugar
1 sm. package vanilla pudding and pie filling mix
1/2 c. chopped pecans

Separate . . . . each roll into 3 pieces.
Arrange . . . . . in greased bundt pan.
Pour . . . . butter over dough.
Mix . . . . brown sugar, pudding mix and pecans in bowl.
Sprinkle . . . . over dough.
Let . . . . stand overnight.
Bake . . . . at 350 degrees for 30 minutes.
Invert . . . . . . onto serving plate.

Joann Carter, Adviser
Kingston H. S., Kingston

BAKED ALMOND DOUGHNUTS

3/4 c. milk, scalded
1/3 c. sugar
1 1/2 tsp. salt
1/2 c. oil
2 pkg. dry yeast
2 eggs, beaten

3/4 tsp. nutmeg
4 1/4 to 4 1/2 c. sifted flour
1 to 1 1/4 c. chopped roasted almonds
1/2 c. melted butter
1/4 c. corn syrup
1 6-oz. package chocolate chips

Combine . . . . first 3 ingredients and 6 tablespoons oil; cool to lukewarm.
Dissolve . . . . yeast in 1/4 cup warm water in large bowl.
Stir . . . . in milk mixture, eggs and nutmeg.
Add . . . . flour and 1/2 cup almonds gradually, mixing well.
Knead . . . . . . on floured surface until smooth and elastic.
Roll . . . . 1/2 inch thick; cut with doughnut cutter.
Place . . . . 2 inches apart on greased baking sheet.
Brush . . . . . . with half the butter.
Let . . . . rise in warm place for 20 to 30 minutes.
Bake . . . . at 425 degrees for 8 to 10 minutes or until brown.
Brush . . . . . . with remaining butter.
Bring . . . . syrup, 2 tablespoons oil and 3 tablespoons water to a boil in saucepan; remove from heat.
Stir . . . . in chocolate chips until melted.
Dip . . . . slightly cooled doughnuts in chocolate mixture; then in remaining almonds.

Photograph for this recipe on page 5.

FROSTED DOUGHNUTS

3 pkg. yeast
3/4 c. sugar
1 tsp. salt
2 eggs, beaten
6 c. (about) flour
3/4 c. shortening
Oil for deep frying
1 c. packed brown sugar
1 c. coffee
1 16-oz. package confectioners' sugar, sifted
Mapleline flavoring to taste

Dissolve . . . . yeast in 3 cups lukewarm water in bowl.

Mix . . . . in sugar, salt, eggs and half the flour.

Add . . . . shortening and enough remaining flour to make stiff dough, mixing well.

Let . . . . rise in warm place until doubled in bulk.

Roll . . . . out on floured surface; cut with doughnut cutter.

Let . . . . rise for 5 minutes.

Deep-fry . . . . until golden brown.

Drain . . . . . . on paper towels.

Boil . . . . brown sugar and coffee in saucepan for 4 minutes.

Pour . . . . over confectioners' sugar in bowl.

Stir . . . . in flavoring.

Drizzle . . . . . over doughnuts.

Yields . . . . . . 50 servings.

Shirley Absher
Cement H. S., Cement

OLD RANCH-STYLE FRIED BREAD

1 pkg. dry yeast
2 tbsp. sugar
2 tbsp. shortening
2 c. flour
2 tsp. salt
Oil for deep frying

Dissolve . . . . yeast in 1 cup warm water in bowl.

Stir . . . . in sugar and shortening.

Sift . . . . in flour and salt, mixing well.

Let . . . . rise in warm place for 30 minutes.

Roll . . . . . . to 1/2-inch thickness on floured surface; cut into strips.

Deep-fry . . . . until golden brown on both sides.

Drain . . . . . . on paper towels.

Yields . . . . . . 8-10 servings.

Cement FHA
Cement H. S., Cement

PEANUT BUTTER MUFFINS

1 c. milk, scalded
1/2 c. sugar
1 tsp. salt
5 tbsp. margarine
2 pkg. dry yeast
2 eggs, beaten
4 c. flour
1/2 c. crunchy peanut butter

Combine . . . . milk, sugar, salt and 1/4 cup margarine in bowl; cool to lukewarm.

Dissolve . . . . yeast in 1/2 cup warm water in large warm bowl.

Stir . . . . in milk mixture, eggs and 3 cups flour; beat until smooth.

Add . . . . remaining flour, mixing well.

Let . . . . rise, covered, in warm place for 1 hour or until doubled in bulk.

Stir . . . . batter down.

Blend . . . . . . peanut butter and 1 tablespoon margarine in bowl.

Swirl . . . . into batter.

Spoon . . . . . . into greased muffin cups.

Bake . . . . at 350 degrees for 20 to 25 minutes or until muffins test done.

Yields . . . . . . 20 muffins.

Photograph for this recipe above.

Breads

HOT PAN ROLLS

1 tbsp. yeast
2 eggs, beaten
1/2 c. oil
5 to 6 c. Hot Roll Master Mix

Dissolve .... yeast in 1 1/2 cups lukewarm water in bowl.
Mix .... in eggs, oil and master mix.
Knead ...... on floured surface for 5 minutes or until smooth and elastic.
Place .... in greased bowl, turning to grease surface.
Let .... rise, covered, in warm place for 1 hour or until doubled in bulk.
Punch ...... dough down.
Shape ...... into small rolls.
Place .... in greased 9 x 13-inch baking pan.
Let .... rise, covered, for 30 minutes or until doubled in bulk.
Bake .... at 375 degrees for 20 to 25 minutes or until golden brown.

Hot Roll Master Mix

Mix 5 pounds flour, 1 1/4 cups sugar, 4 teaspoons salt and 1 cup dry milk powder in bowl. Store in airtight container.

Toni Chance
Ringwood H. S., Ringwood

SOFT PRETZELS

1 pkg. dry yeast
1 tbsp. sugar
1/2 tsp. salt
3 1/2 to 4 c. flour
1 egg
2 tbsp. coarse salt

Dissolve .... yeast in 1 1/3 cups warm water in bowl.
Stir .... in sugar, salt and 3 1/2 cups flour.
Knead ...... in 1/2 cup flour for 5 to 7 minutes or until dough is smooth and elastic.
Roll .... into six 15-inch ropes.
Place .... on baking sheet.
Shape ...... into pretzels.

Brush ...... with mixture of egg and 1 tablespoon water.
Sprinkle .... with coarse salt.
Bake .... at 425 degrees for 15 to 20 minutes or until golden brown.
Yields ...... 6 servings.

Laurie Tune
Vinita H. S., Vinita

HERBED TOMATO BREAD

2 tbsp. brown sugar
2 tsp. salt
2 pkg. dry yeast
5 1/2 c. flour
1 c. milk
5 tbsp. butter
1 c. chopped peeled seeded tomatoes
2 eggs
1/2 tsp. basil
3/4 tsp. thyme

Mix .... brown sugar, salt, yeast and 1 cup flour in large mixer bowl.
Heat .... milk and 3 tablespoons butter in saucepan until very warm.
Beat .... into dry ingredients at low speed until just moistened.
Beat .... at medium speed for 2 minutes, scraping bowl occasionally.
Add .... tomatoes, eggs, spices and 1 1/2 cups flour.
Beat .... for 2 minutes, scraping bowl frequently.
Add .... enough remaining flour to make soft dough.
Knead ...... on floured surface for about 10 minutes or until smooth and elastic, adding additional flour as needed.
Place .... in greased bowl, turning to grease surface.
Let .... rise, covered, in warm place for 1 1/2 hours or until doubled in bulk.
Punch ...... dough down on floured surface.
Let .... rise, covered, for 15 minutes.
Roll .... half the dough into 8 x 12-inch rectangle.
Roll .... as for jelly roll from short side; pinch seams and press under.

Place .... seam side down in greased 5 x 9-inch loaf pan.

Repeat ..... with remaining dough.

Let .... rise in warm place for 1 hour or until doubled in bulk.

Brush ...... with 2 tablespoons melted butter.

Bake .... at 400 degrees for 25 to 30 minutes or until bread tests done.

Cool .... on wire racks.

Carrie Gardnee
Sharon-Mutual, Sharon

SOURDOUGH BREAD

1 pkg. dry yeast
1 c. Sourdough Starter
2 tsp. salt
2 tsp. sugar
5 1/2 to 6 c. flour
1/2 tsp. soda
Melted butter

Soften ...... yeast in 1 1/2 cups warm water in mixer bowl.

Mix .... in Sourdough Starter, salt and sugar.

Add .... 2 1/2 cups flour.

Beat .... for 3 to 4 minutes.

Let .... rise, covered, for 1 1/2 hours or until doubled in bulk.

Mix .... in soda and enough remaining flour to form stiff dough.

Knead ...... on floured surface for 5 to 7 minutes or until smooth and elastic.

Divide ...... dough in half.

Let .... rest, covered, for 10 minutes.

Shape ...... into round loaves on greased baking sheets.

Cut .... diagonal slashes over surface.

Let .... rise for 1 to 1 1/2 hours or until doubled in bulk.

Bake .... at 400 degrees for 35 to 40 minutes or until bread tests done.

Brush ...... with butter.

Sourdough Starter

Dissolve 1 package dry yeast in 1/2 cup warm water in bowl. Mix in 1 tablespoon sugar, 2 cups water and 2 cups flour until smooth. Let stand, covered, at room temperature for 5 to 10 days, stirring 2 or 3 times a day. Chill until ready to use. Add 3/4 cup water, 3/4 cup sifted flour and 1 teaspoon sugar to keep starter going. Let stand at room temperature for 1 day or until bubbly and fermented. Store in refrigerator. Add 1 teaspoon sugar if starter is not used within 10 days. Repeat process, adding sugar every 10 days.

Cathy Kitchens
Crowder FHA, Crowder

CRACKED WHEAT BREAD

2 pkg. yeast
3 tbsp. sugar
1 c. fine cracked wheat
1 c. Bran Buds
1 stick margarine
4 tsp. salt
1/3 c. honey
1 c. dry milk powder
2 1/2 c. whole wheat graham flour
4 to 5 c. all-purpose flour

Dissolve .... yeast and sugar in 1 cup warm water.

Mix .... next 4 ingredients and 2 cups boiling water in bowl; cool to lukewarm.

Add .... yeast mixture, honey, milk powder and graham flour, mixing well.

Let .... rise, covered, in warm place or until doubled in bulk.

Knead ...... in all-purpose flour until smooth and elastic.

Place .... in greased bowl, turning to grease surface.

Let .... rise, covered, until doubled in bulk.

Punch ...... dough down.

Let .... rise again.

Fill .... 4 or 5 greased 1-pound coffee cans 1/2 full; cover with lid.

Let .... rise until dough rises above rim.

Bake .... at 375 degrees for 25 to 30 minutes or until bread tests done.

Remove .... from pans; cool on wire rack.

Yields ...... 4-5 loaves.

Sheri Lynn McCampbell
Norman H. S., Norman

Breads

MONKEY BREAD

1 c. milk
1/4 c. sugar
1 tsp. salt
2 sticks butter
1 pkg. dry yeast
3 1/2 c. flour

Heat .... milk, sugar, salt and 1 stick butter in saucepan until butter melts; cool to lukewarm.
Stir .... in yeast.
Place .... flour in large bowl; make well in center.
Pour .... yeast mixture into well, stirring constantly.
Let .... rise, covered, in warm place for 1 hour and 20 minutes or until doubled in bulk.
Roll .... 1/4 inch thick on floured surface; cut into 3-inch squares.
Melt .... remaining butter in saucepan.
Dip .... squares in remaining melted butter; layer in bundt pan.
Let .... rise in warm place for 40 minutes.
Bake .... at 350 degrees for 20 minutes.
Yields ...... 6-8 servings.

Durene French
Cameron H. S., Cameron

HAWAIIAN SWEET BREAD

6 1/2 to 7 c. flour
3/4 c. instant mashed potato flakes
1 tsp. salt
2/3 c. sugar
1/2 tsp. ginger
2 tsp. vanilla extract
2 pkg. dry yeast
1 c. milk
1 stick margarine
1 c. pineapple juice
3 eggs

Combine .... 3 cups flour, potato flakes, salt, sugar, ginger, vanilla and yeast in mixer bowl.
Heat .... milk, 1/2 cup water and margarine in saucepan until very warm.
Blend ...... into dry ingredients with pineapple juice and eggs at low speed until moistened.
Beat .... at medium speed for 4 minutes.
Stir .... in 3 cups flour.
Knead ...... in 1/2 to 1 cup flour for 5 to 8 minutes or until smooth.
Place .... in greased bowl, turning to grease surface.
Let .... rise, covered, in warm place for 1 to 1 1/2 hours or until doubled in bulk.
Shape ...... into 3 balls.
Place .... in greased 8-inch cake pans.
Let .... rise, covered, for 1 hour or until doubled in bulk.
Bake .... at 375 degrees for 25 to 30 minutes or until bread tests done; remove from pans immediately.
Yields ...... 3 loaves.

Janie Vardy
Wakita Public School, Wakita

SOPAPILLAS

2 c. flour
3/4 tsp. salt
1/2 tsp. baking powder
1 tbsp. sugar
1/2 c. shortening
1 pkg. dry yeast
1/2 c. scalded milk, cooled
Oil for deep frying

Combine .... first 4 ingredients in bowl, mixing well.
Cut .... in shortening until crumbly; make well in center.
Dissolve .... yeast in 1/4 cup warm water.
Add .... to scalded milk in bowl, mixing well.
Pour .... into dry ingredients, mixing well.
Knead ...... 15 to 20 times.
Let .... stand for 10 minutes.
Roll .... 1/4-inch thick on floured surface; cut into squares or triangles.
Deep-fry .... at 420 degrees until puffed and golden brown.
Yields ...... 24 servings.

Lana Carpenter, Adviser
Asher H. S., Asher

Desserts

PEACHY CHOCOLATE CHEESECAKE, recipe on page 139. CHOCOLATE MOUSSE, recipe on page 141.

Desserts

MOCK ANGEL FOOD CAKE

1 c. sugar
1/4 tsp. salt
1 1/3 c. flour
1 tbsp. baking powder
2/3 c. milk, scalded
2 egg whites, stiffly beaten
1 tsp. vanilla extract

Sift . . . . dry ingredients into bowl.
Stir . . . . in hot milk gradually.
Fold . . . . in egg whites and vanilla.
Pour . . . . into tube pan.
Bake . . . . at 350 degrees for 45 minutes.

Robyn Grammont
Moore H. S., Moore

ANGELA'S CAKE

1 pkg. cake mix
1 sm. package gelatin
1 carton whipped topping

Prepare . . . . . and bake cake according to package directions for 9 x 13-inch pan.
Dissolve . . . . gelatin in 1 cup boiling water; stir in 1 cup cold water.
Poke . . . . holes over surface of cake.
Pour . . . . gelatin over hot cake.
Chill . . . . for 2 hours or until set.
Frost . . . . with whipped topping.

Angela Nossaman
Ringwood H. S., Ringwood

APPLE CHIP CAKE

1 1/2 c. oil
2 1/2 c. sugar
2 eggs, beaten
3 c. chopped unpeeled apples
1 c. chopped pecans
3/4 tsp. soda
1 tbsp. vanilla extract
1 tsp. cinnamon
1/4 tsp. nutmeg
3 c. flour
1 c. packed brown sugar
1/3 c. milk
1 tbsp. light corn syrup
1/4 c. butter

Combine . . . . oil, 2 cups sugar, eggs, apples and pecans in bowl.
Mix . . . . in 1/2 teaspoon soda, 2 teaspoons vanilla, cinnamon, nutmeg and flour.
Spoon . . . . . . into bundt pan.
Bake . . . . at 350 degrees for 50 to 60 minutes or until cake tests done.
Combine . . . . brown sugar, milk, corn syrup, remaining 1/2 cup sugar and butter in saucepan.
Boil . . . . for 3 minutes.
Stir . . . . in 1 teaspoon vanilla and 1/4 teaspoon soda; cool.
Beat . . . . until of spreading consistency.
Spread . . . . . over cake when cool.

Edna Crow
State FHA/HERO Adviser
State Dept. of Vo-Tech., Stillwater

CARROT CAKE

2 c. sugar
1 1/2 c. oil
2 c. sifted flour
2 tsp. baking powder
1 tsp. each soda, salt
2 tsp. cinnamon
5 eggs
3 jars baby food carrots
1 c. chopped walnuts
1 recipe cream cheese frosting

Mix . . . . sugar and oil in bowl.
Add . . . . sifted dry ingredients by halves, mixing well after each addition.
Beat . . . . in eggs.
Stir . . . . in carrots and walnuts.
Pour . . . . into greased 9 x 13-inch pan.
Bake . . . . at 350 degrees for 1 hour or until cake tests done.
Spread . . . . . with cream cheese frosting.

Jolene Munsey
Beggs H. S., Beggs

CHERRY-PECAN CAKE

1 pkg. cherry cake mix
1 4-oz. package vanilla instant pudding mix
1 1/4 c. buttermilk
4 eggs

1/2 c. oil
1 c. flaked coconut
1 c. finely chopped pecans
Confectioners' sugar (opt.)

Prepare ..... cake mix according to package directions using pudding mix, 1 1/4 cups buttermilk, 4 eggs and 1/2 cup oil.
Stir .... in coconut and pecans.
Spoon ...... into greased and floured bundt pan.
Bake .... at 350 degrees for 50 to 60 minutes, or until cake tests done.
Cool .... in pan for 1 hour.
Let .... stand overnight.
Sift .... confectioners' sugar over top.

Dee Dee Bradshaw
Choctaw Jr. H. S., Choctaw

CHOCOLATE ANGEL CAKE

1 1/2 c. egg whites
1/2 tsp. cream of tartar
1/4 tsp. salt
1 1/2 tsp. vanilla extract
14 tbsp. sugar
1/4 c. cocoa
3/4 c. sifted cake flour

Beat .... egg whites, cream of tartar, salt and vanilla in bowl until foamy.
Add .... sugar 2 tablespoons at a time, beating until stiff.
Fold .... in mixture of cocoa and flour 3 tablespoons at a time.
Spoon ...... into tube pan.
Bake .... at 375 degrees for 35 minutes or until cake tests done.

Christine Bidwell
Okeene H. S., Hitchcock

CHOCOLATE FUDGE CAKE

1/2 c. butter, softened
1/2 c. shortening
2 c. sugar
2 eggs
1 tsp. vanilla extract
1/2 c. cocoa
2 1/4 c. flour
1 1/4 tsp. soda
1/2 tsp. salt

Cream ...... butter, shortening and sugar in bowl.
Mix .... in eggs and vanilla.
Add .... combined dry ingredients alternately with 1 1/3 cups water, mixing well after each addition.
Spoon ...... into 2 greased and floured 9-inch cake pans.
Bake .... at 350 degrees for 35 to 40 minutes or until cake tests done.
Cool .... in pan for 10 minutes before removing to cool completely.
Frost .... cake as desired.

Marsha Butler
Checotah H. S., Checotah

FAVORITE CHOCOLATE CAKE

1/2 c. shortening
2 sticks butter
7 to 8 tbsp. cocoa
2 c. flour
2 c. sugar
2 eggs, beaten
1/2 c. buttermilk
1 tsp. soda
2 tsp. vanilla extract
5 1/3 to 6 tbsp. milk
1 16-oz. box confectioners' sugar
1 c. chopped nuts

Combine .... shortening, 1 stick butter, 1/4 cup cocoa and 1 cup water in saucepan, mixing well.
Bring .... to a boil.
Stir .... into sifted flour and sugar in bowl, mixing well.
Beat .... in eggs, buttermilk, soda and 1 teaspoon vanilla until smooth.
Spoon ...... into large baking pan.
Bake .... at 400 degrees for 20 minutes.
Combine .... 1 stick butter, 4 tablespoons cocoa and milk in saucepan.
Bring .... to a boil.
Stir .... in confectioners' sugar, 1 teaspoon vanilla and nuts.
Spread ..... over hot cake.

Linda Wood
Eisenhower H. S., Lawton
Donna Henson
Vinita H. S., Vinita
Sarah Carman
Talihina H. S., Talihina

Desserts

QUICK CHOCOLATE CAKE

2 c. sugar
2 c. flour
1/2 c. cocoa
1/2 tsp. salt
2 eggs
1 c. oil
2 tsp. soda
1 c. buttermilk

Combine .... sugar, flour, cocoa and salt in bowl.
Add .... eggs, oil, soda, 1 cup boiling water and buttermilk, mixing well.
Pour .... into 9 x 13-inch pan.
Bake .... at 350 degrees for 25 to 30 minutes or until cake tests done.

Robyn Wilson
Boise City H. S., Boise City

CINNAMON CHOCOLATE CAKE

1 c. margarine
1/2 c. cocoa
1/2 c. oil
2 c. sugar
2 c. self-rising flour
1/2 c. buttermilk
1 tsp. soda
2 eggs
1 tsp. cinnamon
1 tsp. vanilla extract
6 tbsp. milk
1 16-oz. box confectioners' sugar

Bring .... 1/2 cup margarine, 1/4 cup cocoa, oil and 1 cup water to a boil in saucepan.
Add .... to sugar and flour in bowl.
Stir .... in mixture of buttermilk, soda, eggs, cinnamon and vanilla.
Spoon ...... into greased and floured 9 x 13-inch baking pan.
Bake .... at 375 degrees for 20 to 25 minutes or until cake tests done.
Bring .... 1/2 cup margarine, 1/4 cup cocoa and milk to a boil in saucepan.
Stir .... in confectioners' sugar.
Spread ..... over cooled cake.

Sherri Cox
Noble Jr. H. S., Noble

CHOCOLATE SHEET CAKE

1/2 c. cocoa
1 1/2 c. margarine, softened
2 c. flour, sifted
2 c. sugar
1 tsp. each soda, cinnamon
2 eggs, beaten
Buttermilk
1 16-oz. package confectioners' sugar

Heat .... 1/4 cup cocoa, 1 cup margarine and 1 cup water in saucepan until margarine is melted.
Add .... to mixture of flour, sugar, soda and cinnamon in bowl.
Add .... eggs and 1/2 cup buttermilk, mixing well.
Pour .... into greased sheet cake pan.
Bake .... at 350 degrees for 20 minutes or until cake tests done.
Melt .... 1/2 cup margarine in 1/3 cup buttermilk in saucepan.
Add .... to mixture of confectioners' sugar and 1/4 cup cocoa in bowl, mixing well.
Spread ..... over hot cake.
Yields ...... 20 servings.

Valerie Riggs
Ringwood H. S., Ringwood

CHOCOLATE MAYONNAISE CAKE

2 c. flour
1 1/2 tsp. each soda, baking powder
2 c. sugar
1/2 c. cocoa
1 c. Miracle Whip
4 tsp. vanilla extract
1/4 c. milk
1/4 c. butter

Mix .... flour, soda, baking powder, 1 cup sugar and 1/4 cup cocoa in bowl.
Blend ...... in Miracle Whip, 2 teaspoons vanilla and 1 cup cold water.
Pour .... into 2 greased layer cake pans.
Bake .... at 350 degrees for 25 to 30 minutes, or until cake tests done.
Boil .... milk, butter, 1 cup sugar and 1/4 cup cocoa in saucepan for 1 minute.

Stir . . . . in 2 teaspoons vanilla.
Beat . . . . until cool and thickened.
Spread . . . . . between layers and over top of
cake.

Carin Cochran
Gould H. S., Gould

RICH TURTLE CAKE

1 pkg. German chocolate cake mix
1 c. evaporated milk
1 stick margarine, softened
1 egg
1 14-oz. package caramels
1 c. chopped nuts
1 6-oz. package chocolate chips

Beat . . . . cake mix, 3/4 cup evaporated
milk, margarine and egg together
in bowl.
Pour . . . . half the batter into 9 x 13-inch
baking dish.
Bake . . . . . . at 350 degrees for 15 to 20 min-
utes or until nearly set.
Melt . . . . . . caramels in 1/4 cup evaporated
milk in saucepan.
Pour . . . . over top of cake.
Sprinkle . . . . with nuts and chocolate chips.
Top . . . . with remaining batter.
Bake . . . . for 18 minutes longer.
Cut . . . . into squares when cool.

DeeAnn Goodall
Macomb H. S., Tecumseh

FAVORITE TURTLE CAKE

1 pkg. German chocolate cake mix
3/4 c. margarine
1/2 c. evaporated milk
1 14-oz. package caramels
1 c. chopped nuts
1 6-oz. package chocolate chips

Prepare . . . . . cake mix, using package
directions.
Spoon . . . . . . half the batter into greased and
floured 9 x 13-inch baking pan.
Bake . . . . at 350 degrees for 15 minutes.
Heat . . . . margarine, evaporated milk and
caramels in saucepan until cara-
mels melt, stirring constantly.
Spread . . . . . over cake.
Sprinkle . . . . with nuts and chocolate chips.

Pour . . . . remaining batter over top.
Bake . . . . at 350 degrees for 20 minutes or
until cake tests done.
Yields . . . . . . 20 servings.

Laurie Adam
Okeene H. S., Okeene

COMPANY TURTLE CAKE

1 14-oz. package vanilla caramels
Evaporated milk
1 pkg. German chocolate cake mix
3/4 c. melted margarine
1 c. milk chocolate chips
1 c. pecans

Melt . . . . caramels in 1/3 cup evaporated
milk in saucepan; set aside.
Mix . . . . cake mix, margarine and 3/4 cup
evaporated milk in bowl.
Pour . . . . half the batter in prepared 9 x
13-inch baking pan.
Bake . . . . . . at 350 degrees for 15 minutes.
Spread . . . . caramel mixture over top.
Sprinkle . . . . with chocolate chips and pecans.
Spoon . . . . . . remaining batter over top.
Bake . . . . for 15 to 20 minutes longer or
until cake tests done.
Cut . . . . into squares when cool.

Karen Creekbaum
Checotah H. S., Checotah

MOTHER'S CAKE

2 sticks margarine
2 c. sugar
3 c. flour
2 tsp. baking powder
1 c. cocoa
1 c. milk
3 eggs
1 tsp. vanilla extract

Cream . . . . . . margarine and sugar in bowl.
Add . . . . combined dry ingredients alter-
nately with milk and eggs, mix-
ing well after each addition.
Stir . . . . in vanilla.
Spoon . . . . . . into greased tube pan.
Bake . . . . at 350 degrees for 1 hour.
Cool . . . . in pan for 10 minutes before re-
moving to cool completely.

Karlene Oxford
Wagoner H. S., Wagoner

Desserts

NUTTY DEVIL'S FOOD CAKE

1/2 c. shortening
2 c. sugar
4 eggs, separated
2 oz. unsweetened chocolate, melted
2 1/2 c. cake flour
1 tbsp. baking powder
1/2 tsp. salt
1 c. milk
1 c. chopped nuts
1 tsp. vanilla extract

Cream . . . . . . shortening and sugar in bowl.
Beat . . . . in beaten egg yolks for 30 seconds.
Add . . . . chocolate, beating well.
Add . . . . sifted dry ingredients alternately with milk, mixing well after each addition.
Stir . . . . in nuts and vanilla.
Fold . . . . in stiffly beaten egg whites.
Spoon . . . . . . into 3 greased and floured 9-inch cake pans.
Bake . . . . at 350 degrees for 30 minutes.

Michelle Morris
Bray-Doyle, Foster

FROSTED MISSISSIPPI MUD CAKE

4 eggs
2 c. sugar
3 sticks margarine
2 tsp. vanilla extract
Cocoa
1 1/2 c. flour
1 tsp. baking powder
1 1/2 c. flaked coconut
1 c. chopped nuts
1 9-oz. jar marshmallow creme
1 16-oz. box confectioners' sugar
1/3 c. evaporated milk

Mix . . . . eggs, sugar, 2 sticks margarine and vanilla in bowl.
Add . . . . 3 tablespoons cocoa, flour and baking powder, mixing well.
Stir . . . . in coconut and nuts.
Spread . . . . . in greased and floured 9 x 13-inch cake pan.
Bake . . . . at 350 degrees for 30 to 40 minutes or until cake tests done.
Spread . . . . . marshmallow creme over warm cake.

Combine . . . . 1 stick margarine, confectioners' sugar, 1/3 cup cocoa, evaporated milk and 1 teaspoon vanilla in saucepan.
Heat . . . . and stir until blended.
Spread . . . . . over cooled cake.

Stephanie Lorenz
Okeene H. S., Okeene

COCONUT MISSISSIPPI MUD CAKE

1 1/4 c. margarine
2 c. sugar
5 tbsp. cocoa
4 eggs
2 tsp. vanilla extract
1 1/2 c. flour
1 1/3 c. flaked coconut
1 1/2 c. chopped pecans
1 9-oz. jar marshmallow creme
1 c. confectioners' sugar
1/4 c. Milnot

Cream . . . . . . 1 cup margarine, sugar and 2 tablespoons cocoa in mixer bowl.
Beat . . . . in eggs, 1 teaspoon vanilla and flour for 1 or 2 minutes or until smooth.
Stir . . . . in coconut and pecans.
Spoon . . . . . . into baking pan.
Bake . . . . at 350 degrees for 30 minutes.
Spread . . . . . marshmallow creme on warm cake; cool.
Mix . . . . 1/4 cup margarine, confectioners' sugar, 3 tablespoons cocoa, Milnot and 1 teaspoon vanilla in bowl.
Spread . . . . . over top.

D'Ann Ingram
Tomlinson Jr. H. S., Lawton

EASY MISSISSIPPI MUD CAKE

2 c. sugar
1 c. shortening
4 eggs
1 1/2 c. flour
1/3 c. cocoa
1 1/2 tsp. salt
1 tbsp. vanilla extract
1 c. chopped nuts
1 6 1/4-oz. package marshmallows

Cream . . . . . . sugar, shortening and eggs in bowl.

Sift . . . . in flour, cocoa and salt, mixing well.

Stir . . . . in vanilla and nuts.

Pour . . . . into greased 9 x 13-inch baking pan.

Bake . . . . at 300 degrees for 30 minutes.

Top . . . . with marshmallows.

Bake . . . . . . for 10 minutes longer, or until marshmallows are melted.

Charlotte Scott
Chickasha H. S., Chickasha

REALLY WACKY CAKE

1 1/2 c. sifted flour
1 c. sugar
3 tbsp. cocoa
1/2 tsp. soda
1/2 tsp. salt
1 tbsp. vinegar
5 tbsp. butter, melted
1 tsp. vanilla extract

Sift . . . . flour and next 4 dry ingredients into 8-inch square baking pan.

Make . . . . 3 wells in mixture.

Pour . . . . vinegar into 1 well, butter into 1 well and vanilla into remaining well.

Pour . . . . 1 cup water over all.

Stir . . . . until smooth.

Bake . . . . at 350 degrees for 30 to 35 minutes or until cake tests done.

Marsha Davidson
Checotah H. S., Checotah

QUICK WACKY CAKE

3/4 c. oil
2 tbsp. vinegar
2 tsp. vanilla extract
3 c. flour
6 tbsp. cocoa
2 c. sugar
2 tsp. soda
1 tsp. salt

Mix . . . . oil, vinegar, vanilla and 2 cups cold water in bowl.

Add . . . . sifted dry ingredients, mixing well.

Pour . . . . into 9 x 13-inch baking pan.

Bake . . . . at 350 degrees for 30 minutes.

Yields . . . . . . 12 servings.

Kristin Veldhuizen
Eisenhower H. S., Lawton

CHOCOLATE CHIP CAKE

1 sm. package chocolate pudding and pie filling mix
2 1/2 c. milk
1 pkg. dark chocolate cake mix
1 sm. package chocolate chips
1 c. chopped nuts

Mix . . . . pudding mix with milk in large saucepan.

Cook . . . . using package directions.

Stir . . . . in cake mix gradually. Batter will be very stiff.

Spread . . . . . in greased and floured jelly roll pan.

Sprinkle . . . . chocolate chips and nuts over top; press into batter.

Bake . . . . at 350 degrees for 35 to 40 minutes or until cake tests done.

Yields . . . . . . 24 servings.

Beverly Perry
Putnam City Central Jr. H. S., Oklahoma City

CHOCOLATE OREO CAKE

15 Oreo cookies, crushed
1 chocolate cake mix
5 c. peanut butter
14 lg. chocolate candy bars

Press . . . . cookie crumbs into bottom of greased 9 x 13-inch pan.

Prepare . . . . . cake mix according to package directions, adding only enough water to make very thick batter; mix well.

Layer . . . . . . half the peanut butter, half the candy bars, all the cake batter, remaining peanut butter and candy bars over crumbs.

Bake . . . . at 350 degrees for 25 to 30 minutes or until cake tests done.

Yields . . . . . . 24 servings.

Samantha Moore
Checotah H. S., Checotah

Desserts

WHAM BROWNIE CHOCOLATE CAKE

2 c. sugar
2 c. flour
1/2 c. buttermilk
1 tsp. soda
2 eggs
2 tsp. vanilla extract
1/2 c. cocoa
1/2 c. shortening
2 sticks margarine
6 tbsp. milk
1 box confectioners' sugar
1 c. chopped nuts

Sift . . . . sugar and flour into bowl.
Combine . . . . buttermilk, soda, eggs and 1 teaspoon vanilla in small bowl, mix-
ing well.
Stir . . . . into flour mixture.
Bring . . . . 1/4 cup cocoa, shortening and 1
stick margarine to a boil in
saucepan.
Add . . . . to flour mixture, mixing well.
Pour . . . . into greased and floured oblong
baking dish.
Bake . . . . at 400 degrees for 20 minutes,
shaking each time cake begins to
rise.
Combine . . . . remaining 1 stick margarine, remaining 1/4 cup cocoa and milk
in saucepan.
Bring . . . . to a boil, stirring frequently; remove from heat.
Beat . . . . in confectioners' sugar, remaining 1 teaspoon vanilla and nuts.
Spread . . . . . over hot cake.
Yields . . . . . . 30 servings.

Oneta Adams
Macomb H. S., Macomb

GERMAN SWEET CHOCOLATE CAKE

4 oz. German's chocolate
2 tsp. vanilla extract
1 1/2 c. butter, softened
3 c. sugar
4 eggs, separated
2 1/2 c. sifted cake flour
1 tsp. soda
1/2 tsp. salt
1 c. buttermilk
1 c. evaporated milk

3 egg yolks, slightly beaten
1 1/3 c. flaked coconut
1 c. chopped pecans

Melt . . . . chocolate in 1/2 cup boiling
water; cool.
Stir . . . . in 1 teaspoon vanilla.
Cream . . . . . . 1 cup butter and 2 cups sugar in
bowl.
Beat . . . . in 4 egg yolks 1 at a time.
Stir . . . . in chocolate mixture.
Add . . . . sifted flour, soda and salt alternately with buttermilk, mixing
well after each addition.
Fold . . . . in stiffly beaten egg whites.
Pour . . . . into 3 waxed paper-lined 9-inch
cake pans.
Bake . . . . at 350 degrees for 30 to 40 minutes or until cake tests done;
cool.
Combine . . . . evaporated milk, beaten egg
yolks, 1/2 cup butter, 1 cup
sugar and 1 teaspoon vanilla in
saucepan.
Cook . . . . over medium heat for 12 minutes or until thickened, stirring
constantly.
Stir . . . . in coconut and pecans.
Spread . . . . . frosting between layers and over
top of cake.

Jackie Moler
Beggs H. S., Beggs

CHOCOLATE POTATO CAKE

4 oz. semisweet chocolate, melted
1/2 c. milk
1 c. mashed potatoes
3/4 c. unsalted butter, softened
1 c. sugar
1 tsp. vanilla extract
4 eggs, separated
2 c. cake flour
2 tsp. baking powder
1/2 tsp. salt
1 recipe chocolate frosting

Melt . . . . chocolate in hot milk in
saucepan.
Stir . . . . into mashed potatoes.
Cream . . . . . . butter with 1/2 cup sugar and
vanilla in bowl.
Stir . . . . in chocolate mixture.

Add . . . . beaten egg yolks alternately with sifted dry ingredients, mixing well after each addition.
Beat . . . . 1/2 cup sugar gradually into softly beaten egg whites, beating until stiff.
Fold . . . . into batter.
Spoon . . . . . . into greased and floured 9 x 13-inch baking pan.
Bake . . . . at 350 degrees for 35 to 40 minutes, or until cake tests done; cool.
Frost . . . . with chocolate frosting.
Yields . . . . . . 12 servings.

Amy Harris
Elmore City H. S., Elmore City

BLACK BOTTOM CUPCAKES

1 1/2 c. flour
1 tsp. soda
1/3 c. cocoa
1 1/3 c. sugar
Salt
1/3 c. oil
1 tsp. vinegar
1 tsp. vanilla extract
1 8-oz. package cream cheese, softened
1 egg
1 c. miniature chocolate chips
1/3 c. chopped walnuts

Sift . . . . flour, soda, cocoa, 1 cup sugar and 1/2 teaspoon salt into bowl.
Beat . . . . 1 cup water, oil, vinegar and vanilla in bowl.
Add . . . . to dry ingredients gradually, mixing well.
Fill . . . . 18 paper-lined muffin cups 1/2 full.
Beat . . . . cream cheese, egg, 1/8 teaspoon salt and 1/3 cup sugar in bowl until creamy.
Stir . . . . in chocolate chips.
Spoon . . . . . . 1 tablespoon mixture into each muffin cup.
Top . . . . each with 1/2 teaspoon walnuts.
Bake . . . . at 350 degrees for 25 minutes.
Yields . . . . . . 18 servings.

Kim Berg
Barnsdall H. S., Barnsdall

COCONUT CAKE

1/2 c. shortening
2 1/4 c. flour, sifted
1 1/2 c. sugar
3 tsp. baking powder
1 tsp. salt
1 c. milk
2 eggs
1 1/2 tsp. vanilla extract
2 c. coconut
1 recipe butter frosting

Beat . . . . shortening in mixer bowl.
Sift . . . . in flour, sugar, baking powder and salt.
Add . . . . 2/3 cup milk, mixing until moistened.
Beat . . . . at high speed for 2 minutes.
Add . . . . remaining 1/3 cup milk, eggs and vanilla.
Beat . . . . for 2 minutes longer.
Stir . . . . in 1 cup coconut.
Pour . . . . into 2 greased and floured 9-inch cake pans.
Bake . . . . at 350 degrees for 30 minutes or until cakes test done; cool.
Stir . . . . remaining 1 cup coconut into butter frosting.
Spread . . . . . between layers and over top and side of cake.

Marie Edwards
Michelle Edwards
Macomb H. S., Macomb

ICEBOX FRUITCAKE

1 1-lb. package graham crackers, crushed
4 c. pecans
1 1-lb. package raisins
1/3 lb. candied maraschino cherries
1/3 lb. candied pineapple
1 can sweetened condensed milk
1 c. coconut
1 tsp. vanilla extract

Combine . . . . all ingredients in bowl, mixing well.
Press . . . . into 9 x 12-inch dish.
Chill . . . . until serving time.
Yields . . . . . . 24 servings.

Evelyn Matthews
Grove H. S., Grove

Desserts

FROSTED OATMEAL CAKE

1 c. oats
1/2 c. shortening
1 c. packed brown sugar
1 c. sugar
1 1/3 c. flour
1 tsp. salt
1 tsp. cinnamon
1 tsp. soda
2 eggs, beaten
6 tbsp. butter
1 tsp. vanilla extract
1 1/2 c. confectioners' sugar
4 tsp. cream

Mix . . . . oats with 1 1/4 cups boiling water in bowl.
Let . . . . stand for 20 minutes.
Cream . . . . . . shortening with sugars in bowl.
Sift . . . . in next 4 dry ingredients.
Add . . . . oats and eggs, beating well.
Pour . . . . into greased and floured 9-inch square pan.
Bake . . . . at 350 degrees for 30 to 35 minutes, or until cake tests done; cool.
Invert . . . . . . onto serving plate.
Brown . . . . . . butter in saucepan.
Stir . . . . in vanilla, confectioners' sugar and enough cream to make of spreading consistency.
Spread . . . . . over top and side of cake.

Charmarie Henson
Bray Doyle H. S., Marlow

LAZY DAISY OATMEAL CAKE

1 c. oats
3/4 c. butter
1 c. sugar
1 1/2 c. packed brown sugar
1 tsp. vanilla extract
2 eggs
1 1/2 c. flour
1 tsp. soda
1/2 tsp. salt
1/4 tsp. nutmeg
3/4 tsp. cinnamon
3 tbsp. cream
1/2 c. chopped nuts
3/4 c. coconut

Pour . . . . 1 1/4 cups boiling water over oats in bowl.
Let . . . . stand, covered, for 20 minutes.
Cream . . . . . . 1/2 cup softened butter, sugar and 1 cup brown sugar in bowl.
Add . . . . vanilla, eggs and oats.
Mix . . . . in flour, soda, salt, nutmeg and cinnamon.
Spread . . . . . in greased and floured 9 x 13-inch pan.
Bake . . . . at 350 degrees for 50 to 55 minutes or until cake tests done.
Blend . . . . . . 1/4 cup melted butter, 1/2 cup brown sugar and cream in bowl.
Stir . . . . in nuts and coconut.
Spread . . . . . over cake.
Broil . . . . until bubbly.
Yields . . . . . . 18 servings.

Peggy Glenn
Heavener H. S., Howe

ORANGE SLICE CAKE

4 c. sugar
1 c. shortening
4 eggs
1 tbsp. soda
1 1/2 c. buttermilk
1/2 tsp. salt
4 c. flour
4 c. finely chopped candy orange slices
1 c. chopped dates
1 c. chopped pecans
1 1/2 c. orange juice
2 tsp. grated orange rind

Cream . . . . . . 2 cups sugar and shortening in bowl.
Beat . . . . in eggs 1 at a time.
Dissolve . . . . soda in buttermilk.
Add . . . . with salt to creamed mixture.
Stir . . . . in flour, candy, dates and pecans.
Spoon . . . . . . into tube pan.
Bake . . . . at 300 degrees for 1 1/2 hours.
Invert . . . . . . onto serving plate.
Blend . . . . . . orange juice, 2 cups sugar and orange rind in bowl.
Pour . . . . over hot cake gradually.

Nevaleen Selmat
Assistant Professor of Home Economics
NWOSU, Alva

Desserts

CHOCOLATE PEANUT-FROSTED CAKE

1 pkg. yellow cake mix
1 lb. chocolate-covered peanuts

Prepare ..... and bake cake according to package directions for 9 x 13-inch baking pan.
Sprinkle .... chocolate-covered peanuts over hot cake.
Bake .... for 5 minutes longer; cool.
Yields ...... 12 servings.

Photograph for this recipe above.

PINEAPPLE DREAM CAKE

1 pkg. butter-recipe yellow cake mix
1 11-oz. can mandarin oranges
4 eggs
1/2 c. oil
1 pkg. vanilla instant pudding mix
1 sm. can crushed pineapple
1 lg. carton whipped topping
Chopped nuts

Prepare ..... cake mix in bowl according to package directions using mandarin oranges, 4 eggs and 1/2 cup oil.
Spoon ...... into 2 greased and floured 9-inch cake pans.
Bake .... at 350 degrees for 30 minutes.
Combine .... pudding mix and pineapple in bowl, mixing well.

Fold .... in whipped topping.
Spread ..... between layers and over top and side of cake.
Sprinkle .... with nuts.

Yvonne Praytor
Vinita H. S., Vinita

PINEAPPLE PRALINE CAKE

2 c. flour
2 1/4 c. sugar
1/4 tsp. salt
2 tsp. soda
1 20-oz. can crushed pineapple
3/4 c. packed brown sugar
3/4 c. chopped nuts
1 stick margarine, softened
1 sm. can evaporated milk

Sift .... flour, 1 1/2 cups sugar, salt and soda into bowl.
Stir .... in pineapple.
Spoon ...... into 9 x 13-inch baking pan.
Sprinkle .... with brown sugar and nuts.
Bake .... at 350 degrees for 35 minutes.
Blend ...... margarine, 3/4 cup sugar and evaporated milk in saucepan.
Bring .... to a boil.
Cook .... for 10 minutes.
Pour .... over hot cake.

Barbara Jeanguneat
Tuttle H. S., Tuttle

GRANNY'S POUND CAKE

2 c. sugar
1 c. butter, softened
1 tsp. vanilla extract
6 eggs
2 c. flour
1 tsp. salt

Cream ...... sugar, butter and vanilla in mixer bowl for 6 minutes.
Add .... eggs, 1 at a time, beating for 2 minutes after each addition.
Mix .... in combined flour and salt until flour is just moistened.
Spoon ...... into bundt pan.
Bake .... at 350 degrees for 1 hour.

Karen Garrett
Midwest City H. S., Midwest City

115

Desserts

LEMONADE CAKE

1 pkg. lemon cake mix
1 lg. package lemon instant pudding mix
4 eggs
1/3 c. oil
1 sm. can frozen lemonade concentrate,
    thawed
2 1/2 c. confectioners' sugar

Combine .... cake mix, pudding mix, eggs, oil and 17 tablespoons water in mixer bowl.
Beat .... for 2 minutes.
Pour .... into greased 9 x 13-inch pan.
Bake .... at 350 degrees for 35 minutes.
Pierce ...... cake with fork.
Spread ..... mixture of lemonade and confectioners' sugar over top.
Bake .... for 5 minutes longer.
Yields ...... 16 servings.

Stacy Pulse
Porum H. S., Porum

NEVER-FAIL POUND CAKE

1/2 lb. butter, softened
1 1/2 c. sugar
2 c. flour
1/2 tsp. baking powder
Pinch of soda
6 eggs
1 1/2 tsp. vanilla extract

Cream ...... butter and sugar in bowl.
Add .... sifted dry ingredients alternately with eggs, mixing well after each addition.
Stir .... in vanilla.
Spoon ...... into greased and floured 10-inch tube pan.
Bake .... at 350 degrees for 50 to 60 minutes or until cake tests done.
Cool .... in pan for several minutes before removing to rack to cool completely.

Dale Archer
Byng H. S., Ada

HERSHEL'S POUND CAKE

1 c. butter, softened
1/2 c. shortening

3 c. sugar
5 eggs
3 c. flour
1 c. milk
1 c. flaked coconut
1 tsp. vanilla extract
1 tsp. coconut flavoring

Cream ...... butter, shortening and sugar in bowl.
Beat .... in eggs 1 at a time.
Add .... flour and milk alternately, beating well after each addition.
Stir .... in coconut and flavorings.
Pour .... into greased bundt pan.
Bake .... at 300 degrees for 1 1/2 hours.
Cool .... in pan for several minutes before removing to serving plate to cool completely.

Deanna Hardesty
Tuttle H. S., Tuttle

SOUR CREAM POUND CAKE

1 c. butter, softened
3 c. sugar
6 eggs
2 tsp. vanilla extract
1/2 tsp. almond extract
3 c. sifted flour
1/4 tsp. each salt, soda
1 8-oz. carton sour cream

Cream ...... butter in large mixer bowl.
Beat .... in sugar gradually.
Add .... eggs 1 at a time, beating well after each addition.
Stir .... in flavorings.
Add .... sifted flour, salt and soda alternately with sour cream, beating well after each addition.
Pour .... into greased and floured 10-inch tube pan.
Bake .... at 350 degrees for 1 1/4 hours.
Cool .... in cake pan for 15 minutes.

Annika Martinez
Eisenhower Sr. H. S., Lawton

RAINBOW CAKE

2 baked 8-in. white cake layers
1 3-oz. package cherry gelatin
1 3-oz. package lime gelatin
1 container whipped topping

Place .... each cake layer in 8-inch cake pan.
Prick .... with fork at 1/2-inch intervals.
Dissolve .... cherry gelatin in 1 cup boiling water in small bowl.
Spoon ...... over 1 layer.
Repeat ..... with lime gelatin and second layer.
Chill .... for 3 or 4 hours or until set.
Dip .... layers in warm water; unmold.
Spread ..... whipped topping between layers and over top and side of cake.
Chill .... in refrigerator.
Yields ...... 12 servings.

Debbie Beck
Indian Capitol Area Vo-Tech, Muskogee

PUMPKIN-PECAN ROLL

3 eggs
1 c. sugar
2/3 c. pumpkin
1 tsp. lemon juice
3/4 c. flour
2 tsp. cinnamon
1/2 tsp. salt
1 tsp. baking powder
1/2 tsp. nutmeg
1 c. finely chopped pecans
Confectioners' sugar
1/4 c. butter, softened
2 3-oz. packages cream cheese, softened
1/2 tsp. vanilla extract

Beat .... eggs in mixer bowl at high speed for 5 minutes.
Add .... sugar gradually, beating constantly.
Stir .... in pumpkin and lemon juice.
Fold .... in next 5 combined dry ingredients.
Spread ..... in generously greased and floured jelly roll pan.
Sprinkle .... with pecans.
Bake .... at 375 degrees for 15 minutes.
Turn .... onto towel.
Sprinkle .... with confectioners' sugar.
Roll .... towel and cake as for jelly roll from wide end; cool.
Beat .... 1 cup confectioners' sugar, butter, cream cheese and vanilla in bowl until smooth.

Unroll ...... cake; spread with cream cheese mixture.
Reroll ...... and chill.

Jane Nusz
Geary H. S., Geary

PUMPKIN-WALNUT ROLL

2/3 can pumpkin
3 eggs
1 c. sugar
1 tsp. soda
1/2 tsp. cinnamon
3/4 c. flour
1 c. chopped walnuts
Confectioners' sugar
2 tbsp. margarine, softened
1 8-oz. package cream cheese, softened
3/4 tsp. vanilla extract

Combine .... pumpkin and next 5 ingredients in bowl, mixing well.
Spread ..... in greased and waxed paper-lined jelly roll pan.
Sprinkle .... with walnuts.
Bake .... at 350 degrees for 15 minutes.
Turn .... cake onto towel sprinkled with confectioners' sugar.
Roll .... towel and cake as for jelly roll from wide end; cool.
Blend ...... margarine, cream cheese, vanilla and 1 cup confectioners' sugar in bowl.
Unroll ...... cake, removing waxed paper.
Spread ..... with cream cheese filling.
Reroll ...... and chill.

Jodi Crow
Gould H. S., Gould

RESCUE THE CAKE

1 c. packed brown sugar
1/2 c. chopped nuts
3 egg whites, stiffly beaten
1 fallen cake

Fold .... brown sugar and nuts into egg whites.
Spoon ...... over cake, mounding in center.
Bake .... at 350 degrees until brown.
Yields ...... 8 servings.

Hope Grimes
Moore H. S., Moore

Desserts

RED PLUM CAKE

1 1/2 c. sugar
1 c. oil
3 eggs
2 tsp. red food coloring
1 lg. jar strained baby food plums
2 c. flour
1 tsp. each cloves, cinnamon, nutmeg
1/2 tsp. each soda, salt
1 c. chopped nuts

Mix . . . . sugar, oil and eggs in bowl.
Stir . . . . in food coloring and plums.
Add . . . . combined dry ingredients, mixing well.
Stir . . . . in nuts.
Spoon . . . . . . into greased and floured bundt pan.
Bake . . . . at 350 degrees for 40 to 50 minutes or until cake tests done.

Brenda Oney
Okeene H. S., Okeene

RED VELVET CAKE

1 1/2 c. sugar
1/2 c. shortening
1/4 tsp. salt
2 eggs
2 c. sifted flour
1 tsp. cinnamon
1 c. buttermilk
1 tsp. each lemon, orange extracts
1 oz. red food coloring
1 tsp. vinegar
1 tsp. soda

Cream . . . . . . sugar, shortening and salt in bowl.
Beat . . . . in eggs.
Add . . . . flour, cinnamon, buttermilk, flavorings and food coloring, mixing well.
Stir . . . . in combined vinegar and soda.
Spoon . . . . . . into greased and floured heart-shaped cake pan.
Bake . . . . at 350 degrees for 25 minutes.

Sheri R. Gervin
Eisenhower H. S., Lawton

MICHELE'S ICING

1/4 lb. butter, softened
4 c. sugar
1 pt. heavy cream
1 pt. half and half
1 tbsp. lemon juice
2 tbsp. orange extract

Blend . . . . . . butter and sugar in saucepan.
Add . . . . next 3 ingredients, mixing well.
Cook . . . . until thickened, stirring constantly.
Stir . . . . in flavoring.

Michele Cohlma
Waynoka H. S., Waynoka

COOKED CARAMEL FROSTING

1 1/3 c. packed brown sugar
1/4 tsp. salt
1/2 c. milk
3 tbsp. butter, melted
1 tsp. vanilla extract
3 c. confectioners' sugar

Bring . . . . brown sugar, salt and milk to a boil in saucepan.
Cook . . . . over low heat for 5 minutes or until thickened, stirring constantly; remove from heat.
Stir . . . . in butter and vanilla; cool slightly.
Beat . . . . in confectioners' sugar until smooth.
Spread . . . . . over cake.

Regina McClendon
Byng H. S., Ada

BUTTERSCOTCH PINWHEELS

1 6-oz. package chocolate chips
6 tbsp. shortening
1 lg. can sweetened condensed milk
1 c. flour
1 tsp. vanilla extract
Confectioners' sugar
1 12-oz. package butterscotch chips
1/2 c. chopped pecans

Melt . . . . chocolate chips and 2 tablespoons shortening in double boiler.

Stir	in condensed milk, flour and vanilla.
Spread	in greased jelly roll pan lined with greased waxed paper.
Bake	at 325 degrees for 8 minutes.
Invert	onto towel sprinkled with confectioners' sugar.
Melt	butterscotch chips and 4 tablespoons shortening in double boiler.
Spread	over chocolate layer.
Sprinkle	with pecans.
Roll	with towel as for jelly roll from wide end.
Chill	wrapped in towel until firm.
Unwrap	and slice.

Cleta M. Sandlin
Jarman Jr. H. S., Midwest City

HARD CINNAMON CANDY

1 1/2 c. light corn syrup
3 3/4 c. sugar
1 tsp. cinnamon liquid
Red food coloring
Confectioners' sugar

Heat	corn syrup, sugar and 1 cup water in saucepan until sugar dissolves, stirring constantly.
Boil	until mixture reaches hard-crack stage or to 310 degrees on candy thermometer; do not stir.
Stir	in cinnamon and food coloring.
Pour	into 12 x 24-inch foil-lined pan sprinkled with confectioners' sugar.
Break	into pieces when cool.

Lesa Jennings
State FHA President 1984-85
Rush Springs H. S., Rush Springs

CAROB NUGGET SNACK

1 c. bite-sized cereal
1/2 c. chow mein noodles
2 tsp. butter, melted
1 tsp. Worcestershire sauce
3 drops of Tabasco sauce
1/2 c. dried apricots
1/4 c. carob nuggets
1/2 c. salted peanuts

Combine	cereal and noodles in bowl.
Blend	butter, Worcestershire sauce and Tabasco sauce in bowl.
Pour	over noodle mixture; mix well.
Add	remaining ingredients; toss lightly.
Store	in airtight container.

Photograph for this recipe above.

HERSHEY'S COCOA FUDGE

2/3 c. cocoa
3 c. sugar
1/8 tsp. salt
1 1/2 c. milk
1/4 c. butter
1 tsp. vanilla extract

Combine	cocoa, sugar and salt in 4-quart saucepan, mixing well.
Stir	in milk.
Bring	to a boil, stirring constantly.
Cook	to soft-ball stage or 234 degrees on candy thermometer. Do not stir.
Remove	from heat.
Add	butter and vanilla. Do not stir.
Cool	to room temperature.
Beat	until fudge thickens and loses gloss.
Spread	in lightly buttered pan.

Donna Ramsey
Vinita H. S., Vinita

Desserts

NUTTY CHOCOLATE FUDGE

2 c. sugar
1/4 c. cocoa
1 c. heavy cream
1/2 tsp. salt
2 tbsp. corn syrup
2 tbsp. butter
1 tsp. vanilla extract
1/2 c. chopped nuts

Bring . . . . sugar and next 4 ingredients to a boil in saucepan.
Cook . . . . until mixture reaches soft-ball stage or to 234 degrees on candy thermometer.
Stir . . . . in butter and vanilla; cool slightly.
Beat . . . . until mixture loses gloss.
Stir . . . . in nuts.
Spread . . . . . in buttered 9-inch square pan.
Yields . . . . . . 32 servings.

Sandra Allen
Howe H. S., Howe

HONEY FUDGE

2/3 c. evaporated milk
1/2 c. honey
1/4 tsp. salt
1/4 c. butter
1 c. peanut butter
2 c. chocolate chips
1 7-oz. jar marshmallow creme

Boil . . . . milk and next 3 ingredients in saucepan for 5 minutes.
Stir . . . . in peanut butter, chocolate chips and marshmallow creme.
Pour . . . . into greased 9 x 13-inch pan.
Chill . . . . for 1 hour.
Yields . . . . . . 60 servings.

Teri Douglas
Lindsay H. S., Lindsay

FUDGE KRISPIES

1 to 2 c. chocolate chips
1 stick margarine
1/2 c. light corn syrup
2 tsp. vanilla extract
1 c. sifted confectioners' sugar
4 c. Rice Krispies

Combine . . . . first 3 ingredients in medium saucepan.
Cook . . . . over low heat until smooth, stirring frequently; remove from heat.
Add . . . . vanilla and confectioners' sugar, mixing well.
Stir . . . . in Rice Krispies.
Spread . . . . . evenly in 9 x 13-inch baking dish.
Chill . . . . until firm.
Cut . . . . into 1 1/2-inch squares.
Store . . . . in refrigerator.

Shannon Miller
Waynoka H. S., Waynoka

WHITE FUDGE

3 c. sugar
1 c. milk
1 stick margarine
1 7-oz. jar marshmallow creme
12 oz. flaked coconut
1 tsp. vanilla extract
1 c. nuts

Boil . . . . sugar, milk and margarine in saucepan for 7 minutes; remove from heat.
Stir . . . . in marshmallow creme.
Beat . . . . until cooled and thickened.
Stir . . . . in coconut, vanilla and nuts.
Pour . . . . into 9-inch square buttered pan.
Yields . . . . . . 36 servings.

Willene Walsh
State Home Economics Teacher of the Year 1984
Union City H. S., Union City

MINT PATTIES

1 stick butter, softened
1 16-oz. package confectioners' sugar
1/3 c. corn syrup
2 tsp. peppermint flavoring
1 12-oz. package chocolate chips
1/2 bar paraffin

Cream . . . . . . butter and confectioners' sugar in bowl.
Mix . . . . in corn syrup and flavoring.
Pat . . . . out to desired thickness on waxed paper.
Cut . . . . into small circles.

Chill . . . . for 1 hour.
Melt . . . . chocolate chips and paraffin in double boiler.
Dip . . . . patties in chocolate mixture.
Place . . . . on waxed paper to set.
Yields . . . . . . 5 dozen.

Barbie Lamle
Okeene H. S., Okeene

MICROWAVE QUICK PENUCHE

1 7-oz. jar marshmallow creme
1 sm. can evaporated milk
6 tbsp. margarine
1 3/4 c. sugar
1/4 tsp. salt
1 6-oz. package butterscotch chips
1 c. chopped walnuts

Combine . . . . first 5 ingredients in large glass bowl.
Microwave . . on High for 6 minutes or until mixture boils, stirring twice.
Microwave . . on Medium for 3 minutes, stirring once.
Stir . . . . in butterscotch chips until melted.
Add . . . . walnuts.
Spoon . . . . . . into buttered, foil-lined 8-inch square pan.
Chill . . . . until firm.
Yields . . . . . . 24 servings.

Judy Adler
Snyder H. S., Snyder

PEANUT BRITTLE

2 c. sugar
1 c. light corn syrup
2 c. raw peanuts
1/2 tsp. salt
2 tsp. vanilla extract
1 tsp. butter
1 tsp. soda

Cook . . . . sugar, corn syrup and 1/2 cup water in saucepan for 5 to 10 minutes, or to hard-crack stage.
Add . . . . peanuts.
Cook . . . . until peanuts pop, stirring constantly.
Stir . . . . in salt, vanilla and butter; remove from heat.

Mix . . . . in soda.
Spread . . . . . on buttered foil to cool.
Break . . . . . . into pieces.

Lisa Garrett
Geary H. S., Geary

PEANUT PATTIES

2 1/2 c. sugar
2/3 c. light corn syrup
1 c. evaporated milk
3 c. raw peanuts
1 tsp. butter
1 tsp. vanilla extract
Red food coloring (opt.)

Combine . . . . sugar, syrup, milk and peanuts in 3-quart saucepan, mixing well.
Simmer . . . . . for 1 hour.
Beat . . . . in butter, vanilla and food coloring until creamy.
Drop . . . . by spoonfuls onto waxed paper; shape into patties.
Cool . . . . until firm.
Yields . . . . . . 24 servings.

Monica Gross and Christy Johnson
Wagoner H. S., Wagoner

CHUNKY PEANUT BUTTER BALLS

1/2 c. margarine, softened
2 c. chunky peanut butter
2 c. confectioners' sugar
3 c. crisp rice cereal
1 8-oz. chocolate bar
1 12-oz. package chocolate chips
1/4 bar paraffin

Mix . . . . margarine, peanut butter and confectioners' sugar in bowl.
Stir . . . . in cereal.
Shape . . . . . . into balls; place on waxed paper.
Chill . . . . for 15 minutes or until set.
Melt . . . . chocolate, chocolate chips and paraffin in double boiler.
Dip . . . . balls in chocolate mixture.
Chill . . . . until set.
Store . . . . in refrigerator.
Yields . . . . . . 4 dozen.

Stephanie Sorge
OCCC, Tuttle

Desserts

FAVORITE PEANUT BUTTER CUPS

2 sticks margarine, melted
2 c. peanut butter
1 1/2 boxes confectioners' sugar
1   12-oz. package chocolate chips
1/2 bar paraffin

Mix . . . . margarine, peanut butter and sugar in bowl.
Shape . . . . . . into balls.
Chill . . . . overnight.
Melt . . . . chocolate chips and paraffin in double boiler.
Dip . . . . peanut butter balls in chocolate mixture.
Cool . . . . on waxed paper.
Yields . . . . . . 2 1/2 dozen.

Shannon Mann
Checotah H. S., Checotah

EASY PEANUT BUTTER BALLS

3/4 c. margarine
1 1/2 c. peanut butter
1   16-oz. package confectioners' sugar
1/3 bar paraffin
1   12-oz. package chocolate chips

Melt . . . . margarine and peanut butter in saucepan over low heat, stirring constantly.
Stir . . . . in confectioners' sugar.
Shape . . . . . . into small balls.
Chill . . . . on waxed paper for 30 minutes or until set.
Melt . . . . paraffin and chocolate chips in double boiler.
Dip . . . . peanut butter balls in chocolate mixture.
Cool . . . . on waxed paper until set.
Store . . . . in refrigerator.

Kim Neale
FHA President 1983, 1984, Westville H. S.

BUCKEYES

1 stick butter, softened
1 1/2 c. peanut butter
3/4 lb. confectioners' sugar
1 tsp. vanilla extract
1 pkg. chocolate chips
1/2 block paraffin

Cream . . . . . . butter, peanut butter, confectioners' sugar and vanilla in bowl.
Shape . . . . . . into small balls.
Melt . . . . chocolate chips and paraffin in double boiler.
Dip . . . . balls in chocolate mixture.
Cool . . . . on waxed paper.

Kelly Sellers
Mustang H. S., Mustang

PEANUT BUTTER SQUARES

1/3 c. graham cracker crumbs
2 3/4 c. confectioners' sugar
2 sticks margarine, melted
1 c. peanut butter
2 c. chocolate chips

Combine . . . . all ingredients except chocolate chips in bowl, mixing well.
Press . . . . into 12 x 18-inch dish.
Melt . . . . chocolate chips in saucepan.
Spread . . . . . on top of graham cracker mixture.
Chill . . . . in refrigerator.

Angie Pepper
Waynoka H. S., Waynoka

QUICK PEANUT BUTTER CUPS

1 stick margarine, melted
2 c. confectioners' sugar
1/2 c. peanut butter
1   6-oz. package chocolate chips, melted

Combine . . . . all ingredients except chocolate chips in bowl, mixing well.
Spread . . . . . in bottom of greased 8-inch square pan.
Spread . . . . . chocolate on top.
Chill . . . . until firm.
Yields . . . . . . 16 servings.

Connie Harvey
Macomb H. S., Macomb

PRALINES

2 c. packed light brown sugar
3/4 c. light cream
1 tbsp. butter
1/8 tsp. salt
2 c. pecan halves

Heat . . . . brown sugar, cream, butter and salt in saucepan until sugar is dissolved, stirring constantly.

Cook . . . . until mixture reaches soft-ball stage or 238 degrees on candy thermometer, stirring constantly; remove from heat.

Cool . . . . for 5 minutes.

Stir . . . . until mixture loses gloss and coats spoon.

Place . . . . pecans in clusters of 3 on greased baking sheet.

Spoon . . . . . . mixture over pecans; cool completely.

Store . . . . in airtight container.

Yields . . . . . . 2 1/2-3 dozen.

Virginia Searles
Westville Schools, Westville

SUPER KISSES

1 10-oz. package marshmallows
1/4 c. margarine
5 c. chocolate rice cereal

Heat . . . . marshmallows with margarine in saucepan until melted, stirring constantly.

Cook . . . . for 3 minutes over low heat, stirring constantly; remove.

Stir . . . . in cereal until coated; cool slightly.

Press . . . . into large, buttered funnels; cool.

Unmold . . . . and wrap in plastic.

Yields . . . . . . 2-4 servings.

Paula Owens
Barnsdall H. S., Barnsdall

ALMOND TOFFEE

1 c. butter
1 c. sugar
1 tbsp. light corn syrup
1 c. chopped almonds
1 8-oz. chocolate bar, broken

Cook . . . . butter, sugar and corn syrup mixed with 3 tablespoons hot water in saucepan to 300 degrees on candy thermometer.

Stir . . . . in 2/3 cup finely chopped almonds.

Spread . . . . . on greased baking sheet.

Sprinkle . . . . with chocolate pieces while hot.

Spread . . . . . melting chocolate to cover.

Sprinkle . . . . with 1/3 cup almonds.

Cool . . . . completely before breaking into squares.

Amy Ford
Okeene H. S., Okeene

CARAMEL POPCORN BALLS

1 1/4 c. sugar
1 1/4 c. packed brown sugar
1/2 c. light corn syrup
1 tbsp. butter
5 qt. lightly salted popped popcorn

Heat . . . . sugar, brown sugar, corn syrup and 2/3 cup water in saucepan until sugars dissolve, stirring constantly.

Stir . . . . in butter.

Cook . . . . to soft-crack stage or 270 degrees on candy thermometer; do not stir.

Add . . . . popcorn, stirring until coated.

Shape . . . . . . into balls.

Yields . . . . . . 24 servings.

Pat Kellner
Okeene Public Schools, Okeene

EASY CARAMEL POPCORN

3 3/4 qt. popped popcorn
1 c. packed brown sugar
1/2 c. margarine
1/4 c. light corn syrup
1/2 tsp. salt
1/2 tsp. soda

Place . . . . popcorn on ungreased baking sheet.

Mix . . . . brown sugar, margarine, corn syrup and salt in bowl.

Warm . . . . . . in 200-degree oven for 5 minutes.

Stir . . . . in soda.

Drizzle . . . . . over popcorn.

Bake . . . . at 200 degrees for 1 hour, stirring every 15 minutes.

David Hasenbeck
Tomlinson Jr. H. S., Lawton

Desserts

SUPER BROWNIES

2 sticks margarine, melted
4 sq. chocolate, melted
2 c. sugar
4 eggs
2 c. flour
1/2 tsp. salt
2 tsp. vanilla extract
1/2 c. chopped nuts

Combine .... margarine, chocolate and sugar in bowl, mixing well.
Beat .... in eggs, 1 at a time, mixing well after each addition.
Stir .... in flour, salt, vanilla and nuts.
Pour .... into greased cake pan.
Bake .... at 350 degrees for 20 minutes or until brownies test done.

Tracey Earls
Gould H. S., Gould

COCOA BROWNIES

3/4 c. melted butter
1 1/2 c. sugar
1 1/2 tsp. vanilla extract
3 eggs
3/4 c. flour
1/2 c. cocoa
1/2 tsp. baking powder
1/2 tsp. salt

Cream ...... butter, sugar and vanilla in bowl.
Beat .... in eggs.
Stir .... in mixture of flour, cocoa, baking powder and salt.
Spread ..... in greased 8-inch square baking pan.
Bake .... at 350 degrees for 40 to 45 minutes, or until brownies test done; cool.
Yields ...... 1 dozen.

Lanetta Mann
Checotah H. S., Checotah

BLOND BROWNIES

1 stick butter, melted
2/3 c. packed brown sugar
1 egg
1 tsp. vanilla extract
3/4 c. flour
1 tsp. baking powder

1/2 c. chopped pecans
1 6-oz. package chocolate chips

Heat .... butter and brown sugar in saucepan until sugar dissolves, stirring constantly.
Cool .... for 5 minutes.
Stir .... in egg and vanilla.
Blend ...... in combined dry ingredients.
Stir .... in pecans and 3/4 cup chocolate chips.
Spread ..... in greased 8-inch baking pan.
Sprinkle .... with remaining chocolate chips.
Bake .... at 350 degrees for 25 minutes.
Cool .... in pan on rack.
Yields ...... 16 servings.

Marcy Fox
Checotah H. S., Checotah

COMPANY BUTTERSCOTCH BROWNIES

2 c. packed light brown sugar
1/2 c. melted shortening
2 eggs
1 1/2 c. sifted flour
2 tsp. baking powder
1 tsp. salt
1 tsp. vanilla extract
1 c. chopped nuts

Stir .... brown sugar into shortening in bowl; cool.
Mix .... in eggs, flour, baking powder and salt.
Stir .... in vanilla and nuts.
Pour .... into greased and floured 9 x 13-inch baking pan.
Bake .... at 350 degrees for 25 minutes or until brownies test done.

Judith Hays
Ringwood H. S., Ringwood

MICROWAVE SAUCEPAN BROWNIES

1/2 c. butter
2 sq. unsweetened chocolate
1 c. sugar
2 eggs
3/4 c. flour
1 tsp. vanilla extract
3/4 c. chopped nuts

Melt	.... butter and chocolate in sauce-pan; remove from heat.
Stir	.... in remaining ingredients in order listed.
Spread	..... in greased 9-inch square glass baking pan.
Microwave	.. on High for 4 to 6 minutes or until brownies test done; cool in pan.
Yields	...... 16 servings.

Janelle Howard
Elmore City H. S., Pauls Valley

PEANUT BUTTER AND JELLY BROWNIES

1 lg. package brownie mix
1 c. chocolate chips
3/4 to 1 c. peanut butter
3/4 c. jelly, heated

Prepare	..... brownie mix, using package directions.
Pour	.... into 9 x 13-inch baking pan.
Sprinkle	.... with chocolate chips; press into batter.
Bake	.... according to package directions.
Spread	..... peanut butter over hot brownies.
Drizzle	..... jelly over top.
Yields	...... 24 servings.

Christy Long
Chickasha H. S., Chickasha

CHOCOLATE-CARAMEL BARS

1/3 c. butter
1 18-oz. package oatmeal cookie mix
1 6-oz. package semisweet chocolate chips
32 caramels
1 5 1/3-oz. can evaporated milk

Cut	.... butter into cookie mix in bowl until crumbly.
Press	.... into bottom of greased 9 x 13-inch pan, reserving 1 cup.
Bake	.... at 350 degrees for 12 minutes.
Sprinkle	.... with chocolate chips.
Melt	.... caramels in evaporated milk in saucepan, stirring constantly.
Spread	..... over chocolate chips.
Sprinkle	.... with reserved crumb mixture.

Bake	.... for 15 minutes longer; cool.
Chill	.... for 1 hour or until set.
Yields	...... 12-15 servings.

Betty Blackburn
South Intermediate H. S., Broken Arrow

HELLO DOLLIES

6 c. crushed graham crackers
1/2 c. melted margarine
1 pkg. semisweet chocolate chips
1 pkg. pecans
1 pkg. flaked coconut
1 can sweetened condensed milk, warmed

Line	.... bottom of 9 x 13-inch pan with cracker crumbs.
Pour	.... margarine over crumbs.
Layer	...... with chocolate chips, pecans and coconut over crumbs.
Pour	.... condensed milk evenly over top.
Bake	.... at 375 degrees for 7 to 10 minutes or until coconut is browned.
Yields	...... 12 servings.

Tracy Jones
Ringwood H. S., Meno

MAGIC COOKIE BARS

1 1/2 c. graham cracker crumbs
1/2 c. margarine, melted
1 14-oz. can sweetened condensed milk
1 6-oz. package semisweet chocolate chips
1 3 1/2-oz. can flaked coconut
1 c. chopped nuts

Sprinkle	.... graham cracker crumbs over margarine in 9 x 13-inch baking pan.
Pour	.... condensed milk over crumbs.
Layer	...... chocolate chips, coconut and nuts over top, pressing firmly into pan.
Bake	.... at 350 degrees for 25 to 30 minutes or until lightly browned; cool.
Store	.... loosely covered, at room temperature.
Yields	...... 24 servings.

Kim Turner
Chickasha H. S., Chickasha

Desserts

CHOCOLATE CHIP BARS

1 c. melted margarine
3/4 c. sugar
3/4 c. packed brown sugar
2 eggs
1 tsp. vanilla extract
2 c. flour
1 tsp. each soda, salt
1 c. chocolate chips
1 c. chopped nuts (opt.)

Mix . . . . margarine and sugars in bowl.
Add . . . . . . eggs and vanilla, mixing well.
Mix . . . . in flour, soda and salt.
Stir . . . . in chocolate chips and nuts.
Spread . . . . . in greased baking pan.
Bake . . . . at 350 degrees for 25 minutes.

Patty Holub
Ringwood H. S., Ringwood

COCONUT BARS

1/2 c. butter
1 1/2 c. packed brown sugar
3/4 tsp. salt
Flour
2 tsp. baking powder
2 eggs
1 tsp. vanilla extract
1 c. flaked coconut

Combine . . . . butter, 1/2 cup brown sugar, 1/2 teaspoon salt and 1 cup flour in bowl; mix well.
Press . . . . into bottom of baking pan.
Bake . . . . at 350 degrees for 25 minutes.
Mix . . . . 1 cup brown sugar, 1/4 teaspoon salt, 2 tablespoons flour and remaining ingredients in bowl.
Spread . . . . . over crust.
Bake . . . . at 350 degrees for 25 minutes.
Cut . . . . into squares when cool.
Yields . . . . . . 24 servings.

Virginia Darnell, Teacher
Apache H. S., Apache

GERMAN COOKIES

4 eggs
2 c. packed brown sugar
2 1/2 c. flour
1/8 tsp. salt
1 tsp. cinnamon
1/2 tsp. cloves
1 c. chopped nuts
1 c. confectioners' sugar
1/2 tsp. vanilla extract

Beat . . . . eggs and brown sugar in bowl.
Add . . . . flour, salt and spices, mixing well.
Stir . . . . in nuts.
Spread . . . . . in 12 x 15-inch baking pan.
Bake . . . . at 375 degrees for 20 minutes.
Cool . . . . for 1 minute.
Mix . . . . confectioners' sugar, vanilla and 3 tablespoons water in bowl.
Spread . . . . . over cookies.

Bernice Duncan, Adviser
Gould FHA, Gould

CHEWY CHOCOLATE COOKIES

1 1/4 c. butter
2 c. sugar
2 eggs
2 tsp. vanilla extract
2 c. flour
3/4 c. cocoa
1 tsp. soda
1/2 tsp. salt
1 c. finely chopped nuts (opt.)

Cream . . . . . . butter and sugar in bowl.
Mix . . . . in eggs and vanilla.
Add . . . . combined dry ingredients, mixing well.
Stir . . . . in nuts.
Drop . . . . by teaspoonfuls onto cookie sheet.
Bake . . . . at 350 degrees for 8 or 9 minutes or until lightly browned.
Cool . . . . on cookie sheet for 1 minute; cool completely on wire rack.

Susan Mowdy
Lindsay H. S., Lindsay

FAVORITE CHOCOLATE CHIP COOKIES

1 /3 c. margarine
1 c. sugar
1 c. packed light brown sugar
1/3 c. unsalted butter
2/3 c. shortening

2 eggs
2 tsp. vanilla extract
3 c. unbleached flour
1 tsp. each soda, salt
3 c. miniature chocolate chips

Cream . . . . . . margarine, sugars, butter and shortening in bowl.
Beat . . . . in eggs and vanilla.
Sift . . . . in dry ingredients, mixing well.
Stir . . . . in chocolate chips.
Drop . . . . by teaspoonfuls onto cookie sheet.
Bake . . . . at 375 degrees for 8 to 10 minutes or until lightly browned.

Charlene Meyer
Tuttle H. S., Tuttle

NUTTY CHOCOLATE CHIP COOKIES

1/2 c. butter, softened
1 tsp. vanilla extract
3/4 c. packed light brown sugar
1 egg
1 c. sifted flour
1/2 tsp. baking powder
1/8 tsp. each soda, salt
1 6-oz. package semisweet chocolate chips
1/2 c. chopped nuts

Cream . . . . . . butter, vanilla and brown sugar in bowl.
Beat . . . . in egg.
Mix . . . . in combined dry ingredients.
Stir . . . . in chocolate chips and nuts.
Drop . . . . by teaspoonfuls onto baking sheet.
Bake . . . . at 375 degrees for 10 to 12 minutes or until lightly browned.
Cool . . . . on wire rack.
Yields . . . . . . 4 dozen.

Kristi Rutledge
Granite Jr. H. S., Granite

FORGOTTEN COOKIES

1 tsp. vanilla extract
2 egg whites, stiffly beaten
2/3 c. sugar
1 c. chocolate chips
1 c. chopped nuts

Combine . . . . all ingredients in bowl, mixing well.
Drop . . . . by teaspoonfuls on foil-covered baking sheet.
Place . . . . in 350-degree oven; turn oven off.
Let . . . . stand in closed oven overnight.
Yields . . . . . . 3 dozen.

Rhonda Sheffield
Waurika Jr. H. S., Waurika

INK DOT COOKIES

3/4 c. butter
1 1/2 c. sugar
1 tsp. vanilla extract
2 eggs
2 1/4 c. flour
1 tsp. each soda, salt
2 c. chocolate chips

Cream . . . . . . butter, sugar and vanilla in bowl.
Beat . . . . in eggs.
Add . . . . mixture of flour, soda and salt.
Stir . . . . in chocolate chips.
Drop . . . . by teaspoonfuls onto ungreased cookie sheet.
Bake . . . . at 375 degrees for 8 to 10 minutes or until lightly browned.
Cool . . . . slightly before removing from sheet.
Yields . . . . . . 6 dozen.

Peggy Glenn
Heavener H. S., Howe

EASY M AND M COOKIES

1 1/2 c. plain M and M candies
1 c. shortening
1 c. packed brown sugar
1/2 c. sugar
2 tsp. vanilla extract
2 eggs
1 tsp. soda
1 tsp. salt
2 1/2 c. flour

Combine . . . . M and M candies with remaining ingredients in bowl, mixing well.
Drop . . . . by spoonfuls onto ungreased cookie sheet.
Bake . . . . at 375 degrees for 10 minutes.

Candy Smith
Checotah H. S., Checotah

Desserts

M AND M PARTY COOKIES

1 c. shortening
1 c. packed brown sugar
1/2 c. sugar
2 tsp. vanilla extract
2 eggs
2 1/4 c. sifted flour
1 tsp. soda
1/2 tsp. salt
2 c. plain M and M candies

Cream ...... shortening and sugars in bowl.
Beat .... in vanilla and eggs.
Sift .... flour, soda and salt into egg mixture, blending well.
Stir .... in 1 1/2 cups candies.
Drop .... by teaspoonfuls onto ungreased cookie sheet.
Sprinkle .... with remaining 1/2 cup candies.
Bake .... at 375 degrees for 10 minutes.
Yields ...... 6 dozen.

Robin Praytor
Vinita H. S. Vinita

MONSTER COOKIES

1 lb. butter, softened
2 lb. brown sugar
4 c. sugar
12 eggs
1 tbsp. vanilla extract
1 tbsp. corn syrup
8 tsp. soda
1 c. flour
18 c. oats
3 lb. peanut butter
1 pkg. chocolate chips
1 pkg. M and M's

Cream ...... butter and sugars in large bowl.
Beat .... in eggs.
Add .... vanilla, corn syrup and soda, mixing well.
Mix .... in flour, oats and peanut butter.
Stir .... in chocolate chips and M and M's.
Drop .... by heaping spoonfuls onto baking sheet.
Bake .... at 350 degrees for 12 minutes.

Monica Kauffman
Pryor Jr. H. S., Pryor

CHOCOLATE CHIP-OATMEAL COOKIES

1 c. shortening
3/4 c. sugar
3/4 c. packed brown sugar
2 eggs, beaten
1 tsp. vanilla extract
1 tsp. soda
1 1/2 c. flour
1 tsp. salt
2 c. oats
1/2 c. chopped nuts
1 6-oz. package chocolate chips

Cream ...... shortening and sugars in bowl.
Add .... eggs, vanilla and soda dissolved in 1 tablespoon hot water, mixing well.
Stir .... in remaining ingredients.
Drop .... by spoonfuls onto cookie sheet.
Bake .... at 350 degrees for 10 to 12 minutes, or until browned.

Tim Beegle
Checotah H. S., Checotah

CHOCOLATE OATMEAL COOKIES

1/2 c. milk
2 c. sugar
1/4 c. cocoa
1 stick butter
3 c. quick-cooking oats
1/2 c. peanut butter
1 tsp. vanilla extract

Heat .... milk, sugar and cocoa in saucepan.
Stir .... in butter.
Boil .... for 2 minutes, stirring constantly; remove from heat.
Add .... oats, peanut butter and vanilla, mixing well.
Drop .... by spoonfuls onto waxed paper.
Yields ...... 2 dozen.

Sharon Funburg
Checotah H. S., Checotah

NO-BAKE OATMEAL COOKIES

1/2 c. milk
1 stick butter
2 c. sugar
3 tbsp. cocoa

1 tsp. vanilla extract
1/2 c. peanut butter
3 c. oats

Combine . . . . first 5 ingredients in saucepan.
Boil . . . . for 1 minute; remove from heat.
Stir . . . . in peanut butter and oats.
Drop . . . . by teaspoonfuls onto waxed paper.

Cheryl Overacker
Barnsdall H. S., Barnsdall

GOLDEN THUMBPRINT COOKIES

1/2 c. butter, softened
1/3 c. packed brown sugar
1 egg, beaten
1 c. flour
1/4 tsp. salt
3/4 c. chopped walnuts
1/4 c. candied cherries

Cream . . . . . . butter and sugar in bowl.
Add . . . . egg, flour and salt, mixing well.
Stir . . . . in walnuts and cherries.
Drop . . . . by spoonfuls onto baking sheet.
Bake . . . . at 350 degrees for 10 minutes.
Yields . . . . . . 2 dozen.

Melanie Riggs
Ringwood H. S., Ringwood

GUMDROP JUMBLES

4 c. gumdrops, chopped
2 3/4 c. flour
1 1/2 c. packed brown sugar
1 tsp. salt
1/2 tsp. soda
1 8-oz. carton sour cream
1/2 c. shortening
2 eggs
1 tsp. vanilla extract

Combine . . . . all ingredients in bowl, mixing well.
Drop . . . . by tablespoonfuls 2 inches apart onto greased and floured baking sheet.
Bake . . . . at 350 degrees for 10 minutes or until firm.
Remove . . . . from baking pan immediately.
Yields . . . . . . 6 dozen.

Tammy York
Elmore City H. S., Elmore City

GRANDMA'S RANGER COOKIES

1 c. shortening
1 c. sugar
1 c. packed brown sugar
2 eggs
2 tsp. vanilla extract
2 c. oats
2 c. cornflakes
2 c. flour
2 tsp. soda
1 tsp. baking powder
1/2 tsp. salt
1 c. flaked coconut

Cream . . . . . . shortening, sugars, eggs and vanilla in bowl.
Stir . . . . in oats and cornflakes.
Sift . . . . in dry ingredients.
Add . . . . coconut, mixing well.
Roll . . . . into balls.
Place . . . . on greased cookie sheet; flatten.
Bake . . . . at 375 degrees for 15 to 20 minutes.

Judy Holsapple
Canton H. S., Oakwood

CHEWY OATMEAL COOKIES

1 c. sifted flour
3/4 tsp. each soda, salt
1/2 tsp. cinnamon
1/4 tsp. nutmeg
3/4 c. shortening
1 1/3 c. packed brown sugar
2 eggs
1 tsp. vanilla extract
2 c. oats
1 c. raisins (opt.)

Sift . . . . flour, soda, salt, cinnamon and nutmeg in mixer bowl.
Add . . . . shortening, brown sugar, eggs and vanilla.
Beat . . . . for 2 minutes or until smooth.
Stir . . . . in oats and raisins.
Drop . . . . by heaping teaspoonfuls onto greased baking sheet.
Bake . . . . at 350 degrees for 12 to 15 minutes or until lightly browned.
Yields . . . . . . 3 dozen.

Peggy Jantzen
Ringwood H. S., Ringwood

Desserts

OATMEAL CRISPIES

1 c. shortening
1 c. packed brown sugar
1 c. sugar
2 eggs, beaten
1 tsp. vanilla extract
1 1/2 c. flour
1 tsp. soda
1/2 tsp. salt
2 c. oats
1/2 c. chopped pecans
1/2 c. flaked coconut (opt.)

Cream ...... shortening and sugars in bowl.
Beat .... in eggs and vanilla.
Sift .... in flour, soda and salt.
Add .... oats, pecans and coconut, mixing well.
Drop .... by teaspoonfuls onto cookie sheet.
Bake .... at 350 degrees for 10 to 12 minutes, or until light golden brown.
Yields ...... 5-6 dozen.

Dadrian McNeill
Elmore City H. S., Pauls Valley

RAISIN-OATMEAL COOKIES

1 c. raisins
1/2 c. shortening
1 c. sugar
2 eggs, beaten
1/4 c. milk
1 2/3 c. oats
1 1/2 c. flour
1 tsp. soda
1/2 tsp. salt
1 tsp. cinnamon

Cover ...... raisins with hot water in bowl; drain.
Cream ...... shortening and sugar in bowl.
Mix .... in eggs and milk.
Stir .... in oats and raisins.
Sift .... in flour, soda, salt and cinnamon.
Drop .... by spoonfuls onto greased baking sheet.
Bake .... at 350 degrees for 12 minutes.
Yields ...... 3 dozen.

Tona Lovelace
Crescent H. S., Crescent

ORANGE OATMEAL COOKIES

1 c. shortening
1 c. sugar
1 tsp. vanilla extract
2 eggs
1/4 c. orange juice
2 tsp. grated orange rind
2 c. flour
1/2 tsp. salt
1 tsp. soda
2 c. oats
1/2 c. chopped nuts
1/2 c. raisins

Cream ...... shortening, sugar, vanilla, eggs, orange juice and rind in bowl.
Mix .... in dry ingredients, oats, nuts and raisins.
Drop .... by spoonfuls onto baking sheet.
Bake .... at 350 degrees for 8 to 16 minutes or until lightly browned.

Brenda Oney
Okeene H. S., Okeene

MOLASSES CRINKLES

3/4 c. shortening
1 c. packed brown sugar
1 egg
1/4 c. molasses
2 1/4 c. sifted flour
2 tsp. soda
1/4 tsp. salt
1/2 tsp. cloves
1 tsp. each ginger, cinnamon
Sugar

Cream ...... shortening, brown sugar, egg and molasses in bowl.
Sift .... in next 6 ingredients, mixing well.
Chill .... in refrigerator.
Shape ...... into balls.
Dip .... tops in sugar.
Place ...... 3 inches apart on greased baking sheet.
Sprinkle .... tops with water.
Bake .... at 375 degrees for 8 to 10 minutes or until set, but not hard.
Yields ...... 3-4 dozen.

Carla Grizzle
Stuart H. S., McAlester

Desserts

PECAN DREAM COOKIES

3 sticks butter, softened
3 c. flour
1 1/2 c. confectioners' sugar
1/2 tsp. salt
1 tbsp. vanilla extract
1/4 c. milk
1 c. chopped pecans

Cream ...... butter, flour, confectioners' sugar and salt in bowl.
Stir .... in remaining ingredients.
Roll .... into small logs; place on baking sheet.
Bake .... at 400 degrees for 10 minutes.
Roll .... warm cookies in additional confectioners' sugar.
Store .... in refrigerator.

Terri Brock
Waynoka H. S., Waynoka

RAISIN BARS

1 c. shortening
2 c. sugar
2 c. raisins
1 tsp. each cinnamon, cloves, nutmeg
3 1/2 c. flour
2 tsp. soda
1/8 tsp. salt

Bring .... 2 cups water, shortening, sugar, raisins and spices to a boil in saucepan; cool.
Stir .... in flour, soda and salt.
Spoon ...... into 9 x 13-inch pan.
Bake .... at 350 degrees for 25 to 30 minutes or until firm.
Yields ...... 2 dozen.

Esther Moorhead
Buffalo Public Schools, Tulsa

ROCK CAKES

1 c. self-rising flour
Pinch of salt
6 tbsp. margarine
6 tbsp. caster sugar
6 tbsp. dried fruit
1 egg, beaten
Milk

Sift .... flour and salt into bowl.
Cut .... in margarine until crumbly.
Mix .... in sugar, fruit, egg and enough milk to make stiff dough.
Drop .... by heaping spoonfuls onto greased baking sheet.
Bake .... at 450 degrees for 15 minutes.

Izumi Hayashi
Thomas H. S., Thomas

PARTY ROCKS

2 tbsp. cocoa
1 c. sugar
1/4 c. milk
1/4 c. butter
1/2 tsp. vanilla extract
1 1/2 c. oats
1/4 c. coconut (opt.)

Bring .... cocoa, sugar, milk and butter to a boil in saucepan.
Boil .... for 2 minutes; remove from heat.
Let .... stand for 1 minute.
Stir .... in vanilla, oats and coconut.
Drop .... quickly by spoonfuls on waxed paper.

Dawn Roberts
Choctaw Jr. H. S., Choctaw

PARTY PEANUT BUTTER COOKIES

1 c. butter, softened
1 c. peanut butter
1 c. sugar
1 c. packed brown sugar
2 eggs
2 1/2 c. flour
1/2 tsp. each salt, soda

Cream ...... butter, peanut butter and sugars in bowl.
Beat .... in eggs.
Add .... combined dry ingredients, mixing well.
Drop .... by teaspoonfuls onto cookie sheet; flatten with fork.
Bake .... at 375 degrees for 10 to 15 minutes, or until lightly browned.

Dean Dorsett
Geary H. S., Geary

Desserts

SUGARLESS PEANUT BUTTER COOKIES

1/4 c. diet margarine
8 pkg. Sweet N' Low
1/2 c. peanut butter
1 egg
1/3 c. milk
Vanilla extract to taste
1 c. flour
1/4 tsp. salt
1 tsp. baking powder

Cream . . . . . . margarine, sweetener and peanut butter in bowl.
Mix . . . . in egg, milk and vanilla.
Sift . . . . in flour, salt and baking powder, mixing well.
Drop . . . . by spoonfuls on foil-lined baking sheet.
Flatten . . . . . with fork.
Bake . . . . at 375 degrees for 10 minutes; cool on wire rack.
Yields . . . . . . 3 dozen.

Mendie Adam
Okeene H. S., Okeene

JAMIE'S SUGAR COOKIES

1 c. margarine
1 1/2 c. sifted confectioners' sugar
1 egg
1 tsp. vanilla extract
1/2 tsp. almond flavoring
1 tsp. soda
1 tsp. cream of tartar
2 1/2 c. flour
Sugar

Cream . . . . . . margarine and confectioners' sugar in bowl.
Beat . . . . in egg and flavorings.
Sift . . . . in dry ingredients except sugar, mixing well.
Chill . . . . for 2 to 3 hours.
Roll . . . . to 3/16-inch thickness on floured surface.
Cut . . . . with cookie cutter; sprinkle with sugar.
Place . . . . on lightly greased baking sheet.
Bake . . . . at 375 degrees for 7 or 8 minutes or until lightly browned.
Yields . . . . . . 5 dozen.

Jamie Christy
Beggs H. S., Okmulgee

SANTA'S WHISKERS

1 c. butter
1 c. sugar
2 tbsp. milk
1 tsp. vanilla extract
2 1/2 c. sifted flour
3/4 c. finely chopped red and green candied cherries
1/2 c. finely chopped pecans
3/4 c. flaked coconut

Cream . . . . . . butter and sugar in bowl.
Blend . . . . . . in milk and vanilla.
Stir . . . . in flour, cherries and pecans.
Shape . . . . . . into two 8-inch rolls.
Roll . . . . in coconut.
Chill . . . . wrapped in foil, for several hours.
Slice . . . . 1/4 inch thick; place on baking sheet.
Bake . . . . at 375 degrees for 12 minutes or until edges are golden brown.
Yields . . . . . . 5 dozen.

Tammy Daniels
Bray-Doyle H. S., Rush Springs

ORANGE-PECAN REFRIGERATOR COOKIES

1 c. shortening
1/2 c. packed brown sugar
1/2 c. sugar
1 egg, beaten
1 1/2 tsp. grated orange rind
2 tbsp. orange juice
2 3/4 c. sifted flour
1/4 tsp. each soda, salt
1/2 c. chopped pecans

Cream . . . . . . shortening and sugars in bowl.
Mix . . . . in egg, orange rind and orange juice.
Sift . . . . in flour, soda and salt.
Stir . . . . in pecans.
Shape . . . . . . into rolls 2 inches in diameter; wrap in waxed paper.
Chill . . . . for several hours.
Cut . . . . into thin slices.
Place . . . . on baking sheet.
Bake . . . . at 400 degrees for 10 minutes or until lightly browned.

Shirley Teske
State Dept. of Vo-Tech., Stillwater

ALL-AMERICAN APPLE PIE

> 6 med. apples, sliced
> 3/4 c. sugar
> 2 tbsp. flour
> 1 tsp. cinnamon
> 1 recipe 2-crust pie pastry
> 1 tbsp. butter

Toss . . . . apples in mixture of sugar, flour and cinnamon in bowl until coated.

Arrange . . . . . in pastry-lined 9-inch pie plate.

Dot . . . . with butter.

Top . . . . with remaining pastry; seal edges and cut vents.

Bake . . . . at 400 degrees for 30 to 40 minutes, or until crust is browned.

Anita Dutton
Elmore City H. S., Elmore City

APPLE-PECAN PIE

> 1 c. sugar
> 1 tbsp. flour
> 1 1/2 tsp. cinnamon
> Dash of salt
> 4 c. coarsely grated apples
> 1/4 c. melted margarine
> 1 egg, beaten
> 1 unbaked 9-in. pie shell
> 1 c. chopped pecans

Mix . . . . sugar, flour, cinnamon and salt in bowl.

Stir . . . . in apples.

Mix . . . . in margarine and egg.

Spoon . . . . . . into pie shell.

Sprinkle . . . . with pecans.

Bake . . . . at 400 degrees for 10 minutes; reduce temperature to 350 degrees.

Bake . . . . at 350 degrees for 45 to 50 minutes longer or until set.

Sue Reynolds
Bartlesville H. S., Bartlesville

TWO-CRUST APPLE PIE

> 1 c. sugar
> 1/2 tsp. ginger
> 1 tsp. cinnamon
> 1/4 tsp. each nutmeg, salt
> 2 tbsp. flour

> 3 tbsp. strong tea
> 1 tbsp. lemon juice
> 4 c. sliced apples
> 1 recipe 2-crust pie pastry
> 2 tbsp. butter

Mix . . . . sugar, spices, salt, flour, tea and lemon juice in bowl.

Layer . . . . . . apples and sugar mixture in pastry-lined pie plate alternately, heaping filling slightly in center.

Dot . . . . with butter.

Cover . . . . . with remaining pastry; flute edges and cut vents.

Bake . . . . at 425 degrees for 40 to 50 minutes or until golden brown.

Yields . . . . . . 6 servings.

Sherry Farmer
Snyder H. S., Snyder

BUTTERSCOTCH CREAM-PEANUT PIE

> 1/4 c. cornstarch
> 1/2 c. packed brown sugar
> 1/2 tsp. salt
> 2 1/2 c. milk
> 3 egg yolks, beaten
> 1 tsp. vanilla extract
> 2 tbsp. margarine
> 1/2 c. unsalted roasted peanuts, chopped
> 1 baked 9-in. pie shell
> 1 recipe 3-egg meringue

Mix . . . . first 3 ingredients in saucepan.

Blend . . . . . . in milk.

Cook . . . . over medium heat until thickened, stirring constantly; cool.

Stir . . . . a small amount of hot mixture into egg yolks; stir egg yolks into hot mixture.

Cook . . . . for 2 minutes over low heat; remove.

Stir . . . . in vanilla, margarine and peanuts.

Spoon . . . . . . into pie shell.

Top . . . . with meringue.

Bake . . . . at 400 degrees until lightly browned.

Yields . . . . . . 6 servings.

Shelly Lee
Bluejacket H. S., Bluejacket

Desserts

BUTTERSCOTCH PECAN PIE

1/2 c. dark corn syrup
2 eggs
1/4 tsp. salt
1 6-oz. package butterscotch chips, melted
1/2 c. pecans
1 unbaked 9-in. pie shell

Mix . . . . corn syrup, eggs and salt in bowl.
Stir . . . . in butterscotch and pecans.
Pour . . . . into pie shell.
Bake . . . . at 350 degrees for 45 minutes.
Yields . . . . . . 6 servings.

Suzie Brown
Bray-Doyle H. S., Rush Springs

BLUEBERRY CHEESECAKE PIE

1 8-oz. package cream cheese, softened
1 c. sifted confectioners' sugar
1 tsp. vanilla extract
1 c. whipping cream, whipped
1 9-in. baked pie shell
1 can blueberry pie filling

Beat . . . . cream cheese, confectioners' sugar and vanilla in bowl until smooth.
Fold . . . . in whipped cream.
Spoon . . . . . . into pie shell.
Top . . . . with pie filling.
Chill . . . . until set.

Angie Hernandez
Porum H. S., Porum

BLUEBERRY SKY PIES

1 8-oz. package cream cheese, softened
1 6-oz. can frozen lemonade concentrate
1 can sweetened condensed milk
1 lg. carton whipped topping
1 can blueberry pie filling
2 graham cracker crust pie shells
1 c. chopped pecans (opt.)

Beat . . . . cream cheese in bowl.
Add . . . . concentrate and condensed milk, mixing well.
Fold . . . . in 3/4 of the whipped topping and 2/3 of the pie filling.
Spoon . . . . . . into pie shells.

Top . . . . with remaining whipped topping and pie filling.
Sprinkle . . . . with pecans.
Chill . . . . until set.

Judy McDaris
Beggs H. S., Beggs

BAKED CHEESECAKE PIE

1 8-oz. package cream cheese, softened
Sugar
1 tbsp. lemon juice
1/2 tsp. vanilla extract
Pinch of salt
2 eggs
1 8-in. graham cracker pie shell
1 8-oz. carton sour cream

Combine . . . . cream cheese, 1/2 cup sugar, lemon juice, 1/4 teaspoon vanilla and salt in bowl, mixing well.
Add . . . . eggs, 1 at a time, mixing well after each addition.
Pour . . . . into pie shell.
Bake . . . . on baking sheet at 325 degrees for 25 to 30 minutes, or until set.
Combine . . . . sour cream, 2 tablespoons sugar and 1/4 teaspoon vanilla in bowl.
Spread . . . . . over pie.
Bake . . . . for 10 minutes longer; cool.
Chill . . . . until firm.
Garnish . . . . . with fruit.

Sabrina Snyder
Duncan H. S., Duncan

MICROWAVE CHOCOLATE PIE

1/4 c. flour
3 tbsp. cocoa
1/2 tsp. salt
3/4 c. sugar
2 c. milk
3 egg yolks, beaten
2 tbsp. margarine
1/2 tsp. vanilla extract
1 baked pie shell
1 recipe meringue

Mix . . . . flour, cocoa, salt and sugar in bowl.
Microwave . . milk in glass bowl on High for 3 minutes.

134

Stir .... flour mixture into milk until sugar dissolves.

Mix .... a small amount of mixture into egg yolks; stir egg yolks into milk mixture.

Microwave .. on High for 3 minutes longer or until mixture thickens.

Stir .... in margarine and vanilla.

Pour .... into pie shell.

Top .... with meringue.

Bake .... at 400 degrees until lightly browned.

Deanna Reeves
Granite H. S., Granite

CUSTARD PIE

4 eggs, slightly beaten
2 egg whites
1/2 c. sugar
1/4 tsp. salt
2 c. milk, scalded
1 unbaked 9-in. pie shell
1/2 tsp. nutmeg

Combine .... eggs, egg whites, sugar and salt in bowl, beating well.

Stir .... milk into egg mixture very gradually.

Pour .... into pie shell.

Bake .... at 350 degrees for 30 minutes or until set.

Sprinkle .... with nutmeg.

Yields ...... 8 servings.

Teri Lyn Stringer
Waurika H. S., Waurika

OREO PIE

3 egg whites
1/2 c. sugar
1/2 c. chopped nuts
12 Oreo cookies, crushed
Whipped topping

Beat .... egg whites and sugar in bowl until stiff peaks form.

Fold .... in nuts and crushed Oreos.

Spoon ...... into buttered 8-inch pie plate.

Bake .... at 350 degrees for 30 minutes.

Spread .... whipped topping over top.

Sherri Lynn Olson
Waynoka H. S., Waynoka

COCONUT DREAM PIE

1 pkg. whipped topping mix
2 3/4 c. milk
1 pkg. vanilla instant pudding mix
1 can flaked coconut
1 baked 9-in. pie shell

Prepare ..... whipped topping mix in mixer bowl according to package directions, using 1 cup milk.

Beat .... in remaining 1 3/4 cups milk and pudding mix at high speed for 2 minutes, scraping bowl occasionally.

Stir .... in coconut.

Spoon ...... into pie shell.

Chill .... for 4 hours or longer.

Sheila Dromgoole
Geary H. S., Geary

LEMONADE PIES

1 sm. carton whipped topping
1 can sweetened condensed milk
1 sm. can frozen pink lemonade concentrate, thawed
2 9-in. graham cracker pie shells

Blend ...... whipped topping, condensed milk and lemon concentrate in bowl.

Spoon ...... into pie shells.

Freeze ...... until firm.

Felicia D. Winfrey
Eisenhower Sr. H. S., Lawton

EASY PECAN PIES

1 c. sugar
2 tbsp. flour
3 eggs
1 c. dark corn syrup
2 tbsp. melted butter
1 tsp. vanilla extract
1 c. pecans
2 unbaked 9-in. pie shells

Mix .... sugar and flour in bowl.

Beat .... in next 4 ingredients with fork.

Spread ..... pecans over bottom of pie shells.

Pour .... corn syrup mixture over pecans.

Bake .... at 350 degrees for 45 minutes.

Dina Scribner
Bray-Doyle H. S., Foster

Desserts

MAPLE PECAN PIE

5 tbsp. cornstarch
1/3 c. packed brown sugar
2/3 c. sugar
2 1/2 c. milk
1/4 c. margarine
2 egg yolks
1/2 tsp. salt
1/2 c. chopped pecans
1/2 tsp. maple flavoring
1 9-in. baked pie shell
1/2 pt. whipping cream

Blend ...... cornstarch, brown sugar and 1/3 cup sugar in saucepan.
Mix .... in milk, margarine, egg yolks and salt.
Cook ...... until thickened; remove from heat.
Stir .... in pecans and flavoring; cool.
Spoon ...... into pie shell.
Spread ..... with cream whipped with 1/3 cup sugar.

Brenda Oney
Okeene H. S., Okeene

PECAN PIE WITH MIXER PIE CRUST

3 eggs
2/3 c. sugar
1/2 tsp. salt
1/3 c. butter, softened
1 c. corn syrup
1 c. pecans
1/2 recipe Mixer Pie Crust

Beat .... first 5 ingredients in bowl.
Stir .... in pecans.
Pour .... into pastry-lined pie plate.
Bake .... at 375 degrees for 40 to 50 minutes, or until set.

Mixer Pie Crust

Beat 2 cups flour, 1 teaspoon salt and 2/3 cup shortening in mixer bowl until crumbly. Stir in 1 tablespoon vinegar. Stir in water, 1 tablespoon at a time, until dough forms ball. Roll into two 8-inch circles between sheets of waxed paper.

Brenda Stegall
Gould H. S., Gould

FAVORITE FROZEN PEANUT BUTTER PIE

4 oz. cream cheese, softened
1 c. confectioners' sugar
1/3 c. peanut butter
1/2 c. milk
1/2 12-oz. carton whipped topping
1 graham cracker pie shell

Beat .... cream cheese and confectioners' sugar in bowl until smooth.
Mix .... in peanut butter and milk.
Fold .... in whipped topping.
Spoon ...... into pie shell.
Freeze ...... for 6 to 8 hours or overnight.
Yields ...... 6-8 servings.

Amber Leach
Sharon-Mutual H. S., Mutual

CREAMY PEANUT BUTTER PIE

1/2 c. sugar
1/2 c. flour
1/4 tsp. salt
3 c. milk
4 eggs, separated
1/4 c. creamy peanut butter
1/4 c. coarsely chopped peanuts (opt.)
1 baked 9-in. pie shell
1 recipe meringue

Mix .... sugar, flour and salt in saucepan.
Stir .... in milk gradually.
Cook .... until thickened, stirring constantly; reduce heat.
Simmer ..... for 2 minutes longer, stirring constantly; remove from heat.
Stir .... 1 cup hot mixture into beaten egg yolks; stir egg yolks into hot mixture.
Bring .... to a boil.
Cook .... for 2 minutes longer, stirring constantly; remove from heat.
Stir .... in peanut butter until smooth.
Mix .... in peanuts.
Pour .... into pie shell.
Top .... with meringue.
Bake .... at 450 degrees for 10 to 12 minutes, or until lightly browned.

Stephanie Harrel
Elmore City H. S., Elmore City

VANILLA PEANUT BUTTER PIE

1/2 c. peanut butter
3/4 c. confectioners' sugar
1 baked 9-in. pie shell
1 sm. package French vanilla instant
*   pudding mix*
1 sm. carton whipped topping

Cut . . . . peanut butter into confectioners' sugar in bowl until crumbly.
Sprinkle . . . . 2/3 of the mixture in bottom of pie shell.
Prepare . . . . . pudding mix using package directions.
Spoon . . . . . . over peanut butter layer.
Top . . . . with whipped topping and remaining peanut butter mixture.
Chill . . . . . . until set.
Yields . . . . . . 6-8 servings.

Sue Lawson
Haworth H. S., Haworth

PINEAPPLE CHESS PIES

3/4 c. margarine, softened
3 c. sugar
1/2 c. flour
4 eggs, beaten
3 c. crushed pineapple, drained
1 1/2 c. flaked coconut
2 unbaked pie shells

Cream . . . . . . margarine, sugar and flour in bowl.
Mix . . . . in eggs.
Stir . . . . in pineapple and coconut.
Spoon . . . . . . into pie shells.
Bake . . . . at 350 degrees for 50 to 60 minutes or until pies are set.

Debra Thompson Hamilton
Mountain View H. S., Mountain View

MILLIONAIRE PIES

1 lg. carton whipped topping
1 can sweetened condensed milk
2 tsp. lemon juice
1 lg. can crushed pineapple, drained
1 sm. jar maraschino cherries, drained,
*   chopped*

1 c. chopped pecans
2 graham cracker pie shells

Blend . . . . . . whipped topping, condensed milk and lemon juice in bowl.
Stir . . . . in pineapple, cherries and pecans.
Spoon . . . . . . into pie shells.
Chill . . . . for several hours.
Yields . . . . . . 2 pies.

Rochelle Craig
Indian Capital Vo-Tech., Muskogee

ELEGANT MILLION DOLLAR PIE

1 can sweetened condensed milk
1/4 c. lemon juice
1   15-oz. can crushed pineapple, drained
Maraschino cherries, chopped
1/2 c. chopped pecans
1 lg. carton whipped topping
1   8-in. graham cracker pie shell

Blend . . . . . . condensed milk and lemon juice in bowl.
Stir . . . . in next 4 ingredients.
Spoon . . . . . . into pie shell.
Chill . . . . in refrigerator.
Yields . . . . . . 6-8 servings.

Louise Cooks
Macomb H. S., Tecumseh

QUANTITY PIE DOUGH

1 c. light corn syrup
1/3 c. sugar
1 tbsp. salt
1   3-lb. can shortening
1   5-lb. package flour

Mix . . . . corn syrup, sugar and salt in 1-quart container.
Add . . . . enough water to fill container; mix well.
Cut . . . . shortening into flour in bowl until crumbly.
Mix . . . . in corn syrup mixture.
Shape . . . . . . into balls.
Freeze . . . . . . in freezer storage bags.
Yields . . . . . . 20 pie crusts.

Tangee Hughes
Boise City H. S., Boise City

Desserts

KIM'S PIE CRUST

15 tbsp. shortening
2 c. flour
1 tsp. salt

Cut .... shortening into flour and salt in bowl until crumbly.
Mix .... a small amount of flour mixture and 1/4 cup water in bowl until smooth.
Stir .... into flour mixture; mix well.
Roll .... on floured surface.

Kim Ogg
Byng H. S., Ada

FAVORITE BANANA SPLIT CAKE

1 1/4 c. margarine
2 c. graham cracker crumbs
2 eggs
2 c. confectioners' sugar
1 tsp. vanilla extract
1 20-oz. can crushed pineapple, drained
4 bananas, sliced
1 8-oz. carton whipped topping
1/2 c. chopped nuts

Combine .... 1/2 cup melted margarine and graham cracker crumbs in bowl, mixing well.
Press .... mixture into 9 x 13-inch pan.
Beat .... eggs in mixer bowl until fluffy.
Add .... confectioners' sugar, 3/4 cup margarine and vanilla.
Beat .... at medium speed for 5 minutes.
Spoon ...... over crumb crust.
Chill .... for 30 minutes.
Layer ...... pineapple, bananas and whipped topping over creamed layer.
Sprinkle .... with nuts.
Chill .... for 6 hours.

Beverly Hasenbeck
Tomlinson Jr. H. S., Lawton

PARTY BANANA SPLIT DESSERT

2 c. crushed graham crackers
Butter
2 eggs
2 c. confectioners' sugar
1 tbsp. vanilla extract
1 lg. can crushed pineapple
3 lg. bananas, sliced

1 16-oz. carton whipped topping
Chopped nuts
Maraschino cherries

Combine .... graham cracker crumbs and 2/3 cup melted butter in bowl, mixing well.
Press .... in bottom of 9 x 13-inch baking pan.
Cream ...... 1 cup softened butter, eggs, confectioners' sugar and vanilla in bowl.
Drain ...... pineapple, reserving juice.
Dip .... banana slices in pineapple juice.
Layer ...... creamed mixture, bananas, pineapple, whipped topping, nuts and maraschino cherries over crumb layer.
Chill .... for 8 hours.

Donna Pleere
Gould H. S., Gould

BLACKBERRY BUCKLE

1/2 c. butter, softened
1 c. sugar
1 egg, beaten
1 1/3 c. flour
1 1/2 tsp. baking powder
1/8 tsp. salt
1/3 c. milk
1 tsp. vanilla extract
2 c. blackberries, sweetened
1/2 tsp. cinnamon

Cream ...... 1/4 cup butter and 1/2 cup sugar in bowl.
Beat .... in egg.
Sift .... in 1 cup flour, baking powder and salt alternately with milk and vanilla, mixing well after each addition.
Pour .... into greased and floured 7-inch pan.
Top .... with blackberries.
Combine .... 1/4 cup butter and 1/2 cup sugar in bowl.
Stir .... in 1/3 cup flour and cinnamon until crumbly.
Sprinkle .... over blackberries.
Bake .... at 375 degrees for 45 minutes or until set.

Thedia Beesley
Beggs H. S., Beggs

HEAVENLY BLUEBERRY DESSERT

1 1/2 sticks margarine, melted
1 1/2 c. flour
2 tbsp. sugar
1 c. chopped pecans
2 pkg. whipped topping mix, prepared
2 8-oz. packages cream cheese, softened
1 16-oz. package confectioners' sugar
2 cans blueberry pie filling

Combine .... margarine, flour, sugar and pecans in bowl, mixing well.
Press .... into 9 x 13-inch baking pan.
Bake .... at 300 degrees for 20 minutes; cool.
Mix .... whipped topping, cream cheese and confectioners' sugar in bowl.
Spoon ...... over baked layer.
Chill .... for 20 to 30 minutes or until set.
Spread ..... pie filling over top.
Chill .... until firm.

Renee Ford
Heavener H. S., Heavener

CHEESECAKE REGENCY

1 1/2 c. graham cracker crumbs
2 1/4 c. sugar
1/2 c. melted butter
1/8 tsp. salt
3 8-oz. packages cream cheese, softened
4 eggs
2 tsp. vanilla extract
1 16-oz. carton sour cream
1 sm. can crushed pineapple in heavy syrup
2 tbsp. cornstarch

Combine .... crumbs, 1/4 cup sugar and butter in bowl, mixing well.
Press .... into bottom and 1 1/2 inches up side of springform pan.
Cream ...... 1 1/2 cups sugar, salt and cream cheese in bowl.
Add .... eggs, 1 at a time, mixing well after each addition.
Beat .... in 1 teaspoon vanilla.
Pour .... into prepared pan.
Bake .... at 350 degrees for 50 minutes; remove from oven.
Let .... stand for 15 minutes.
Blend ...... sour cream, 1/4 cup sugar and 1 teaspoon vanilla in bowl.
Spread ..... over cheesecake.
Bake .... at 450 degrees for 15 minutes; cool.
Combine .... pineapple, 1/2 cup sugar and cornstarch in saucepan, mixing well.
Cook .... until thickened.
Spread ..... over top of cooled cheesecake.
Yields ...... 12 servings.

Donna L. Smith
Union H. S., Tulsa

PEACHY CHOCOLATE CHEESECAKE

1 c. ground toasted almonds
3/4 c. vanilla wafer crumbs
1/4 c. confectioners' sugar
1/2 c. butter
Sugar
11 oz. cream cheese, softened
1 1/4 c. semisweet chocolate chips, melted
2 1/2 tsp. vanilla extract
2 c. whipping cream, whipped
1 tsp. unflavored gelatin
1/2 c. chopped sweetened peaches, drained

Combine .... almonds, crumbs, confectioners' sugar and 1/4 cup melted butter in bowl, mixing well.
Press .... over bottom and up side of 9-inch springform pan.
Cream ...... 1/3 cup sugar, 1/4 cup softened butter and cream cheese in bowl.
Beat .... in melted chocolate and 1 1/2 teaspoons vanilla.
Fold .... in half the whipped cream.
Spoon ...... into prepared pan.
Chill .... in refrigerator.
Soften ...... gelatin in 1 tablespoon cold water.
Add .... 2 tablespoons boiling water, stirring until dissolved.
Beat .... 2 tablespoons sugar into remaining whipped cream.
Blend ...... in gelatin and 1 teaspoon vanilla.
Fold .... in chopped peaches.
Spoon ...... over chocolate layer.
Chill .... until firm.
Garnish ..... with sliced peaches and chocolate curls.

Photograph for this recipe on page 105.

Desserts

CHOCOLATE-CHOCOLATE CHIP CHEESECAKE

3 tbsp. butter, melted
1 c. crushed chocolate wafers
Sugar
4 8-oz. packages cream cheese, softened
4 eggs
1 1/2 c. sour cream
Vanilla to taste
1 c. miniature chocolate chips
8 oz. semisweet chocolate, melted

Mix . . . . butter, wafer crumbs and 2 tablespoons sugar in bowl.
Press . . . . . . into bottom of greased 9-inch springform pan; freeze.
Combine . . . . cream cheese and 1 cup sugar in mixer bowl.
Beat . . . . on high until smooth.
Add . . . . eggs 2 at a time, mixing well after each addition.
Stir . . . . in sour cream, vanilla, chocolate chips and chocolate.
Spoon . . . . . . into prepared pan.
Wrap . . . . sides of pan with foil.
Place . . . . in 2 inches water in large pan.
Bake . . . . at 275 degrees for 1 1/2 to 2 hours or until firm.
Unwrap . . . . . and cool on wire rack for 45 minutes.
Chill . . . . covered, for 5 hours or longer.
Garnish . . . . . with chocolate curls.
Yields . . . . . . 16 servings.

Jo Ann Cochran
Shawnee H. S., Shawnee

MARBLE CHEESECAKE

1 pkg. graham crackers, crushed
Sugar
1/3 c. butter, softened
1 6-oz. package semisweet chocolate chips
2 8-oz. packages cream cheese, softened
1/2 c. sour cream
Vanilla extract to taste
3 eggs

Combine . . . . graham cracker crumbs, 2 tablespoons sugar and butter in bowl, mixing well.
Press . . . . in bottom and 1 inch up side of 9-inch springform pan.

Melt . . . . chocolate chips with 1 cup sugar in double boiler; set aside.
Beat . . . . cream cheese in mixer bowl on high speed until light and fluffy.
Add . . . . sour cream, vanilla, 3/4 cup sugar and eggs; beat on high speed after each addition.
Stir . . . . chocolate chip mixture into half the batter.
Spoon . . . . . . into prepared pan.
Pour . . . . remaining batter over top, swirling to marbleize.
Bake . . . . at 325 degrees for 50 minutes or until nearly set.
Cool . . . . and remove side of pan.
Chill . . . . in refrigerator.
Yields . . . . . . 8-12 servings.

Kay Eggleton
Caddo H. S., Caddo

CHOCOLATE ALMOND RING

1/2 c. margarine
1 c. sifted flour
4 eggs
4 1/2 c. milk
1 lg. package chocolate instant pudding mix
1 sm. package vanilla instant pudding mix
2 3-oz. packages cream cheese, softened
1 8-oz. carton whipped topping
3/4 c. confectioners' sugar
1/2 c. sliced almonds

Bring . . . . 1 cup water and margarine to a boil in saucepan.
Stir . . . . in flour.
Cook . . . . for 1 minute or until mixture forms ball, stirring constantly; remove from heat.
Beat . . . . in eggs 1 at a time.
Spread . . . . . into 9-inch ring on baking sheet.
Bake . . . . at 400 degrees for 45 to 50 minutes or until dry; cool.
Slice . . . . off top; scoop out soft dough.
Beat . . . . milk and pudding mixes in mixer bowl on low speed for 2 minutes.
Blend . . . . . . cream cheese, half the whipped topping and confectioners' sugar in bowl.
Stir . . . . into pudding mixture.

Spoon . . . . . . 3/4 of the pudding mixture into ring.

Swirl . . . . half the remaining whipped topping over top.

Sprinkle . . . . with half the almonds; replace top.

Layer . . . . . . remaining pudding and whipped topping over ring.

Sprinkle . . . . with remaining almonds.

Balko FHA, Balko

CHOCOLATE ANGEL FOOD DESSERT

1 lg. package chocolate chips, melted
4 eggs, separated
1 pt. whipping cream
1/2 c. sugar
2 c. chopped pecans
1 angel food cake, broken into sm. pieces

Mix . . . . melted chocolate chips and beaten egg yolks in bowl.

Fold . . . . in stiffly beaten egg whites.

Whip . . . . cream with sugar in bowl.

Fold . . . . into chocolate mixture.

Stir . . . . in pecans.

Layer . . . . . . half the cake and chocolate mixture in 9 x 13-inch dish.

Repeat . . . . . layers with remaining ingredients.

Chill . . . . in refrigerator.

Allison Evans
Binger H. S., Binger

CHOCOLATE MOUSSE

1 3-oz. package cream cheese, softened
2/3 c. sugar
1/3 c. cocoa
1/4 c. milk
1 tsp. vanilla extract
1 1/2 c. whipping cream, whipped

Beat . . . . cream cheese and sugar in mixer bowl until smooth.

Blend . . . . . . in cocoa, milk and vanilla.

Fold . . . . in whipped cream.

Spoon . . . . . . into dessert dishes.

Chill . . . . until firm.

Garnish . . . . . with fresh fruit. Mousse may be frozen.

Photograph for this recipe on page 105.

FROSTED CHOCOLATE ECLAIR DESSERT

2 pkg. vanilla instant pudding mix
3 c. milk
1 8-oz. carton whipped topping
Graham crackers
3/4 stick butter, melted
2 tbsp. cocoa
1 tsp. vanilla extract
1/4 c. hot coffee
1 1/2 c. confectioners' sugar

Prepare . . . . . pudding mix according to package directions, using 3 cups milk.

Fold . . . . in whipped topping.

Layer . . . . . . graham crackers and pudding mixture alternately in greased 9 x 13-inch pan, ending with crackers.

Blend . . . . . . remaining ingredients in bowl.

Spread . . . . . over top layer.

Yields . . . . . . 25 servings.

Tracey Laubach
Okeene H. S., Okeene

MAKE-AHEAD CHOCOLATE ECLAIR CAKE

Milk
2 pkg. vanilla instant pudding mix
1 8-oz. carton whipped topping
Graham crackers
2 sq. chocolate, melted
3 tbsp. butter, melted
2 tbsp. light corn syrup
1 tbsp. vanilla extract
1 1/2 c. confectioners' sugar

Mix . . . . 3 cups milk and pudding mix in bowl.

Fold . . . . in whipped topping.

Layer . . . . . . graham crackers and pudding mixture alternately in 9 x 13-inch pan, ending with graham crackers.

Blend . . . . . . remaining ingredients and 3 tablespoons milk in bowl.

Spread . . . . . over top.

Chill . . . . for 24 hours.

Amy Fast
Weatherford H. S., Weatherford

Desserts

PARTY CHOCOLATE DESSERT

1 c. flour
1 stick margarine, melted
Sugar
1 lg. package cream cheese, softened
1 pkg. each vanilla, chocolate instant
    pudding mix
2 c. milk
1/2 lg. carton whipped topping
1 chocolate candy bar, grated (opt.)

Combine .... flour, margarine and 2 table-spoons sugar in bowl, mixing well.
Press .... in bottom of 9 x 12-inch baking pan.
Bake .... at 350 degrees for 8 minutes.
Mix .... cream cheese and 1 cup sugar in bowl.
Mix .... pudding mixes with milk in bowl.
Layer ...... cream cheese mixture and pudding mixture over crust.
Top .... with whipped topping and grated chocolate.
Yields ...... 8 servings.

Stephanie Arnold
Choctaw Jr. H. S., Choctaw

CRISPY CREAMY FREEZE

1/4 c. oil
1 3/4 c. M and M's plain chocolate
    candies
1 1/2 c. crisp rice cereal
1 qt. ice cream, slightly softened

Combine .... oil and 1 1/2 cups candies in saucepan.
Cook .... over very low heat, stirring constantly and crushing candies until chocolate melts but color coating is visible; remove from heat.
Stir .... in cereal.
Press .... into 9-inch square baking pan lined with oiled foil extending several inches beyond edge.
Freeze ...... for 30 minutes.
Spread ..... ice cream over crust.
Sprinkle .... with 1/4 cup chopped candies.
Freeze ...... covered, overnight.
Lift .... from pan using foil liner.
Cut .... into squares.

Photograph for this recipe on this page.

LAYERED PUDDING CAKE

1 stick margarine
1 c. flour
1 c. chopped pecans
1 c. sifted confectioners' sugar
1 8-oz. package cream cheese, softened
2 1/2 c. whipped topping
1 lg. package each chocolate, vanilla
    instant pudding mix
6 c. milk
1 chocolate candy bar, grated

Combine .... margarine, flour and pecans in bowl, mixing well.
Press .... in bottom of 9 x 13-inch baking dish.
Bake .... at 350 degrees for 20 minutes; cool.
Cream ...... confectioners' sugar, cream cheese and 1 cup whipped topping in bowl.
Prepare ..... pudding mixes according to package directions using 3 cups milk for each.

Layer ...... cream cheese mixture, chocolate pudding, vanilla pudding and 1 1/2 cups whipped topping over crust.

Sprinkle .... with grated chocolate.

Chill .... in refrigerator.

Diane Selman
W. District State Vice President
Arapaho H. S., Arapaho

ELEGANT FOUR-LAYER DESSERT

1 1/2 c. flour
1/4 tsp. salt
1 1/2 sticks margarine, melted
1 c. chopped pecans
1 c. confectioners' sugar
1 8-oz. package cream cheese, softened
1 c. whipped topping
1 lg. package chocolate instant pudding
   mix

Combine .... flour, salt, margarine and pecans in bowl, mixing well.

Press .... into 9 x 13-inch baking pan.

Bake .... at 350 degrees for 20 minutes; cool.

Cream ...... confectioners' sugar and cream cheese in bowl; fold in whipped topping.

Spread ..... over baked layer.

Prepare ..... pudding mix, using package directions.

Spread ..... over cream cheese layer.

Top .... with additional whipped topping and pecans.

Chill .... in refrigerator.

Mary Ann Cleer
Gould H. S., Gould

NEXT DOOR NEIGHBOR CAKE

1 stick margarine, softened
1 c. flour
1 c. finely chopped nuts
1 8-oz. package cream cheese, softened
1 c. confectioners' sugar
1 8-oz. carton whipped topping
1 sm. package each vanilla, chocolate
   instant pudding mix
3 c. milk
1 chocolate candy bar, grated
Chocolate syrup

Combine .... margarine, flour and nuts in bowl, mixing well.

Press .... into bottom of 9 x 13-inch pan.

Bake .... at 350 degrees for 20 minutes; cool.

Blend ...... cream cheese, confectioners' sugar and 1 cup whipped topping in bowl.

Beat .... pudding mixes and milk in bowl until thick.

Layer ...... cream cheese mixture and pudding mixture over crust.

Spread ..... remaining whipped topping over top.

Sprinkle .... with grated chocolate.

Drizzle ..... chocolate syrup in stripes over top.

Julie Bartel
Balko H. S., Balko

THREE-LAYER DESSERT

1 c. flour
1 c. chopped pecans
1 stick margarine, melted
1 8-oz. package cream cheese, softened
2 c. whipped topping
1 c. confectioners' sugar
1 sm. package each vanilla, chocolate
   instant pudding mix
3 c. milk
1 chocolate candy bar, grated

Combine .... flour, pecans and margarine in bowl, mixing well.

Press .... in bottom of 9 x 13-inch pan.

Bake .... at 350 degrees for 15 minutes; cool.

Combine .... cream cheese, whipped topping and confectioners' sugar in mixer bowl.

Beat .... on high until smooth.

Combine .... pudding mixes and milk in mixer bowl.

Beat .... on high until thickened.

Layer ...... cream cheese mixture and pudding mixture over crust.

Top .... with additional whipped topping.

Sprinkle .... with grated chocolate.

Yields ...... 15 servings.

Jennifer Washburn
Berryhill H. S., Tulsa

Desserts

FANTASTIC DESSERT

1 stick butter, melted
1/2 c. chopped pecans
1 1/4 c. confectioners' sugar
1 c. flour
1 8-oz. package cream cheese, softened
1 c. whipped topping
1 pkg. chocolate instant pudding mix
1 3/4 c. milk

Combine .... butter, pecans, 1/4 cup confectioners' sugar and flour in bowl, mixing well.
Press .... in bottom of baking pan.
Bake .... at 325 degrees for 15 minutes.
Blend ...... cream cheese, 1 cup confectioners' sugar and whipped topping in bowl.
Mix .... pudding mix and milk in bowl.
Layer ...... cream cheese mixture and pudding over baked layer.
Spread ..... additional whipped topping over top.

Kaye Hardeman
Checotah H. S., Checotah

RICH FOUR-LAYER PIE

1 stick margarine, melted
1 c. flour
1/2 c. chopped nuts
1 c. confectioners' sugar
1 16-oz. carton whipped topping
1 8-oz. package cream cheese, softened
2 sm. packages chocolate instant pudding mix
3 c. milk

Combine .... margarine, flour and nuts in bowl, mixing well.
Press .... into 12 x 15-inch baking pan.
Bake .... at 375 degrees for 15 minutes.
Cream ...... confectioners' sugar, 1 cup whipped topping and cream cheese in bowl.
Spread ..... over baked layer.
Mix .... pudding mix with milk in bowl.
Pour .... over cream cheese layer.
Top .... with remaining whipped topping and additional nuts.
Chill .... for several hours.

Shannon Skaggs
Checotah H. S., Checotah

CHOCOLATE CREAM CRUNCH

1/2 c. margarine, softened
1 c. flour
1 c. finely chopped pecans
1 8-oz. package cream cheese, softened
1 c. confectioners' sugar
1 c. whipped topping
1 6-oz. package each chocolate, vanilla instant pudding mix
3 c. milk

Combine .... margarine, flour and pecans in bowl, mixing well.
Press .... in bottom of 9 x 13-inch pan.
Bake .... at 350 degrees for 20 minutes; cool.
Beat .... cream cheese and confectoners' sugar in bowl until fluffy.
Fold .... in whipped topping.
Prepare ..... pudding mixes using 1 1/2 cups milk for each.
Layer ...... cream cheese mixture, chocolate and vanilla puddings over crust.
Spread ..... additional whipped topping over top.
Yields ...... 16-20 servings.

Traci Clester
Okeene H. S., Okeene
Linda Boardman
Midwest City H. S., Midwest City

GINGERBREAD WITH LEMON SAUCE

1/2 c. shortening
1/4 c. packed brown sugar
1 egg
1/2 c. light molasses
1 1/2 c. flour
3/4 tsp. each ginger, cinnamon
1/2 tsp. each baking powder, soda
Salt
1 tbsp. cornstarch
1/8 tsp. nutmeg
1/2 c. sugar
2 tbsp. butter
2 tbsp. lemon juice

Cream ...... shortening and brown sugar in bowl.
Mix .... in egg and molasses.
Combine .... next 5 dry ingredients and 1/2 teaspoon salt in bowl.

Add .... to creamed mixture alternately with 1/2 cup boiling water, mixing well after each addition. Do not overbeat.

Pour .... into 9-inch round baking pan.

Bake .... at 350 degrees for 30 to 35 minutes or until gingerbread tests done.

Combine .... cornstarch, 1/8 teaspoon salt, nutmeg and sugar in saucepan.

Stir .... in 1 cup water.

Cook .... until thick and bubbly, stirring constantly.

Stir .... in butter and lemon juice.

Pour .... over gingerbread.

Yields ...... 8 servings.

Juanita Boyce
Lawton H. S., Lawton

COLORFUL ICE CREAMWICHES

3/4 c. margarine, softened
3/4 c. creamy peanut butter
1 1/4 c. packed light brown sugar
1 egg
1 tsp. vanilla extract
1 1/4 c. flour
1 tsp. soda
1/4 tsp. salt
1 c. chopped M and M's plain chocolate candies
3 pt. vanilla or chocolate ice cream, slightly softened

Beat .... first 3 ingredients in mixer bowl until fluffy.

Add .... egg and vanilla, mixing well.

Mix .... in combined flour, soda and salt.

Stir .... in candies.

Shape ...... into 1 1/4-inch balls.

Place .... 3 inches apart on greased cookie sheet; flatten to 1/4-inch thickness.

Sprinkle .... with additional chopped candies; press in lightly.

Bake .... at 350 degrees for 10 to 12 minutes or until edges are lightly browned.

Cool .... on sheet for 3 minutes before removing to wire rack to cool completely.

Spread ..... 1/2 cup ice cream on each of half the cookies.

Top .... with remaining cookies.

Freeze ...... wrapped in foil, until firm.

Photograph for this recipe on page 142.

SUNNY SPRINKLES

1/3 to 1/2 c. chopped toasted almonds
1/3 c. finely chopped dried apricots
1/3 c. finely chopped dried pineapple
1/3 c. raisins
1/2 c. coconut
1/2 c. granola
1/2 c. sunflower seeds
1/2 c. coarsely chopped M and M's plain chocolate candies

Combine .... almonds with choice of any ingredients in any combination.

Sprinkle .... 1 to 2 tablespoonfuls over ice cream.

Photograph for this recipe on page 142.

HEAVENLY HASH AND VIBRANT VANILLA SUPER SCOOPS

1 qt. chocolate ice cream
3/4 c. marshmallow creme
1 c. chopped toasted almonds
3/4 to 1 c. chopped M and M's plain chocolate candies, frozen

Place .... ice cream in bowl.

Let .... stand for 5 minutes or until slightly softened.

Beat .... with wooden spoon until of spreading consistency.

Stir .... in marshmallow creme until marbleized.

Fold .... in almonds and candies.

Spoon ...... into original ice cream container.

Freeze ...... until firm.

Vibrant Vanilla

Prepare as above using 1 quart vanilla ice cream, 3/4 cup chopped M and M's and 1/4 teaspoon orange or lemon extract.

Photograph for this recipe on page 142.

Desserts

BUTTERFINGER ICE CREAM

6 eggs
2 c. sugar
3 pt. half and half, scalded
Milk
5 lg. Butterfinger candy bars, crushed

Beat . . . . eggs and sugar in bowl until fluffy.
Mix . . . . in hot half and half.
Pour . . . . into freezer container.
Add . . . . enough milk to fill 2/3 full; cool.
Add . . . . candy.
Freeze . . . . . . according to freezer directions.
Yields . . . . . . 1 gallon.

Raeanne Carson
Byng H. S., Ada

HEAVENLY CHOCOLATE ICE CREAM

1 can sweetened condensed milk
2 qt. chocolate milk
1/8 tsp. salt
1 lg. carton whipped topping

Blend . . . . . . condensed milk, chocolate milk, salt and whipped topping in bowl.
Spoon . . . . . . into 1 gallon freezer container.
Freeze . . . . . . using freezer directions.
Yields . . . . . . 1 gallon.

Tina Butler
Oney H. S., Albert

PASTEL DESSERT

1 sm. package gelatin
1 sm. package vanilla pudding and pie filling mix
1 8-oz. carton whipped topping

Combine . . . . gelatin and pudding mix in saucepan.
Add . . . . 1 1/2 cups water, mixing well.
Cook . . . . for 5 minutes or until thickened, stirring frequently.
Chill . . . . until partially set.
Fold . . . . in whipped topping.
Spoon . . . . . . into individual serving dishes.
Chill . . . . in refrigerator.
Garnish . . . . . with fruit.

Donna Robinson
Carrier Jr. H. S., Nash

PEACH CAKE COBBLER

1 lg. can peaches
3 tbsp. cornstarch
1/3 c. milk
1 pkg. cake mix

Bring . . . . peaches to a boil in saucepan.
Add . . . . cornstarch blended with milk.
Cook . . . . until thick, stirring frequently.
Spoon . . . . . . into baking pan.
Prepare . . . . . cake mix using package directions.
Pour . . . . over peaches.
Bake . . . . at 350 degrees for 30 to 35 minutes or until cake tests done.
Yields . . . . . . 20 servings.

Kathy Rosebrook
Ringwood H. S., Ringwood

PIZELLES

3 1/2 sticks margarine, softened
12 eggs
3 c. sugar
1 tsp. salt
1 tbsp. vanilla extract
Flour
1 tbsp. almond extract
2/3 tsp. aniseed

Mix . . . . margarine, eggs, sugar, salt and vanilla in bowl.
Stir . . . . in enough flour to make stiff dough.
Add . . . . almond flavoring and aniseed, mixing well.
Bake . . . . 1 tablespoonful at a time in Pizelle iron until lightly browned.

Steve Rohloff
Bray-Doyle H. S., Marlow

SOUTHERN INDIAN PUDDING

1 /2 c. quick-cooking grits
1/4 tsp. salt
1/3 c. sugar
1 tsp. butter
3 eggs, beaten
1/4 c. chopped almonds
1 tsp. vanilla extract
1 1/3 c. milk

1 tsp. cinnamon
1/4 c. raisins

Prepare . . . . . grits in 2 cups boiling water with salt in saucepan according to package directions.
Stir . . . . in sugar and butter.
Combine . . . . remaining ingredients in bowl, mixing well.
Stir . . . . into grits mixture.
Spoon . . . . . . into casserole.
Bake . . . . at 350 degrees for 30 minutes, or until set.

Felicia Young
Eisenhower Sr. H. S., Lawton

LAYERED STRAWBERRY DESSERT

1/2 lb. vanilla wafers, crushed
1/2 c. butter, softened
2 1/2 c. confectioners' sugar
2 eggs
1 qt. strawberries, sliced in half
1/2 pt. whipping cream, whipped
Sugar to taste

Spread . . . . . wafer crumbs in bottom of greased dish.
Beat . . . . butter, confectioners' sugar and eggs in bowl.
Pour . . . . over cookie crumbs.
Arrange . . . . . strawberries over filling.
Top . . . . with whipped cream sweetened with sugar.
Sprinkle . . . . with additional cookie crumbs.
Chill . . . . for 12 hours.

Karen Lytle
Kingston H. S. FHA, Kingston

STRAWBERRY GELATIN SUPREME

1 lg. package strawberry gelatin
1 c. marshmallows
1 pkg. frozen strawberries, thawed
1/2 c. chopped nuts
Whipped topping

Dissolve . . . . gelatin in 2 cups boiling water in bowl.
Stir . . . . in marshmallows until melted; add 1 cup cold water.
Chill . . . . until partially set.
Stir . . . . in strawberries and nuts.
Chill . . . . until partially set.

Fold . . . . in whipped topping.
Chill . . . . until set.
Yields . . . . . . 10 servings.

Julie McDonald
Snyder H. S., Snyder

BABY RUTH TURNOVERS

1 10-count can refrigerator biscuits
1 Baby Ruth candy bar
Oil for deep frying
Confectioners' sugar

Separate . . . . biscuits and roll thin.
Cut . . . . candy bar into 10 pieces.
Place . . . . 1 piece in center of each biscuit; fold over and seal edges.
Deep-fry . . . . until golden brown.
Drain . . . . . . on paper towels.
Sprinkle . . . . with confectioners' sugar.
Yields . . . . . . 10 servings.

LaDeen Loveless
Macomb H. S., Tecumseh

MICROWAVE VANILLA CREAM FILLING

1/4 c. flour
Pinch of salt
3/4 c. sugar
1 1/2 c. milk
2 eggs, beaten
2 tbsp. margarine
2 tsp. vanilla extract

Combine . . . . flour, salt and sugar in glass bowl, mixing well.
Stir . . . . in milk gradually.
Microwave . . on High for 4 minutes, or until mixture boils.
Stir . . . . a small amount of hot mixture into eggs; stir eggs into hot mixture.
Microwave . . for 30 to 60 seconds, until mixture boils.
Blend . . . . . . in margarine and vanilla.
Let . . . . stand, covered, until cool. May add 3 tablespoons cocoa with dry ingredients or fold in 1/2 cup coconut with vanilla.

Sue Hill
Central Jr. H. S., Lawton

Charts

Herb & Spice Chart

Basil can be chopped and added to cold poultry salads. If your recipe calls for tomatoes or tomato sauce, add a touch of basil to bring out a rich flavor.

Bay leaf, the basis of many French seasonings, is nice added to soups, stews, marinades and stuffings.

Bouquet garni, a must in many Creole cuisine recipes, is a bundle of herbs, spices and bay leaf tied together and added to soups, stews or sauces.

Celery seed, from wild celery rather than our domestic celery, adds pleasant flavor to bouillon or stock.

Chervil is one of the traditional *fines herbes* used in French-derived cooking. (The others are tarragon, parsley and chive.) It is particularly good in omelets or soups.

Chives, available fresh, dried or frozen, can be substituted for raw onion in any poultry recipe.

Garlic, one of the oldest herbs in the world, must be carefully handled. When cooking, do not simmer until black or it will create an offensive odor. For best results, press or crush garlic clove against the kitchen table; then cook. If your recipe calls for sliced garlic, substitute grated or pressed garlic. The flavor will improve noticeably.

Marjoram is an aromatic herb of the mint family. It is good in soups, sauces, stuffings and stews.

Mustard (dry) brings a sharp bite to sauces. Sprinkle just a touch over roast chicken for a delightful flavor treat.

Oregano is a staple herb in Italian, Spanish and Mexican cuisines. It is very good in dishes with a tomato foundation; it adds an excellent savory taste.

Paprika, a mild pepper, adds color to many dishes, and it is especially attractive with poultry. The very best paprika is imported from Hungary — there is a world of difference between it and the supermarket variety.

Rosemary, a tasty herb, is an important seasoning in stuffing for duck, partridge and capon.

Sage, the perennial favorite with all kinds of poultry, adds flavor to stuffings. It is particularly good with goose.

Tarragon, one of the *fines herbes,* has wonderful flavor and goes well with all poultry dishes except one; it is too pungent for poultry soups.

Thyme is used in combination with bay leaf in soups and stews.

Allspice, a pungent, aromatic spice, comes in whole or powdered form. It is excellent in marinades, particularly in game marinade, or curries.

Cinnamon, ground from the bark of the cinnamon tree, is important in preparing desserts as well as savory dishes.

Coriander adds an unusual flavor to soups, stews, chili dishes, curries and some desserts.

Cumin is a staple spice in Mexican cooking. To use, rub seeds together and let them fall into the dish just before serving. Cumin also comes in powdered form.

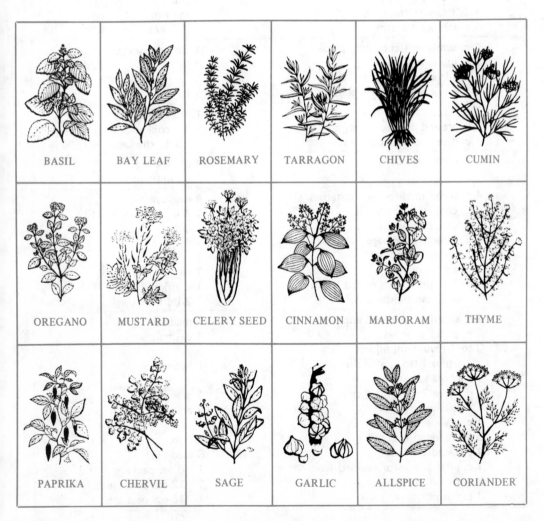

BASIL	BAY LEAF	ROSEMARY	TARRAGON	CHIVES	CUMIN
OREGANO	MUSTARD	CELERY SEED	CINNAMON	MARJORAM	THYME
PAPRIKA	CHERVIL	SAGE	GARLIC	ALLSPICE	CORIANDER

Equivalent Chart

WHEN RECIPE CALLS FOR:	YOU NEED:
BREAD & CEREAL	
1 c. soft bread crumbs	2 slices
1 c. fine dry bread crumbs	4-5 slices
1 c. small bread cubes	2 slices
1 c. fine cracker crumbs	24 saltines
1 c. fine graham cracker crumbs	14 crackers
1 c. vanilla wafer crumbs	22 wafers
1 c. crushed cornflakes	3 c. uncrushed
4 c. cooked macaroni	1 8-oz. package
3 1/2 c. cooked rice	1 c. uncooked
DAIRY	
1 c. freshly grated cheese	1/4 lb.
1 c. cottage cheese or sour cream	1 8-oz. carton
2/3 c. evaporated milk	1 sm. can
1 2/3 c. evaporated milk	1 tall can
1 c. whipped cream	1/2 c. heavy cream
SWEET	
1 c. semisweet chocolate pieces	1 6-oz. package
2 c. granulated sugar	1 lb.
4 c. sifted confectioners' sugar	1 lb.
2 1/4 c. packed brown sugar	1 lb.
MEAT	
3 c. diced cooked meat	1 lb., cooked
2 c. ground cooked meat	1 lb., cooked
4 c. diced cooked chicken	1 5-lb. chicken
NUTS	
1 c. chopped nuts	4 oz. shelled
	1 lb. unshelled
VEGETABLES	
4 c. sliced or diced raw potatoes	4 medium
2 c. cooked green beans	1/2 lb. fresh or 1 16-oz. can
1 c. chopped onion	1 large
4 c. shredded cabbage	1 lb.
2 c. canned tomatoes	1 16-oz. can
1 c. grated carrot	1 large
2 1/2 c. lima beans or red beans	1 c. dried, cooked
1 4-oz. can mushrooms	1/2 lb. fresh
FRUIT	
4 c. sliced or chopped apples	4 medium
2 c. pitted cherries	4 c. unpitted
3 to 4 tbsp. lemon juice plus 1 tsp. grated rind	1 lemon
1/3 c. orange juice plus 2 tsp. grated rind	1 orange
1 c. mashed banana	3 medium
4 c. cranberries	1 lb.
3 c. shredded coconut	1/2 lb.
4 c. sliced peaches	8 medium
1 c. pitted dates or candied fruit	1 8-oz. package
2 c. pitted prunes	1 12-oz. package
3 c. raisins	1 15-oz. package

COMMON EQUIVALENTS

1 tbsp. = 3 tsp.	4 qt. = 1 gal.
2 tbsp. = 1 oz.	6 1/2 to 8-oz. can = 1 c.
4 tbsp. = 1/4 c.	10 1/2 to 12-oz. can = 1 1/4 c.
5 tbsp. + 1 tsp. = 1/3 c.	14 to 16-oz. can (No. 300) = 1 3/4 c.
8 tbsp. = 1/2 c.	16 to 17-oz. can (No. 303) = 2 c.
12 tbsp. = 3/4 c.	1-lb. 4-oz. can or 1-pt. 2-oz. can (No. 2) = 2 1/2 c.
16 tbsp. = 1 c.	1-lb. 13-oz. can (No. 2 1/2) = 3 1/2 c.
1 c. = 8 oz. or 1/2 pt.	3-lb. 3-oz. can or 46-oz. can or 1-qt. 14-oz. can = 5 3/4 c.
4 c. = 1 qt.	6 1/2-lb. or 7-lb. 5-oz. can (No. 10) = 12 to 13 c.

Candy Chart

PRODUCT	TEST IN COLD WATER*	DEGREES F. ON CANDY THERMOMETER			
		SEA LEVEL	2000 FEET	5000 FEET	7500 FEET
FUDGE, PANOCHA, FONDANT	SOFT BALL (can be picked up but flattens)	234° - 240° F.	230° - 236° F.	224° - 230° F.	219° - 225° F.
CARAMELS	FIRM BALL (holds shape unless pressed)	242° - 248° F.	238° - 244° F.	232° - 238° F.	227° - 233° F.
DIVINITY, TAFFY AND CARAMEL CORN	HARD BALL (holds shape though pliable)	250° - 268° F.	246° - 264° F.	240° - 258° F.	235° - 253° F.
BUTTERSCOTCH, ENGLISH TOFFEE	SOFT CRACK (separates into hard threads but not brittle)	270° - 290° F.	266° - 286° F.	260° - 280° F.	255° - 275° F.
BRITTLES	HARD CRACK (separates into hard and brittle threads)	300° - 310° F.	296° - 306° F.	290° - 300° F.	285° - 295° F.

* Drop about 1/2 teaspoon of boiling syrup into one cup water, and test firmness of mass with fingers.

Charts

Substitution Chart

	INSTEAD OF:	USE:
BAKING	1 tsp. baking powder 1 c. sifted all-purpose flour 1 c. sifted cake flour 1 tsp. cornstarch (for thickening)	1/4 tsp. soda plus 1/2 tsp. cream of tartar 1 c. plus 2 tbsp. sifted cake flour 1 c. minus 2 tbsp. sifted all-purpose flour 2 tbsp. flour or 1 tbsp. tapioca

SWEET	1 1-oz. square chocolate
	1 2/3 oz. semisweet
	   chocolate
	1 c. granulated sugar
	
	1 c. honey
		3 to 4 tbsp. cocoa plus 1 tsp. shortening
		1 oz. unsweetened chocolate plus 4 tsp. sugar
		
		1 c. packed brown sugar or 1 c. corn syrup,
		   molasses, honey minus 1/4 c. liquid
		1 to 1 1/4 c. sugar plus 1/4 c. liquid or
		   1 c. molasses or corn syrup

DAIRY	1 c. sweet milk 1 c. sour milk 1 c. buttermilk 1 c. light cream 1 c. heavy cream 1 c. sour cream	1 c. sour milk or buttermilk plus 1/2 tsp. soda 1 c. sweet milk plus 1 tbsp. vinegar or lemon juice of 1 c. buttermilk 1 c. sour milk or 1 c. yogurt 7/8 c. skim milk plus 3 tbsp. butter 3/4 c. skim milk plus 1/3 c. butter 7/8 c. sour milk plus 3 tbsp. butter
	1 c. bread crumbs	3/4 c. cracker crumbs

SEASONINGS	1 c. catsup
	
	1 tbsp. prepared mustard
	1 tsp. Italian spice
	
	1 tsp. allspice
	1 medium onion
	
	1 clove of garlic
	
	1 tsp. lemon juice
		1 c. tomato sauce plus 1/2 c. sugar
		   plus 2 tbsp. vinegar
		1 tsp. dry mustard
		1/4 tsp. each oregano, basil, thyme, rosemary
		   plus dash of cayenne
		1/2 tsp. cinnamon plus 1/8 tsp. cloves
		1 tbsp. dried minced onion or 1 tsp. onion
		   powder
		1/8 tsp. garlic powder or 1/8 tsp. instant
		   minced garlic or 3/4 tsp. garlic salt
		   or 5 drops of liquid garlic
		1/2 tsp. vinegar

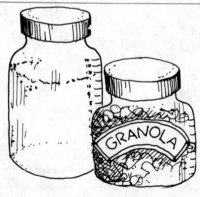

Index

Index

Index

Index

Index

PHOTOGRAPHY CREDITS

Keith Thomas Company; American Spice Trade Association; National Dairy Council; National Macaroni Institute; Ball Corporation; Angostura-Wuppermann Corporation; Florida Tomato Exchange; Spanish Green Olive Commission; Pie Filling Institute; Hershey Foods Corporation; National Dairy Council; California Apricot Advisory Board; National Live Stock and Meat Board; The Tuna Research Foundation; San Giorgio-Skinner Foods; Standard Brands-Fleischmann's Yeast; Diamond Walnut Kitchen; National Peanut Council; El Molino-Cara Coa Brand; and M&M Candies Company.

Order Information

**COMPLETE YOUR COOKBOOK LIBRARY
OR GIVE AS PERFECT GIFTS**

FOR ORDERING INFORMATION
WRITE TO:

FAVORITE RECIPES PRESS
P. O. Box 1408
Nashville, Tennessee 37202

OR CALL:

TOLL FREE Cookbook Hotline
1-800-251-1520